Juran, Quality, and a Century of Improvement

Also Available from ASQ Quality Press:

Six Sigma and Related Studies in the Quality Disciplines: The Best on Quality Book Series, Volume 14
International Academy for Quality

Quality into the 21st Century: Perspectives on Quality and Competitiveness for Sustained Performance
International Academy for Quality

History of Managing for Quality: The Evolution, Trends, and Future Directions of Managing for Quality
J. M. Juran

The Recipe for Simple Business Improvement
David W. Till

Principles and Practices of Organizational Performance Excellence
Thomas J. Cartin

Quality's Greatest Hits: Classic Wisdom from the Leaders of Quality
Zigmund Bluvband

Certified Quality Manager Handbook, Second Edition
Duke Okes and Russell T. Westcott, editors

From Quality to Business Excellence: A Systems Approach to Management
Charles Cobb

The Executive Guide to Improvement and Change
G. Dennis Beecroft, Grace L. Duffy, John W. Moran

Customer Centered Six Sigma: Linking Customers, Process Improvement, and Financial Results
Earl Naumann and Steven H. Hoisington

To request a complimentary catalog of ASQ Quality Press publications, call 800-248-1946, or visit our website at http://qualitypress.asq.org.

Juran, Quality, and a Century of Improvement

The Best on Quality

Book Series of the
International Academy for Quality

Vol. 15

Edited by Dr. Kenneth S. Stephens

ASQ Quality Press
Milwaukee, Wisconsin

American Society for Quality, Quality Press, Milwaukee 53203
© 2005 ASQ
All rights reserved. Published 2004
Printed in the United States of America

12 11 10 09 08 07 06 05 04   5 4 3 2 1

ISSN 0936-160X
ISBN 0-87389-635-1

Publisher: William A. Tony
Acquisitions Editor: Annemieke Hytinen
Project Editor: Paul O'Mara
Production Administrator: Randall Benson
Special Marketing Representative: David Luth

ASQ Mission: The American Society for Quality advances individual, organizational, and community excellence worldwide through learning, quality improvement, and knowledge exchange.

Attention Bookstores, Wholesalers, Schools, and Corporations: ASQ Quality Press books, videotapes, audiotapes, and software are available at quantity discounts with bulk purchases for business, educational, or instructional use. For information, please contact ASQ Quality Press at 800-248-1946, or write to ASQ Quality Press, P.O. Box 3005, Milwaukee, WI 53201-3005.

To place orders or to request a free copy of the ASQ Quality Press Publications Catalog, including ASQ membership information, call 800-248-1946. Visit our Web site at www.asq.org or http://qualitypress.asq.org.

 Printed on acid-free paper

Quality Press
600 N. Plankinton Avenue
Milwaukee, Wisconsin 53203
Call toll free 800-248-1946
Fax 414-272-1734
www.asq.org
http://qualitypress.asq.org
http://standardsgroup.asq.org
E-mail: authors@asq.org

Contents

Preface

Volume 15 of the International Academy for Quality's (IAQ) annual series, *The Best on Quality*, is a tribute issue to the person and works of Joseph M. Juran. It features biographical and bibliographical information on Joe Juran and his longevity in the quality profession, together with enormous contributions to the quality disciplines.

For over three-quarters of a century the quality discipline, which isn't much older than that itself, has been blessed by the person and dynamics of Dr. Joseph M. Juran. His philosophies and contributions to the quality disciplines, his longevity as a contributor, and his vision in managing for quality, have had significant influences on the world of quality, in particular, contributing to make the world a better place via the quality profession.

SECTION I: TRIBUTE TO DR. JOSEPH M. JURAN

The volume is divided into two major sections. The first section, Tribute to Dr. Joseph M. Juran, contains biographical information as well as a brief account of his major contributions via the Juran Institute, the Juran Foundation leading to the Juran Center for Leadership in Quality at the University of Minnesota (his alma mater), and the Juran Medal, established in his honor by the American Society for Quality. These are followed by brief accounts by fellow IAQ academicians of his global influence, especially in Europe (Sweden, in particular) and Japan.

Because these chapters in the first section of this volume contain information that has not been published previously about the life and work of

Joe Juran, they represent valuable reading to gain further insight into and about the "Architect of Quality."

In particular, Chapter 2, "Juran Institute," is an accounting of the formation and growth of the Juran Institute and the man who developed it. The story is told by four authors who have had affiliation with Joe Juran and the Juran Institute.

Another significant legacy that is associated with Joe Juran is The Center for Leadership in Quality in the Carlson School of Management at the University of Minnesota. Chapter 3, "The Juran Center for Leadership in Quality," is a reasonably complete synopsis of the formation of the Center and the continuing work of its namesake being carried out well into the future, with every intention of making the management of quality even better and more effective in serving society in future generations. This chapter contains a biographical sketch of Joe Juran and concludes with an address by Joe Juran as late as 2002 on a "Call for Action in Leadership for Quality." This address goes beyond the time range of the selected papers of Joe Juran presented in Section II (Chapters 6 through 18) and should be studied together with these earlier papers.

Chapter 4, "The Juran Medal and CEO Recipients—An Enduring Monument to Dr. Joseph M. Juran," is about the award medal established in his name by the American Society for Quality. Significant to the work carried out and the contributions made to the disciplines of quality is that this award is intended for corporate CEOs who have made strides in "managing for quality." Already four such CEOs have been recognized via the Juran Medal, and Chapter 4 contains cogent remarks by these executives.

Chapter 5, "Global Influence," is devoted to a brief accounting of the "global" influence of Joe Juran, with papers by two academicians of IAQ who have had frequent and long associations with Joe Juran on two major continents, Europe and Japan.

SECTION II: SELECTED WORKS OF DR. JOSEPH M. JURAN

The second section of this volume is devoted to a selection of papers written and published (and/or presented) by Dr. Joseph M. Juran spanning a period from 1964 through 1994; this is considerably less than his effective contributory span (see also Chapter 3 for a 2002 address). These papers have been selected to demonstrate his contributions, his thinking and philosophy, his growth, and his insights into the field of "managing for quality."

One might argue that one of Joe Juran's greatest achievements during his long and prolific career has been his ability to serve as a go-between, mediator, and ombudsman with quality professional and top management personnel. He was quite at home with a group of quality professionals, with his understanding of the quality discipline and his ability to voice so eloquently its principles, concepts, techniques, and methodologies, many of which he developed. He was equally at home with one or more top management personnel, with his understanding of their language and his ability to translate the language of quality into their terms of reference. He recognized and dealt with top management's deficiencies in understanding the strategic importance of the quality function and of quality to their customers and to their bottom line. It is this unique characteristic of Dr. Juran that is evident in the first selected paper for this tribute volume, namely, his paper in Chapter 6, "The Two Worlds of Quality Control." This paper is both historical and informative and should be read, regardless of its age. Its principles are universal and classic. It is good parallel reading with the paper of Chapter 13.

The paper, "Quality Problems, Remedies and Nostrums," selected for Chapter 7, is interesting from several aspects. For one, it shows that Joe Juran was not afraid to speak out about questionable programs in the quality discipline, in this case the matter of "Zero Defects." It also shows his keen analytical mind examining both the pros and cons of such a program, concluding with a set of criteria that would be required for such a program to have positive benefits. Within this program that he considered highly unlikely to have a major positive impact on actual quality improvement, as opposed to company relations/publicity, he identified at least two benefits to the quality profession at large, namely (1) it achieved wide publicity and set the stage for other "programs" (hopefully with sounder principles and methodologies) to attain this state, and (2) it contributed to a broadened approach to error reduction, "companywide," including white collar areas and nonproduction functions. This paper includes a good discussion of the principles of "self-control," "operator-controllable," and "sporadic versus chronic defects."

The Juran paper in Chapter 8, "The QC Circle Phenomenon," is worthwhile reading today, since there is still a widespread lack of understanding of the quality control circle approach and philosophy among American quality specialists and management. It is one form of team activity that can be used today to deal with the "trivial many" so that they are not swept under the rug.

Chapter 9, "Operator Errors—Time for a New Look," is another example of an early paper that continues to have lessons for today and the future. In this paper, the useful principle, "self-control," is defined and explained, together with related criteria. Associated with this concept are the principles of "operator-controllable" and "management-controllable," also introduced. Juran makes the point that "many companies have been fighting a war without knowing clearly who is the enemy." The phrase, "We have met the enemy, and they are us," comes to mind. Another cogent remark contained in this paper is, "What is lacking is clear, quantitative knowledge about the nature of errors." Juran discusses two theories of interest in this paper, namely, "indifference theory" and "craftsmanship theory," thoughts that are still relevant today. He examines subspecies of operator error as willful errors, lack of skill errors, and inadvertence errors. As we currently face multiple errors, especially in the service sector, the thoughts expressed in this paper are highly relevant for today's quality systems. He displays thoughtful insight in the argument that, "a solution is already in the house, that is, the 'best' operators are in fact solving the problems somehow."

While Chapter 10, "Mobilizing for the 1970s," is understandably written about the 70s decade (as seen in 1969), it contains numerous thoughts and principles applicable for today and the future, again demonstrating Joe Juran's insights and perceptions. We continue to see "revolutions in technology . . . in management of the quality function . . . and in manpower." The visibility of the quality function is still on the rise, with the possible exception of our media. We still need and experience "dikes" of quality control. We still need revision of policies and goals, and many of the elements/ingredients are still the same. We still need to "understand the users' needs and users' economics"; to "measure the effect of quality on income"; to "be wary of perfectionism"; to "examine and use 'motivation,' 'training,' and 'organizational innovations' properly"; to "circumvent the necessity for Government regulation"; to "analyze and innovate 'product liability' "; and to "understand and implement policies and procedures for vendors, new product development, and top management leadership." There are still opportunities for improvement in many areas expounded in this paper of 35 years ago.

The paper appearing in Chapter 11 was published as one of a series of papers under a column entitled, "Management Interface," in *Quality Progress*, May through December, 1973. Dr. Juran assumed an active role as a contributing editor in undertaking this series of papers for *Quality Progress*. The topics covered are as follows: (1) The Taylor system and quality control; (2) The redelegation of quality planning; (3) Inspection returns to its origins; (4) The motivation to meet quality standards; (5) The motivation to improve quality; (6) The future of the inspection department; (7) The quality staff specialist—an emerging role; and (8) The emerging quality control department. These papers are excellent reading, both from an historical viewpoint, as well as to understand how Dr. Juran was developing an emerging grasp on "managing for quality." The reader may want to review all of these papers beyond the first in the series reprinted in this volume.

In Chapter 12, where we have included Juran's paper, "The Non-Pareto Principle—Mea Culpa," the "universal" is seen in the principle of the "vital few" and the "trivial many" so applicable in the quality disciplines. We may yet see a renaming of this principle as the "Juran Principle."

While the title of the paper in Chapter 13, "That Uninterested Top Management," might seem to be aiming at the ills of top management, the paper is must reading for all quality professionals. In it Joe Juran expounds upon why quality managers and other professionals have erroneous opinions of their top management interests. It is certainly must reading for the quality managers who do not believe that their upper management is interested in quality. One sound bit of advice is to "see to it that you engage in both breakthrough and control, and orient these activities to the business objectives of the company." The paper contains a good synopsis of upper management's views of the "control" function.

Much can still be learned from Juran's discussion in Chapter 14 of "Japanese and Western Quality—A Contrast." Using a case example of color television, he examines an analysis of product quality such as aspects of picture quality, function, product appeal, and reliability. He further examines an analysis of process quality such as failures in the development and design of components and in workmanship. He also examines a contrast of governmental policies; of manufacturing, marketing and servicing approaches; and of training of designers by practical experience. He looks at organization and employee relations and discusses national approaches to quality. The paper contains many implications for today and the future.

The paper selected for Chapter 15, "Quality Control in Service Industries," addresses the special application of quality control to the service industries. Dr. Juran looks at the contrasts and similarities between manufacturing and service quality. In his analysis he distinguishes between internal and external conformance; he discusses the measures of service quality; he addresses organization for quality in service industries and how and why it differs from manufacturing industries; and he opines that chronic quality problems, and, hence, the necessity for improvement, abound in service industries. This paper, like others in our selection, provide both historical perspective as well as insights still useful for today's quality applications.

Chapter 16, "Product Quality—A Prescription for the West," summarizes the Japanese revolutionary approach to quality and provides direction for the West. Areas of interest include the habit of annual improvement, universal sequence for making quality improvements, financial analog to quality, massive training, leadership, upper management audits, basic company organizational structures for quality, and QC Circles, to name but a few. There is an interesting discussion of pseudo solutions and nonsolutions.

And there is a prediction of "recovery" in the West in the 1980s and 1990s which did, in fact, take place.

One of the important principles attributed to Joe Juran is his classic, "Quality Trilogy," now well known more affectionately as, "The Juran Trilogy." While appearing in many places over many years, we include his paper, "The Quality Trilogy—A Universal Approach to Managing for Quality," in Chapter 17, which was published in *Quality Progress* in August 1986, based on his presentation at the ASQC 40th Annual Quality Congress in Anaheim, California, on May 20, 1986. This trilogy of planning, control, and improvement was used by Juran to draw a parallel between managing for finance and managing for quality. He used it quite successfully in bridging the quality function with the managerial function in that many top managers were familiar with the language and principles of finance, although not so fluent in quality. The analogy also served in reverse by making quality professionals aware that they should become fluent with the language of management in addition to that of quality if they were to be successful in gaining the ear of management in making proposals related to the quality function. In this sense, this paper is good parallel reading with the one in Chapter 6.

We conclude our limited selection of the works of Joe Juran with his prophetic paper, "The Upcoming Century of Quality," which was initially presented as the keynote address at the ASQC Annual Quality Congress in Las Vegas, May 24, 1994. The paper included here as Chapter 18 is the one by the same title published in *Quality Progress* in August 1994. In this paper, he traces the beginning (of the 20th century) through the various developments during the century to a prognosis for the 21st century, including the label the "Century of Quality." What better quality professional to be asked to deliver such a message than the one who, himself, has had a lifespan throughout the entire century!

About the Editor

Kenneth S. Stephens

Kenneth S. Stephens is an educator, engineer, project manager, statistician, quality practitioner, and author in the fields of quality engineering and management systems, and industrial development, with a professional career spanning over 49 years. He received MS and PhD degrees from Rutgers—The State University of New Jersey under the direction of Dr. Ellis R. Ott and Harold F. Dodge. His bachelor's degree is from LeTourneau Technical Institute. Currently, while enjoying some retirement, Dr. Stephens serves as an adjunct professor in the Department of Industrial Engineering and Management Systems at the University of Central Florida (Orlando) and in the Department of Management and Systems Engineering at the University of South Florida (Tampa). Dr. Stephens served for eight years with Southern Polytechnic State University (SPSU), Marietta, Georgia, where he taught and advised industrial engineering students at the bachelors and masters level. For more than six years he was a principal in the Master of Science in Quality Assurance (MSQA) degree involving Internet studies (see www.msqa.edu). He continues to serve as an adjunct professor teaching Internet courses for SPSU.

For 18 years, Dr. Stephens served with the United Nations Industrial Development Organization (UNIDO) with major assignments in Vienna, China, Pakistan, Ethiopia, Mauritius, Turkey, Nigeria, and Thailand. His career also included five years with the Georgia Institute of Technology and 12 years with the Western Electric Company.

Dr. Stephens is a professional engineer (Pennsylvania), a fellow of ASQ, a certified quality engineer, and an IAQ academician since 1984. He received ASQ's E. L. Grant and E. Jack Lancaster awards, ASQ Metropolitan Section's Ellis R. Ott Award, and AIIE's Book-of-the-Year award (with Dr. Harrison Wadsworth and Dr. A. Blanton Godfrey) for *Modern Methods for Quality Control and Improvement*, John Wiley & Sons, which is now in its second edition (2002). He is author of *The Handbook of Applied Acceptance Sampling* (Quality Press 2001); Volumes 2 and 4 of ASQ's "How to" Series; *Preparing for Standardization, Certification, and Quality Control* (Asian Productivity Organization 1979); numerous book chapters; and scores of papers.

Dr. Stephens now makes his home in Sun City Center, Florida.

Acknowledgements

My sincere thanks go out to all the academicians who have suggested over a span of more than a year that we consider using our IAQ annual publication, *The Best on Quality*, as a tribute volume to Dr. Joseph M. Juran, and especially as his 100th year was approaching. These thanks are extended, in particular, to the IAQ board and officers who sanctioned the proposal. Then, more specifically, sincere thanks are extended to fellow academician Dr. A. Blanton Godfrey for the direct contacts with Joe Juran and the Juran Institute to obtain their agreement for the project.

We are grateful to Joe Juran for his permission to use this medium along with others in recognition of his long and prolific career in the quality and managerial fields. We are further grateful for permission to use the selected works contained in the second section of this volume. We also acknowledge the assistance of the Juran Institute, and in particular, president and CEO, Joe DeFeo, and executive assistant to Dr. J. M. Juran and Juran Institute, Laura Sutherland.

Special acknowledgement and thanks are extended to the contributors of the first section of Volume 15, Tribute to Dr. Joseph M. Juran. Four authors have contributed to Chapter 2 on the Juran Institute, namely, G. Holland Blackiston, Frank Gryna, Blan Godfrey, and Joe DeFeo. We acknowledge the contribution by Dr. Roger Schroeder and Dr. Jim Buckman, co-directors of the Juran Center for Leadership in Quality of the Carlson School of Management of the University of Minnesota and give thanks for permission to use portions of their website. Sincere thanks are extended to fellow academician Greg Watson for his work in compiling Chapter 4, "Juran Medal and the CEO Recipients." And last, but not least, are thanks to fellow academicians Lennart Sandholm and Yoshio Kondo for their contribution to Chapter 5, "Global Influences."

As for the last several volumes of this publication, thanks are again extended to the staff and management of ASQ's Quality Press, Milwaukee, Wisconsin. Acquisitions editor Annemieke Hytinen has been a constant and informative resource for all matters related to the compilation and editing of the material for this volume and has been timely in all correspondence. She has provided the necessary link between the editor deep in Florida and ASQ's headquarters in Milwaukee. We also appreciate the efforts and direction from Quality Press' publisher Bill Tony in extending the facilities and systems to make this volume a published work. Thanks again are also extended to ASQ's project editor, Paul O'Mara, production administrator, Randall Benson, to copy editor, Carolyn Knott Washburn, and to Kate Hawley, the prepress and graphics subcontractor for Volume 15, for their careful, thorough work and cooperation on the task of converting the original manuscript into a published volume.

And again, grateful acknowledgement is made for the day-to-day encouragement, support, tolerance, sacrifices, and love from my wife, Gina, as this project is undertaken during our "retirement."

Ken Stephens
Sun City Center, Florida

Section I

Tribute to Dr. Joseph M. Juran

1

Brief Biographical Synopsis for Dr. Joseph M. Juran

T he following is a brief synopsis of the biography of Dr. Joseph M. Juran highlighting important data and facts in his fruitful life of longevity and service to the quality profession.

Born

December 24, 1904, Braila, Romania

Emigrated to United States, 1912

Naturalized U.S. citizen, 1917

Education

B.S., Electrical Engineering, University of Minnesota, 1924

J.D., Law, Loyola University, 1936

Employment

1924–1941	Engineer, manager, Western Electric Company
1941–1945	Assistant administrator, Lend Lease Administration, Foreign Economic Administration, U.S. Government
1945–1951	Professor and chairman, industrial engineering, New York University
1951–1979	Self-employed consultant

1979–present   Founder, chairman, Juran Institute (Emeritus 1987)

1986   Founder, chairman, Juran Foundation

Honorary Doctorates

Doctor of Engineering, Stevens Institute of Technology, 1988

Doctor of Science, University of Minnesota, 1992

Doctor of Science, Rochester Institute of Technology, 1992

Doctor of Laws, University of New Haven, 1992

Honorary Memberships, United States

American Society for Quality Control (ASQC), Honorary 1981

American Society of Mechanical Engineers (ASME), 1993

International Academy of Management

National Academy of Engineering, 1988

The Academy of the Association for Quality and Participation

Alpha Pi Mu

Sigma Xi, 1946

Tau Beta Pi

Honorary Memberships, International

Australian Organization for Quality Control, 1974

Argentine Organization for Quality Control , 1977

British Institute of Quality Assurance, 1976

European Organization for Quality Control

Philippine Society for Quality Control, 1974

Spanish Association for Quality Control

Romanian Academy, 1992

Society Affiliations, United States

American Association for the Advancement of Science, 1967

American Institute of Industrial Engineers, 1967

American Management Association, 1941

Malcolm Baldrige National Quality Award, Board of Overseers, 1988 to 1991

Member Illinois Bar, 1936–

Professional Engineer, New York, New Jersey

Medals, United States

Alumni Medal, University of Minnesota, 1954

American Management Association, Hall of Fame, 1983

Brumbaugh Award, ASQC, 1958

Chairman's Award, American Association of Engineering Societies, 1988

Edwards Medal, ASQC, 1961

Eugene L. Grant Medal, ASQC, 1967

Gilbreth Award, American Institute of Industrial Engineers, 1981

Managing Automation, Hall of Fame, 1995

National Medal of Technology, 1992

Soichiro Honda Medal, ASME, 1995

Stevens Medal, Stevens Institute of Technology, 1984

Wallace Clark Medal, ASME, AMA, 1967

Worcester Reed Warner Medal, ASME, 1945

Xerox Quality Award

Medals, International

250th Anniversary Medal, Czechoslovakian Higher Institute of Technology, 1965

Medal of Technikhaza, Esztergom, Hungary, 1968

Medal of Honor, Camera Official de la Industria, Madrid, 1970

Order of Sacred Treasure (Emperor of Japan), 1981

Medal of European Organization for Quality, 1993

Placques, Scrolls of Appreciation, United States

American Management Association, Wall of Fame, 1983

Department of the Army

Department of Commerce

Department of Defense

Department of the Navy

Malcolm Baldrige National Quality Award

Placques, Scrolls of Appreciation, International

Scroll of Appreciation, Japanese Union of Scientists and Engineers (JUSE), 1961

Taiwan Productivity Center, 1974

Plaque of Appreciation, Republic of Korea, 1978

Editor's Note: For a more in-depth account of the life and work of Dr. Joseph M. Juran, see the following:

Juran, J. M. 2004. *Architect of quality: The autobiography of Dr. Joseph M. Juran.* New York: McGraw-Hill.
Phillips-Donaldson, D. 2004. Gurus of quality: 100 years of Juran. *Quality Progress* (May) 37(5):25–39.
www.juran.com
See also, Chapters 3, 4, and 5 in this volume.

2

The Juran Institute

G. Howland Blackiston

Dr. Frank M. Gryna

Dr. A. Blanton Godfrey

Dr. Joseph A. DeFeo

The First Few Years

by G. Howland Blackiston
Past President, Juran Institute

SETTING THE STAGE

Let's go back to 1976. The United States was celebrating its 200th birthday, *Rocky* was number one at the box office, and Nadia Comaneci was the star of the summer Olympic games in Montreal.

The year 1976 also marked Dr. Juran's 31st year as an independent consultant, author, and lecturer. Working out of his New York high-rise apartment, the 76-year-old Juran operated pretty much as a one-man gang. His lectures were scheduled and sponsored by the American Management Association. Administrative support was provided, sometimes reluctantly, by Mrs. Juran. Life for Dr. Juran was simple and uncomplicated.

America Turns to Quality

Things were soon to turn more complicated. There was an emerging interest in this country for training in quality matters. Manufacturing companies were sending increasing numbers of managers to Dr. Juran's lectures. These organizations were eager to implement quality improvement within their organizations, motivated by a very real competitive threat from overseas. Japanese industries had swallowed up a number of our companies and were threatening others.

Dr. Juran was convinced there was a need to spread his knowledge in quality management throughout organizations. To be effective, this would have to be done on a scale way beyond what was possible through his public lectures, and it seemed that the medium best suited to accomplish this was via video training cassettes. The idea was to create a video-based series that could be used by companies to train their entire management team. However, this would be a huge project and could not happen without putting some infrastructure in place.

A Company Is Born

Using a million dollars from his own financial resources, Dr. Juran founded Juran Enterprises, in 1979. It was to become the vehicle for creating and marketing this yet-to-be-created video product. He invited his granddaughter's husband, Howland Blackiston, who had experience in advertising and video production, to become the company's first employee and head up this effort. Blackiston would manage the office, provide creative direction for the production of the new videos, and market the tapes when they became available. A seemingly cavernous office was rented in Dr. Juran's apartment building (the first five floors of the building were commercial space) and work began on the big video project.

The Institute's First Product

Approximately one year later, after some extravagant but delightfully exhilarating false starts, *Juran on Quality Improvement* went on the market. The timing was perfect—industry desperately needed the training—and the video production quality was very good. Almost instantly, it was a smashing success. The set of 16 half-hour tapes sold for $15,000, and hundreds of companies were purchasing the series. This ultimately generated over $30 million in sales, eventually giving the company the resources to develop and market additional training materials and courses.

During the time the tapes were being developed, Juran delicensed the American Management Association, which had been sponsoring his two course offerings, Management of Quality and Upper Management and Quality. With an office in place, the newly formed Juran Enterprises began to sponsor and market these courses itself. These two courses, each offered six or seven times a year, accounted for a total of 31 course days. About this time, Juran contracted with Bradley University to attain Dr. Frank Gryna's time (at that time, Gryna was Dean of the College of Engineering and Technology at Bradley). Gryna co-conducted the Management of Quality course with Juran. By the end of 1982, Gryna had joined Juran Enterprises fulltime as the company's first quality professional employee, although he remained in Peoria working out of an office set up at the university—an early experiment in virtual offices. By that time, Juran Enterprises had become Juran Institute, a name change to better reflect the educational focus of its offerings. There were a total of nine employees. Before long, clients were asking for more direct support, in the form of in-company training and counseling. Juran and Gryna would not be able to keep up with the demand, and so Juran Institute took steps to grow its team of quality professionals

An Unexpected Roadblock

It was at this time that the Institute encountered a significant and unwelcome roadblock. In 1982, Juran Institute was based in Manhattan. Yet not a single quality professional that the Institute hoped to recruit was willing to live or work in New York—the grim reality of locating a business in an expensive, noisy, and crime-ridden city.

And so, Juran and Blackiston set out on a top-secret, year-long project to address this problem. "Operation Dogwood" became the code name for the company's efforts to find a more enticing location for the Institute. Without this change, they could not hope to build a world-class staff of quality professionals and support operations. In 1984, the 12 employees of Juran Institute made the move, settling into a handsome facility in Wilton, Connecticut, about 50 miles northeast of New York City.

The Early Years

by Dr. Frank M. Gryna
Former Senior Vice President, Juran Institute

Would you set up a company with a staff of people when you were 74 years old? Most would laugh at the idea. Joe Juran did not—the Institute was incorporated on April 19, 1979. My recollections of the Institute will span from 1982 to 1987; Holland Blackiston, Blan Godfrey, and Joe DeFeo will make further contributions to this subject, some with overlapping years and others filling in some of the other years.

These recollections cover the early location of the Institute and the quality professionals, seminars and consulting work, the *Quality Control Handbook*, the Juran on Quality Improvement tapes, the IMPRO conferences, and lessons learned about quality.

The Beginning

The Institute was originally called Juran Enterprises; later the name was changed to Juran Institute. The first office location was in the building where Juran and his wife resided, United Nations Plaza in New York City, overlooking the United Nations Garden; some mighty famous people lived in that coop apartment house. Later we moved to Wilton, Connecticut, first in a building on Danbury Road and then into larger spaces in a palatial office complex that was formerly part of a research and development facility for a food company.

The original quality professionals in the organization were Juran and myself. I arranged for an early retirement from teaching industrial engineering at Bradley University, and soon we added Dr. John Enell, who had retired as vice president of research at the American Management Association. In the late 1940s and early 1950s Juran, Enell, and I had all been together teaching industrial engineering at New York University. (Yes, at that time NYU had an engineering school at its uptown campus.) Enell and I had been students of Juran. As time went on, we added more and more consultants.

Most of the early work at the Institute was in presenting seminars, updating the *Quality Control Handbook*, developing the *Juran on Quality Improvement* (JQI) tapes, doing consulting, and holding the IMPRO conferences. We wrote simple, handwritten memos, keeping all of us informed of our contacts with various organizations. The collection of those memos could become a book in itself.

Our colleagues were mostly engineers and scientists. Thus, the air was loaded with methodical and precise ideas—with Juran to set the pace. (Insider joke: when the observatory in Greenwich, England, needs to check the precise time, they call Juran. Yes, he is as precise as an arrow.)

Seminars

One of the first seminars Juran developed was a four-day course for quality managers called Management of Quality Control; he had presented earlier versions of this seminar on the NYU campus in the late 1940s. In later years, he and I jointly presented the seminar. This four-day course was packed with information. It opened with a census of the interests of the participants, which guided us on how much time to spend on each topic. We rigidly watched our timetable of topics to be sure of covering the full scope of the seminar. Questions flowed throughout the day, but we were careful that a few individuals did not dominate with their own questions (which sometimes became brief speeches). The seminar ended at 5 p.m. but we also had an open question-and-answer session from 5 to 6 p.m. Each day at breakfast or lunch, attendees were assigned to sit at a separate table with either Juran or me and again had the chance to ask questions.

When an attendee asked a question or made a comment, Juran often made notes, and attendees would ask me why he was taking notes. I replied that he was learning from the question or comment and wanted to retain the learning for the future. (Some of these notes ended up in the *Quality Control Handbook.*) With all of his experience, he was forever learning—the "wisdomkeeper." This made a deep impression on the attendees.

The course notes were a masterpiece of detail and scope—200 pages. In addition, attendees received a copy of the *Quality Control Handbook* and *Quality Planning and Analysis.* Negotiations with a canvas bag manufacturer created a bag that was strong enough to hold all of this knowledge. But then, of course, attendees complained about carrying the cargo home. Another seminar was a one-day course for upper management, Upper Management and Quality, and in the ensuing years, other seminars followed. These seminars were presented throughout the United States, Europe, and other areas. Each year, a three-week trip covered Paris, Stockholm, and London. The European trip was my first experience with simultaneous translation (in Paris). One of my roles in the seminars, in addition to making presentations, was handling the seminar arrangements. You would not believe the detailed checklists for these seminars. (Those of you who know Joe Juran would believe the level of detail.) Hotel managers marveled at these checklists.

We presented seminars and did consulting within companies from a wide variety of industries: Alcoa, AT&T, Dupont, General Motors, Hewlett-Packard, IBM, Kaiser Permanente, Motorola, Eastman Chemical, IRS, Carolina Power and Light, and Shell, to name a few. In the early years, the focus was on the manufacturing industries, but in later years, many clients were from healthcare and other parts of the service sector.

The *Quality Control Handbook*—The Bible of Quality

The first edition in 1951 contained 800 pages; the fifth edition in 1999 topped out at 1,936 pages with a title of *Juran's Quality Handbook*.

The authors for the *Handbook* represent a Who's Who in quality. As associate editor for three editions of the *Handbook*, I benefited from the wonderful cooperation of these experts who shared their rich experience with the rest of us. These authors are top-flight professionals who were generous with their time and patient with the inevitable follow-up of an associate editor (like me).

Quality may be a journey, but creating a handbook is an expedition. An edition typically required three or four years to complete. Sometimes racing to meet deadlines created unusual ploys; for example, at one point, I purposely rode a train to Florida on a business trip to have some undivided time to work on the *Handbook*. Have you ever prepared line graphs (using an ink ruling pen) in a roomette? Some of these graphs can be found in the *Handbook*.

The content of the *Handbook* consisted of three areas: managerial, statistical, and technological. All three areas are essential for achieving quality goals, and we aimed to have the right balance of coverage. We also included separate sections for various industries and different countries.

The *Juran on Quality Improvement* Videocassettes

In the 1980s, the quality circle movement was riding high as a way to involve workforce-level people in the quality movement. Teams (circles) of workers were formed to identify and solve specific quality problems within a department. These teams had some great successes. But management thought the teams could solve all of a company's quality problems. Not so. The major quality problems cut across departments, and it wasn't practical for workers within one department to handle these cross-functional problems. That's where Juran's videocassettes came in. The tapes were not the only way to address cross-functional problems, but the tapes led teams through a problem solving approach—step by step—that achieved results. These tapes were a major impetus for the use of teams in the quality movement. Later we discovered that a facilitator role was vital, and our consultants developed a facilitator's course to supplement the tapes. The facilitator was not a member of the improvement team but served several important roles:

- Explain the company approach to quality improvement.
- Help the team avoid a poor choice of project.
- Provide assistance in team building.
- Assist in training project teams.
- Assist the team leader to solve human relations problems among team members.
- Help the team report progress to management.
- Revitalize a stalled project.
- Provide technical support in quality methodologies.
- Help team members practice the virtue of patience.

Now we would see several levels of facilitators, such as, Six Sigma Green Belt, Six Sigma Black Belt, and Six Sigma Master Black Belt.

Also, the tapes provided the methodology for executing improvement projects, but they were not sufficient to carry out projects year after year at the revolutionary pace required to be competitive. This led to the development of additional seminars on creating the infrastructure for improvement and developing strategies to attain all quality objectives.

The videocassettes were created to document Juran's vast experience in a form that companies could use to have teams work on specific quality problems. They were a smash hit. The technical content, prepared by Juran, was superb and the video production was so good it won an award. Howland Blackiston furnished the expertise on the video production. Juran wanted a favorite classical piece, Beethoven's *Fidelio*, as background music and had to hire an orchestra to record that extract. Many sets of the cassettes were sold to Texas Instruments, General Motors, and Bethlehem Steel. Motorola purchased a license to reproduce the videocassettes and the accompanying workbooks.

At Motorola, quality improvement teams became a ritual. Team members heard *Fidelio* in their sleep. Janet Fiero invited representatives from other companies using the tapes to meet in Chicago and trade experiences in implementing teams with the tapes. I sat in on that meeting. The Institute was so impressed with the value of such a meeting that we decided to sponsor an annual conference, with proceedings, to discuss experiences with the tapes. This was the start of IMPRO—IMPRO for improvement.

IMPRO Conferences

IMPRO was an annual, three-day conference held primarily for users of the JQI tapes to exchange experiences in using the tapes with improvement teams. IMPRO started in 1983 and was held in Chicago, Orlando, or New York City. The staff at Juran Institute did all the groundwork for the conferences—chose a conference theme, issued a call for papers, reviewed and selected papers, made hotel arrangements, handled conference registration, and published the proceedings. Each year it was a huge undertaking, but the resulting papers were an abundant documentation of experiences. Learning was part of the DNA of Juran Institute.

Lessons Learned

Throughout these years, the quality movement was maturing, and lessons learned emerged at the Institute—some obvious, some not so obvious, and some needing emphasis:

- Some obvious lessons:
  - Quality is more than meeting specifications.
  - Focus on the customer.
  - Involve everyone.
  - Upper management must lead.
  - Employees—at all levels—are a rich source of ideas.
- Some not-so-obvious lessons:
  - It's more than teams.
  - Cheerleading gets attention, not results.
  - Start small, go slow, then accelerate.
- Don't overlook these lessons:
  - Make an assessment of quality before selecting techniques.
  - Don't wait to change the culture.

- Emphasize results, not just the process.

- Learn from the reasons for failure.

Later years would bring a steady stream of lessons learned.

All of our work was going on while many quality movements were abounding: statistical quality control, statistical process control, reliability, benchmarking, auditing, total quality control, total quality management, design of experiments, zero defects, quality circles, market research for quality, error proofing, the Baldrige Award, quality functional deployment, business process quality management, ISO 9000, and, of course, Six Sigma. We tried to address all of these movements in the *Handbook* and the seminars.

Fun at the Institute

The early years (and, yes, the later years) involved hard work (and much traveling) at the Institute. But we knew that we were all learning—and we had some fun. The annual summer picnic at Juran's house was always a delight. I still have a t-shirt with the logo "one of the vital few." Our annual Christmas party at the Cobb's Mill Inn in Connecticut helped us unwind.

These were the early days of Juran Institute.

The Creator of Modern Quality Management— Dr. Joseph M. Juran's Contributions, 1987–2000

by Dr. A. Blanton Godfrey
Former CEO, Juran Institute

Dr. Juran and I had become friends during his participation in a number of senior management workshops at AT&T called Managing for Quality and Productivity. These workshops were created in direct response to the increasing competition in telecommunications equipment coming from Japan. After a benchmarking trip to Japan in 1983 by members of my department and Ed Fuchs, director of the Quality Assurance Center, we recommended to the president of Bell Labs, Ian Ross, that we create a three-day workshop to share our findings with the senior staff of the Labs and discuss how to respond. Dr. John Mayo, then a senior vice president of the Labs and, later, president, responded quickly that such a workshop was critically needed and that he wanted to be in the front row at the first workshop. After the first workshop, the senior management of Bell Labs quickly decided that this workshop must include senior leaders from AT&T and AT&T's manufacturing arm, Western Electric, as well as from Bell Labs, the research and development part of AT&T at that time.

My colleagues and I had reviewed seminars by Philip Crosby and Drs. Juran and Deming, and felt that Juran was by far the most suited for these workshops at Bell Labs. His clear logic, fact-based presentation, and careful presentation style were well suited for the audience. We decided to use the first day to set the stage by presenting the findings of our benchmarking visits in Europe, Japan, Korea and the United States. We also invited Professor Earl Sasser from Harvard University to discuss comparisons between Japanese and American product development and manufacturing more broadly. When Sasser was unable to participate in many of the workshops (which grew to number 13 over three years), he recommended Professors Kim Clark of Harvard and Stephen Wheelwright of Stanford University to take his place. Clark and Wheelwright later became dean and head of the MBA program at Harvard, respectively.

During the first day, we set the stage by presenting the findings of our benchmarking studies and having Sasser, Clark or Wheelright give summaries of their worldwide competitive studies. We followed with open discussions of the challenges facing the company. Dr. Juran then presented a one-day version of his well-regarded workshop, Upper Management and Quality. During this day he introduced the concepts of the Juran Trilogy™ and explained how to organize for quality improvement and the basic concepts of implementing quality improvement on an intensive basis. He also gave short descriptions of the "hidden factory" and stressed the need to use the "language of money" at senior management levels and the "language of things" at the shop-floor level.

On the third day we introduced new statistical methods to these vice presidents and directors—at least new to them. Professors Stuart Hunter from Princeton University and William Hunter from the University of Wisconsin–Madison usually presented these sessions on experimental design and reliability. (Dr. Brian Joiner did one session.) Internal speakers from Bell Labs did an additional session on software quality. We quickly decided these three-day workshops should be by business unit with the vice presidents from R&D and manufacturing sponsoring the workshops and key personnel from AT&T, such as finance and purchasing, also participating. During these 13 workshops spread over three years, Dr. Juran and I got to know each other well. We usually met the night before his presentation to discuss the business unit, its products, and its particular challenges. I would share the issues discussed during that day's workshop and the agreements or resistances to change that surfaced. The morning of his presentation, we had breakfast with the two vice presidents from Bell Labs and Western Electric and discussed their views on what needed to happen in their business unit and what they hoped to accomplish during the workshop.

Many things impressed me about Dr. Juran's performance in these workshops. First was his careful preparation. Each time he worked hard to insert small examples and case studies relevant to the business unit and the specific challenges facing the leaders. During the workshops, he would carefully listen to each question, write the question down, repeat the question, answer the question, and then ask if he had answered the question. He often would not answer the question when it was out of his area of expertise, just saying with a smile, "I prefer not to share my ignorance on that subject." Sometimes he would recommend who might have the answer, especially on matters of advanced statistical methods. He knew Stu Hunter well and would suggest they save a particular question for him. Software quality was a new area for him at that time, and he would ask many questions of the leaders in the workshops about the differences between managing software quality and manufacturing or service quality. I shared some articles with him that I had found useful, and he occasionally called to discuss these.

I soon noticed that the answers to questions from previous workshops became part of his presentations to later workshops. He not only was teaching quality improvement, he was practicing it every day. By the 13th workshop, his presentation had become so focused on Bell Labs' problems and needs, it appeared a totally customized course.

During this time, Dr. Juran was also starting the development of what would become his texts, *Juran on Planning for Quality* and *Juran on Quality by Design*, and new videotape series, *Juran on Quality Planning*. While doing the research for these books and videotape series, he had invited representatives from a number of companies he thought were providing leadership in quality management, especially in the area of design quality. These organizations included General Motors, Continental Illinois Bank, Becton Dickinson, AT&T, McDonnell Douglas Electronics, Corning Glass Works, Borg-Warner, Bureau of Labor Statistics, Union Carbide, Perkin-Elmer, DuPont, Bethlehem Steel, Texas Instruments, Florida Power and Light, Dana Corporation, Eastman Kodak, Boeing Aerospace, IBM, Caterpillar, Tenneco, Burlington Industries, the IRS, and Xerox. I was one of the representatives from AT&T Bell Labs. These companies provided ideas, examples of work they were doing in moving quality management upstream, and critiques of his early drafts. Several of these organizations provided test sites for the new methods.

In 1987, Dr. Juran decided that the Institute he had created was "managing him" rather than him managing the Institute. Just the day-to-day running of the Institute was taking him away from the things he really wanted to do. Although founded to sell the videotapes, *Juran on Quality Improvement*, more and more companies were asking for help implementing what was becoming total quality management (TQM). During the three preceding years, Dr. Juran had talked with me several times about joining Juran Institute as head of research, but I had declined each time. I was having too much fun at Bell Labs. But when he asked me to come as Chairman and CEO in 1987, the temptation was too much to resist. He had decided he wanted to focus the remaining years of his life on teaching and writing. This he has done even into his hundredth year.

When I joined the Institute on Monday, August 1, 1987, Dr. Juran had carefully moved out of his office Friday afternoon so I could move in. He wanted to make a clean break with the management of the Institute, although he continued to be actively involved for years to come in consulting, teaching, and writing. He limited his involvement in the management of the Institute during these years to serving as a director on the board of directors and working closely with a number of the senior consultants and research staff on new courses and projects. He was completely involved with the creation of the videotape series on quality planning.

Dr. Juran also focused much of his time during these days on finishing several major projects underway. He and Frank Gryna had been spending considerable time preparing the materials for the Fourth Edition of Juran's *Quality Control Handbook* (1988). During the preparation of this handbook, I had gotten a glimpse of his organizational skills as Robert E. Kerwin and I prepared Section 29, "Electronics Components Industries." Soon after Bob and I had agreed to write this chapter, a huge cardboard box arrived in the mail with several hundred articles about quality in the electronics industry. Not only had Dr. Juran carefully collected articles over the ten-year interval between handbooks for sections he intended to write, he had also collected relevant articles on all potential sections for the next edition. Each author received a remarkably complete literature search. Later I discovered that he would sometimes take as many as three subscriptions to key journals. Two he would cut up, filing the articles in the correct subject files. He explained that some articles needed to be filed in more than one place, for example, industry as well as method. The third journal he kept complete for future reference.

As he slowly withdrew from in-company teaching and consulting, he carefully took me or other senior members of our staff along to make the transition from himself to the Institute. He refused to answer questions about the Institute or its day-to-day management. He continued to add considerable value by developing new courses, books, and products. The members of the Institute had postponed a planned strategy retreat until my arrival. It did not take long for us to decide how to grow the Institute. Companies were asking for more help in implementing total quality management and for services and products we did not have. We quickly decided to provide services for a "total quality system." Two of the first new products were a facilitator course for those leading the quality improvement teams and a tools course covering the ten basic quality improvement statistical and other tools used by the teams. The videotape series, *Juran on Quality Improvement*, was still selling well, but many smaller companies and organizations without professional quality staffs were having trouble using it. They did not have the support available for training team leaders or providing the statistical methods for the teams that larger, more advanced companies had.

Dr. Juran was quite involved in reviewing the plans for the new tools courses, Quality Improvement Tools, and Teaching Quality Improvement Tools and the planned workbooks. Arturo Onias, formerly of Texas Instruments and then working as an independent consultant in Italy, and Paul

Plsek, a colleague of mine from Bell Labs and then an independent consultant, were asked to provide the primary new resource for creating these courses and workbooks under the leadership of John Early, who had just joined us from the Bureau of Labor Statistics. Dr. William Barnard took on the task of creating the facilitator/team leader courses, with external support from what was then Xerox Learning Systems. Dr. Juran was actively involved in the review of the tools courses and made many suggestions about how we should develop and launch them. He was less involved, almost opposed, to the development of the facilitator course as he thought there were other, higher priorities. Both courses and the associated materials were quite successful—the right products and the right time. We were off and running, and the Institute grew quickly, with new people joining and bringing even more new ideas.

Dr. Juran had for some time wanted to update his flagship course, Upper Management and Quality, and now he had time. His process for updating the course was impeccable. He would carefully write a section and send it to the staff for review. He would then call a lunch meeting to listen to critiques, suggestions, and comments. He would listen carefully and take notes. During the next meeting, he would share what had been changed and thank the reviewer, or state why the changes were not made and again thank the reviewer. By the end of this development process he had an entirely new course, Making Quality Happen, that remained the flagship senior management offering of Juran Institute for many years. We taught this course together for several years both in public courses and inside companies. He then withdrew from doing the in-house courses but continued to give the course publicly for a few more years.

Often new professional staff members would join us and teach part of the course as part of their introduction to the materials of the Institute and their transition from management within a large company to consulting. He would patiently give feedback after each session taught by me or another member of our staff. I remember clearly the times he reminded me to repeat the question and to answer only the question and not use it as an excuse to ramble off into another subject. Those of us receiving his usually rather blunt feedback did not always receive it as welcoming, as he himself received feedback and even criticisms from others. I often remarked that one of the skills I would love to learn from him was how to openly ask for and welcome criticism. There is probably no better way to accelerate rapid self-improvement than soliciting critiques and comments from one's colleagues, especially when one's colleagues know that you truly appreciate their giving you carefully thought-out comments and suggestions for improvement.

He was also developing the public course, Juran on Planning for Quality, at this time. He chose Robert Hoogstoel to co-develop and co-teach this course with him. This course was intended to bring the third element of the trilogy into widespread use, as had already happened with quality control and quality improvement. Although Dr. Juran and Bob taught this course numerous times and tens of thousands of the resulting books were purchased, this course never had the impact we had hoped. The other disappointment at this time was the launch in 1989 of the videotape series, *Juran on Quality Planning*. We all had our theories on the relatively modest acceptance of these courses and videotapes (relative to *Juran on Quality Improvement*). Probably the best explanation is a combination of the relative difficulty of the material; the need for cross-functional teams across market research, design, manufacturing, distribution, and sales and service; and the lack of really exciting case studies and examples. In actuality, the products were just too far ahead of their time. Many people have since pointed out the striking similarities between what we now know as Design for Six Sigma (DFSS) and Juran's early work on quality planning. Most of the materials from the research for the videotape series and the workshop were published in book form as *Juran on Planning for Quality* (1988).

On the other hand, the new course for senior management, Making Quality Happen, was a solid hit from its first day. This course was a sellout in the public courses as long as Dr. Juran taught it, and it did extremely well even after he turned it over to me. Our senior consultants taught it time after time in-house, and it formed the foundation course for all companies where we helped implement a complete quality system. The content of this course was published in 1989 as *Juran on Leadership for Quality—An Executive Handbook,* sold in the tens of thousands, and was used extensively in companies throughout the world.

During this time, Dr. Juran also stayed busy giving keynote presentations at conferences throughout the world, serving as a member of the Board of Overseers for the Malcolm Baldrige National Quality Award, and meeting with key groups he felt were accomplishing something, such as The Business Roundtable and Vice President Al Gore's Reinventing Government panel. We also partnered with a number of groups to make his clear thinking and concepts clear to a wider audience. He hosted several panels on satellite broadcasts hosted by the Institute for International Learning and George

Washington University (GWU). As we prepared for one of the GWU broadcasts, we received an interesting phone call from Dr. W. Edwards Deming, who asked if he could attend the live broadcast. We quickly agreed and sent a car to pick Dr. Deming up on the day of the broadcast. It was a classic scene of lifetime learning watching a 91-year-old expert sitting on the front row learning from an 89-year-old expert. A few months later, Dr. Deming was giving a lecture in Danbury, Connecticut, and Dr. Juran was there in the front row.

During the 1990s, Dr. Juran slowly withdrew from international travel and then from most domestic travel. Most people believed this decision was based on his advancing age, but in reality, it was much more predicated on his realization he still had many things he wanted to do and his time was finite. He felt travel just took too much time—most of which was not productive. He became more and more careful about which invitations he would accept. One he could not refuse was the European Organization for Quality Annual Conference in 1989 in Vienna. He had visited and worked in countries all over the world, but somehow he had never been to Vienna. And Vienna was his capital as a young boy. Although his home town is now in Romania, when he was living there, the town was part of the Austrian-Hungarian Empire.

He was asked to give the closing talk for the conference. He disappeared from sight. Some of us thought he must be doing some long-delayed sightseeing. Instead, he had cloistered himself in his room and read every single paper presented at the conference and prepared a detailed summary! Although his talk was exceptional, he could have received the same standing ovation with a mediocre presentation. He had the entire Austrian audience from the beginning. He carefully looked over the crowd and then wondered aloud if anyone else in the room was old enough to have been alive at the time of Emperor Franz Josef. He then proceeded to sing the song—in German—that young children sang each morning at the start of school.

In his same careful fashion he decided to end his domestic lectures with what became a tour of the major cities where he had worked in the United States. These lectures, titled The Last Word, drew huge crowds throughout the country and gave him a chance to summarize in a day the lessons of a long and remarkable life.

In the late 1980s, he had also created the Juran Foundation as a way of stimulating continuing research in quality. Totally separate from Juran Institute, the foundation existed to make significant funding grants in targeted areas. The first major project of the foundation was a worldwide history of quality. The foundation made grants to researchers in an impressive selection of countries to document the history of quality in their region. Published in 1995, *A History of Managing for Quality* remains the seminal book on the long and fascinating history of the subject. Later Dr. Juran turned over all the assets of the foundation to the University of Minnesota, his alma mater. These funds created the basis for what is now the Juran Center for Leadership in Quality in the Carlson School of Management in the University of Minnesota (see Chapter 3).

During the 1990s, Dr. Juran continued to create, teach, and write. A new version of his earlier work on planning for quality, *Juran on Quality by Design*, was published in 1992. With Dr. Frank Gryna, he published *Quality Planning and Analysis* in 1995. At the same time, we started working on the fifth edition of what is now *Juran's Quality Handbook*. When we started, he carefully sat down with me and outlined the work process for creating the handbook. He also shared the notes he and Frank Gryna had compiled when they created the fourth edition. These notes not only documented the process but also revealed their feelings about the different authors. Some were definitely first choices to revise earlier chapters, but some were dropped from consideration.

We spent almost the first year just discussing the sections that would be needed in the new edition, which prior sections could be combined or dropped, and what new sections would have to be created. He selected the sections he would write personally and offered advice on authors for many of the other sections and what should be covered. He also sketched out a plan for creating the sixth and seventh editions. When I jokingly asked if he always made 30-year plans, he went to a file and pulled out the plan he had prepared thirty years before! He then proceeded to go over every item in the plan, explaining what had been published on schedule, what had been combined into one book, what had been split into more than one, and what had been dropped. He also shared with me the story of a novel he had written that never found a publisher. He laughed and said, "It really was pretty bad. But I could write a good one now."

During this time we also published an anniversary edition of his classic, *Managerial Breakthrough*. First published in 1964, this was the book that introduced modern methods of quality improvement to the world. It was the text that I bought numerous copies of to hand out to executives during many of our quality courses at Bell Labs and AT&T. It was also the text I required for the graduate course on quality management I taught for years at Columbia University. Thirty years later the book was still in print, but the plates were wearing out. McGraw-Hill suggested that if they were going to cut new plates, there should be new material in the book. Dr. Juran did not feel he had time to work on this, but he had no objections if we did. Josette Williams took on the lion's share of the work, editing every page and updating the language and examples. We added a new chapter on quality planning, a subject missing from the 1964 book, and a preface explaining the long history of this text. It still remains the book many feel as the classic text in modern quality management.

This period (1987–2000) was a time of great creativity for Dr. Juran even though he was in his 80s and 90s. In addition to the books, videotapes, workbooks, and other materials he produced or contributed to, he also made a number of insightful presentations and published new articles. Some of the most notable were his presentations and articles at the 1990 International Congress of Quality Control Circles in Tokyo, "Worker Participation—Developments in the USA," and the Senior Management Conference on TQC, also in Tokyo, "Total Quality Management (TQM)—Status in the U.S." This same year, 1990, he also presented the summary address at the annual Malcolm Baldrige National Quality Award conference, "Made in the USA: A Break in the Clouds." This paper is still frequently quoted throughout the world.

This was a remarkable time for all of us at Juran Institute. Although we supported many organizations in the quest for certifications under the new ISO 9000 series of standards, we never forgot Dr. Juran's strong criticisms of relying on basic quality systems to define a company's quality approach. We focused most of our efforts on change—first quality improvement and then a more complete leadership approach to total quality management that evolved into Six Sigma. We could always count on serious, well-crafted questions and arguments as we built each new part of what we believed were the necessary components to an integrated system for business excellence. The lessons we learned will remain with all of us for the rest of our lives. His leadership has shaped the management of companies throughout the world and changed the way we think of management in many different dimensions.

Past, Present, and Future

by Dr. Joseph A. DeFeo
President and CEO, Juran Institute

The date was the fall of 1985. I was completing my masters degree in business administration and began my search for a new position. I would be graduating in May 1986. As did most MBA students about to graduate, we believed we could acquire a new job because we had the "degree." This was not the case for me.

I interviewed for the director of training and development position for a well-known elevator company. Out of 200 candidates, it came down to me and one other. I did not get the position because I did not know who Juran and Deming were! I was distraught. I searched for weeks to find someone who knew who these guys were. My search ended with the realization that I might never know. I had already been a high school teacher and technical instructor. I wanted to continue being an educator of adults. One problem: I did not know who Juran was.

It is February 2004; I am president of Juran Institute. What transpired from the time I almost gave up searching for Dr. Juran and today is not too surprising if you know Dr. Juran. He was and still is a man who inspires anyone interested in making a difference—not just a difference in reducing the costs of poor quality, the system that he and Frank Gryna had given birth to, or by learning the Pareto Principle that enabled me and millions of others to focus on the vital few from the useful many—a difference because everything he taught me and us at the Institute was about better serving society.

Fix quality problems, society benefits. Fix inefficient processes, society benefits. How can you beat that? It's infectious.

I have been working for Dr. Juran and the Juran Institute for 15 years. He was 85 when I was hired! I was a mere 30 years old. Young, aggressive, and inaccurate! If you work for Juran, you feel inaccurate. Why? He was meticulous, slow, and methodical, and always accurate.

If he asked what time it was, you'd better state the answer to the precise minute. If you were a co-instructor in a number of public workshops with Dr. Juran, you'd better not have missed the time frames established. Even one minute going over a specified coffee break time would often get a response from Dr. Juran from the back of the classroom. Not a quiet one. He would stand up and state in front of everyone, "You are a minute over the schedule; we made a commitment to our participants to be on time." How can you argue with a man who stood in front of classrooms for so many decades? You didn't. You just sat down and never let it happen again.

26

The Juran Institute was created to provide training in the management of quality. The training materials, workshops, and phone answering had to be done accurately, responsively, and pragmatically. These are three words that I try to live by today. Why? Because when you work for Juran and teach quality, everyone is always looking for a way to challenge you. Slip once and the comments fly. Have a typo in a document and you get letters or nasty feedback forms. You cannot teach quality unless you live quality.

Juran Institute exists today, 25 years later, because of Dr. Juran and these strong principles. It has not always been easy for this organization.

We are an international organization. Headquartered in Connecticut, we have offices in The Netherlands, Spain, and Canada, and partners in China, Malaysia, and other countries around the globe. We are small in size but big in results. We get around. We travel from our homes in many of the countries listed to preach the principles of quality management. We do exactly what our founder did: travel to places that needed our help. Today we deliver the message in 10 different languages. Instead of the videotapes that made Dr. Juran famous, we use "webinars," DVDs, and other means to get the message to our newest zealots for quality—our clients.

The Juran Institute has had its ups and downs, more ups lately. As the current CEO, my memories are the greatest problem I face, memories of working for such an important and humble person as Dr. Juran. Memories such as flying in a Cessna Citation jet sent to pick us up at a local airport so Dr. Juran could deliver a one-day sermon to the executives of the Cessna Aicraft Company and return him home the same evening. Dr. Juran lived in Connecticut and Cessna was in Kansas. That was a long day for a young guy like me. Dr. Juran did this over 150 times per year—at 75, 80, and even 90 years old. I never heard him complain once. We never complained either (at least not when he was around).

Frank Gryna was one of the originators of the IMPRO Conferences. These were high quality events, with speakers from organizations that might have gone out of business if it weren't for the work of Juran, Gryna, Deming and others. They all came together to share their lessons learned. This annual event created by the Juran Institute ran for almost 20 years. At times, there were 800 participants at each conference event. Everyone ate lunch and dinner together. The lunches were always served on time, and the afternoon sessions began on time. Think about it: getting 800 people into a room large enough to feed all of them, eating, listening to a speaker, and then getting back to the sessions, all in 75 minutes. It was remarkable. That is what Juran was about—providing high-quality services that exceeded the needs of his (our) clients.

As president, I am constantly trying to get my new staff to understand what it was like back then. Trying to get them to really understand how good these conferences were. Today's Juran employee is exposed to Internet websites that try to teach quality, conferences that are full of consultants instead of company executives, and so on. I lived through a revolution, a quality revolution. Many of our new employees have not lived through a high-unemployment, poor-quality environment that led to a revolution, but they will.

In 1969, Dr. Juran was presenting a paper to the Annual Quality Congress (AQC) and stated that if the United States did not do something to improve quality, it would be surpassed by the Japanese in the next 10 years. He had just spent almost 20 years visiting Japan and teaching executives how to manage for quality, so he had inside knowledge of this. He observed firsthand what these executives were doing to compete against the United States and Europe. At that time, his statement was hardly noticed.

Then in 1979, when the U.S. economy began to falter, Japanese products flooded our market, and they were of the highest quality available, America began to believe in what Juran had to say. Coincidentally, it was 1979, the year Dr. Juran incorporated the Juran Institute. A revolution began, and in 1988, I joined the Institute and became a part of it.

Today's employees are a part of a revolution; they just do not know it yet. China, India, and Korea are the new Japans. They are taking quality to new levels. It will take a revolution on the part of the United States to fight back and compete at a whole new level of quality—a Six Sigma level. We will win this revolution, not because we are cocky Americans, but because of the tools, techniques, and lessons learned that Dr. Juran will have left behind.

Today's Juran Institute has a mission not much different from when Dr. Juran created us. We will continue to help our clients improve the performance of their products, services, processes, people, and financial results by providing pragmatic solutions to the problems that prevent them from being the best in quality, the key words being "pragmatic" and "best in quality."

Dr. Juran is a very pragmatic person. He never wanted to waste the time of executives. They are busy people. Quality is only one of the issues they are faced with as they manage their organizations. He stressed the importance of providing pragmatic solutions. No jargon, no exhortation, no bull—a give-it-to-me straight attitude. This made its way into our training materials, workshops, and videos.

Can you imagine watching 15, 30-minute videotapes made in 1979 of Dr. Juran talking? Or read a 1900-page *Handbook*? Or attend a four-day workshop taught by a 95-year-old professor? That is what everyone did, and they were fascinated by how he described quality and what an executive had to do to improve quality.

Pragmatic, lessons learned, accurate, high quality, easy to understand—words that the Juran Institute was built on. Words that our founder lived by. The Juran Institute of today and of the future has a tough act to follow. My memory of how it was with Dr. Juran guiding us, leading us, will always get in the way. They were great times.

There will be more great times. There will be more great thinkers, maybe even some new gurus (who knows, maybe even me in 55 more years!). There just will not be another Joseph M. Juran. He is the greatest thinker most of will ever meet. He is humble. He loves his family. He loves his life. He loves his business. Most of all, he loves his customers. Without them, he could not contribute to society. He would not be able to make planes fly longer, cars function well when we drive them, and even surgical procedures work the first time, every time.

He is Dr. Joseph M. Juran. We are the Juran Institute then, now, and well into the future. Thanks, Dr. Juran.

REFERENCES

Juran, J. M., and A. B. Godfrey, eds. 1999. *Juran's quality handbook*, 5th ed. New York: McGraw-Hill.

———. 1999. Quality control. In *Quality handbook*, Chapter 3. New York: McGraw-Hill.

Juran, J. M., ed. 1995. *A history of managing for quality*. Milwaukee: ASQC Quality Press.

——— 1996. Juran y el Calidad por el Diseño. Madrid: Diaz de Santos, S.A.

——— 1995. *Managerial breakthrough*. 30th anniversary ed. New York: McGraw-Hill.

——— 1964. *Managerial breakthrough*. New York: McGraw-Hill.

Juran, J. M. and Frank M. Gryna, eds. 1993. *Quality planning and analysis*. 3rd ed. New York: McGraw-Hill.

Juran, J. M. 1993. Address to the Business Roundtable. Address presented at the Business Roundtable CEO Quality Forum, Washington, DC, April 7.

——— 1992. *Juran on quality by design*. New York: Free Press.

——— 1992. *A look back: 10 years of IMPRO*. Proceedings of IMPRO92, Chicago, IL, November 11–13.

Juran, J. M. and A. B. Godfrey. 1990. *Worker participation: Developments in the U.S.A.* Tokyo: Proceedings of the International Congress of Quality Control Circles (November).

Juran, J. M. and A. B. Godfrey. 1990. Total quality management (TQM): Status in the U.S. Proceedings of the Senior Management Conference on TQC. JUSE, Tokyo, (November).

Juran, J. M. 1990. Made in the U.S.A.: A break in the clouds. Summary address at The Quest for Excellence conference, Washington, DC, February 22-23.

———— 1990. Juran y el Liderazgo para la Calidad—Manual para ejecutivos, Madrid: Diaz de Santos, S.A.

———— 1990. Juran y la Planificacion para la Calidad. Madrid: Diaz de Santos, S.A.

———— 1989. *Juran on leadership for quality: An executive handbook.* New York: The Free Press.

———— 1988. *Juran on planning for quality.* New York: Free Press.

Juran Institute. *Juran's breakthrough for quality improvement teams.* Wilton, CT: Juran Institute.

———— 1981. *Juran on quality improvement.* Videotape training series. Wilton, CT: Juran Institute.

———— 1993. *Quality improvement pocket guide.* Wilton, CT: Juran Institute.

———— 1989. *Juran on quality leadership.* Videotape. Wilton, CT: Juran Institute.

———— 1989. *Juran on quality planning.* Videotape training series. Wilton, CT: Juran Institute.

———— 1989. Quality improvement tools. Course materials developed for Juran Institute by Paul E. Plsek and Arturo Onnias, John F. Early, ed. Wilton, CT: Juran Institute.

3

The Juran Center for Leadership in Quality

Dr. Roger Schroeder

Dr. Jim Buckman

Dr. Roger Schroeder and Dr. Jim Buckman are co-directors of the Juran Center for Leadership in Quality, Carlson School of Management, University of Minnesota.

BACKGROUND

In the mid-1990s, as Dr. Juran was winding down his active career, he was calling for the establishment of a national center for research in quality. At the time, we in the (then-named) Quality Leadership Center of the Carlson School of Management, University of Minnesota, were one of about a dozen research centers in universities across the United States. When the National Science Foundation and the American Society for Quality (ASQ) announced a decently funded research program called Transformations to Quality Organizations, we at Minnesota decided to get serious about competing in this program.

While we did exceptionally well at winning projects and funds in this competition, we decided that the best and most economical thing we were doing was ingraining quality thinking in PhD students. So we got our heads together and asked, "What if we try to do *deliberately* what we've been doing *accidentally?*" (That is, ingrain quality thinking in PhD students.)

We then talked with Blan Godfrey and Howland Blackiston at Juran Institute. We also wrote a proposal letter to Dr. Juran, whom we knew to head up a small foundation named after himself. Dr. Juran liked our ideas, got back to us quickly, and said essentially, "What if I just give you my whole foundation?"

We were obviously delighted and thrilled. But like a dog chasing a sports car, we weren't sure what to do once we caught it. We spent a year traveling the country, talking to leaders like Bob Galvin, Paul O'Neill, Don Petersen, John Pepper, Roger Milliken, David Kearns, Marilyn and Glen Nelson, and many others. Out of those visits came a plan to create a national center, which Dr. Juran had been recommending. During a number of ceremonial events in April of 1998, we became the Juran Center for Leadership In Quality. We are proud to bear Dr. Juran's name and to carry his torch.

In 2004, among our other programs, we have worked with a dozen other universities, providing Juran Fellowships to emerging scholars who will go forth into many fields and, we hope, give those many academic disciplines the benign infection we call "quality thinking." We believe that only in this way will the tenets of disciplined quality thinking make their way into academic journals, into rigorous curricula, and into the heads of leaders of all kinds of enterprises.

We will not be satisfied until every leader, of every kind of enterprise (business, education, government, healthcare, military, transportation, and so on.), who is educated in a leading university, will be a quality leader. Only then will we truly create the vision invoked by Dr. Juran, of a "Century of Quality" (see Chapter 18 for Dr. Juran's paper on this subject). The reader should note that this story is told from Dr. Juran's perspective in his new book, *Architect Of Quality: The Autobiography of Dr. Joseph M. Juran,* Chapter 28.

The following is a description of The Juran Center for Leadership in Quality as it exists today with much of it taken from our website within the Carlson School of Management, www.csom.umn.edu/Page1260.aspx.

THE JURAN CENTER FOR LEADERSHIP IN QUALITY

Housed in the Carlson School of Management at the University of Minnesota, the Juran Center for Leadership in Quality strives to make the university the leading one in quality management research. We are advancing the frontier of quality in business applications, as well as pushing quality principles into the broader society. This is accomplished through:

- Implementing a quality summit that is an opportunity for America's leading quality thinkers, both academic and corporate, to gather, interact, instruct young scholars, examine new research ideas and provide technical assistance to the Juran Center.

- Implementing real-time, project-based approaches in Six Sigma utilizing the Carlson School's MBA and MHA students in deployment of Six Sigma in area companies.

- Granting Juran Fellowships to scholars in various disciplines who incorporate quality principles into their research.

- Constructing a widely accessible collection of articles and books on the topic of quality from a variety of disciplines for use by both academics and practitioners; this is called the Body of Knowledge.

- Researching what it takes to sustain and retain quality through the Quality Leadership Project.

Our *organization's* vision is to be the catalyst for uniting the nation's best universities and leading companies in a learning loop to accelerate the understanding of systems thinking and process excellence by leaders of every kind of enterprise.

DR. JOSEPH M. JURAN'S VISION

A national center for research in quality should:

- Provide an academic home for the field of quality.

- Deepen and clarify the basic disciplines of quality.

- Extend quality principles into nonbusiness segments in the United States (for example, education, government, the environment, healthcare).

- Develop the world's leading quality scholars.

This will be a place where leaders engage with scholars to shape critical questions; where new knowledge is developed, translated, and disseminated; and, above all, where quality scholars are trained. It is my hope that, generations from now, historians will note that we helped create the "Century of Quality."

DEFINITION OF THE QUALITY FIELD

While the research domain associated with "quality" is continually evolving, an emerging consensus includes such universal concepts as:

- *Continuous improvement and learning.* Continuous improvement and learning refers to both incremental and "breakthrough" improvement, and applies to both the individual and organizational levels. Improvement and learning can be directed toward better products and services, to better processes, and to being more responsive, adaptive, and efficient.

- *Involvement of people.* Whether in healthcare, business, education, research, or any other endeavor, quality improvement relies on individuals and teams to carry it out. Organizations depend increasingly on the knowledge, skills, innovation, and motivation of their employees. Their contributions must be integrated and aligned with the organization's strategy.

- *Fact-based decisions.* Improvement within organizations relies upon using data and information to support evaluation and decision-making. Trends, projections, cause-and-effect, and so on, may not be evident without analysis.

- *Systems approach.* The most important problems of a business, an enterprise, and society are systemic, deeply-rooted, and have multiple causes. Coherence of understanding requires a systems view. All elements of that system must be aligned in the same direction to achieve true breakthroughs in quality.

- *Long-range view of the future.* Ideas, products, services, processes, and relationships all suffer when long-term consistency of purpose is sacrificed to expediency. New opportunities, changing expectations, and evolving stakeholder requirements must be considered by the organization. Short-term plans, strategies, and resource allocations need to reflect these long-term influences.

- *Prevention orientation.* In medicine, law, government, and business, the search for quality relies upon the idea that problems can be prevented. It is often less costly to prevent a problem than to correct it "downstream." Accordingly, organizations need to emphasize opportunities for interventions "upstream"—at early stages in a process.

- *Fast response.* A focus on timeliness tends to reduce process steps and costs within the organization. Quality products and services introduce convenience to, and remove delays from, our lives. Time improvements often drive improvements in overall organization, cost, quality, and productivity.

- *External focus.* Students, customers, readers, patients, clients, citizens—some group is the primary recipient of a product or service. It is that group upon whom we must focus. As Peter Drucker said, "The purpose of an organization lies outside itself." A focus on external stakeholders can influence an organization's success because it often increases this group's satisfaction and loyalty.

- *Results orientation.* Balanced and integrated results that pay attention to all stakeholders are the hallmark of a quality enterprise. This will help ensure that the organization's actions meet different stakeholders' needs and avoid adverse impact on any group. Results also offer a way to communicate short- and long-term priorities, to monitor performance, and to marshal support for improvement.

- *Ethics and responsibility.* Quality organizations and individuals see themselves as part of a larger whole, which must be respected. Leadership includes influencing other organizations, private and public, to support the causes in which it believes—such as improved education, resource conservation, community service, or crime reduction.

- *Waste reduction.* Time and materials are wasted extravagantly in many fields. Reducing waste can improve quality and increase the general abundance of time and materials in an organization.

THE LIFE AND CONTRIBUTIONS OF JOSEPH M. JURAN

(The following is adapted from the script for the television documentary, *An Immigrant's Gift*. The film, produced by G. Howland Blackiston [formerly associated with the Juran Institute; see Chapter 2], explores quality's impact on society and the life and career of Dr. J. M. Juran. The script is by John Butman and Jane Roessner.)

Both the life and influence of Joseph M. Juran are characterized by a remarkable span and an extraordinary intensity. Born in 1904, Juran has been active for the bulk of the century, and influential for nearly half of that period. Juran's major contribution to our world has been in the field of management, particularly quality management. Astute observer, attentive listener, brilliant synthesizer, and prescient prognosticator, Juran has been called the "father" of quality, a quality "guru," and the man who "taught quality to the Japanese." Perhaps most important, he is recognized as the person who added the human dimension to quality—broadening it from its statistical origins to what we now call total quality management.

Accurately defining Juran's role in the quality "movement" is as challenging as defining quality itself. Both seem quite basic and yet, on closer inspection, are revealed to be enormously complex. Certainly, Juran's body of work abounds with features that have anticipated and met the needs of his worldwide "customers." A list of only his brightest career highlights swiftly proves that assertion. In 1937, Juran conceptualized the Pareto Principle, which millions of managers rely on to help separate the "vital few" from the "useful many" in their activities. He wrote the standard reference work on quality control, the *Quality Control Handbook*, first published in 1951 and now in its Fifth Edition. In 1954, he delivered a series of lectures to Japanese managers that helped set them on the path to quality. The classic book, *Managerial Breakthrough*, first published in 1964, presented a more general theory of quality management, comprising quality control and quality improvement. It was the first book to describe a step-by-step sequence for breakthrough improvement, a process that has become the basis for quality initiatives worldwide. In 1979, Juran founded Juran Institute to create new tools and techniques for promulgating his ideas. The first was *Juran on Quality Improvement*, a pioneering series of video training programs.

The Quality Trilogy, published in 1986 (see Chapter 17), identified a third aspect to quality management—quality planning. In addition to these accomplishments, there is Juran's seminal role as a teacher and lecturer, both at New York University and with the American Management Association. He also worked as a consultant to businesses and organizations in forty countries, and has made many other contributions to the literature in more than twenty books and hundreds of published papers (translated into a total of 17 languages) as well as dozens of video training programs.

But even the most comprehensive accounting of Juran's achievements (and the many honors and awards they have brought him) cannot express the richness and intensity of Juran's influence. Managers who have learned from Juran—and there are thousands and thousands of them worldwide—speak of his ideas with a respect that transcends appreciation and approaches reverence. Steve Jobs, founder of Apple Computer and NeXT, refers with awe to Juran's "deep, deep contribution." Jungi Noguchi, executive director of the Japanese Union of Scientists and Engineers, states categorically that, "Dr. Juran is the greatest authority on quality control in the entire world." Peter Drucker, the writer and theorist, asserts that, "Whatever advances American manufacturing has made in the last thirty to forty years, we owe to Joe Juran and to his untiring, steady, patient, self-effacing work."

Grim Beginnings

Like many managers who look forward and see only a great struggle in achieving higher quality, Juran's early years were anything but free from trouble. Joseph Moses Juran was born December 24, 1904, in the city of Braila, then and now part of Romania. His father, Jakob, was a village shoemaker. Sometime after 1904, the family moved to Gurahumora, a Carpathian mountain village then a part of the Austria Hungarian Empire. Here, Juran writes, "They had no quality problems. Never had a power failure, never had an automobile fail. Of course, they didn't have power; they didn't have any automobiles." In 1909, Jakob left Romania seeking a better life in America. His father's goodbye to five-year-old Joseph remains one of Juran's earliest memories—the boy would not see his father again for three years, when the entire family joined Jakob in Minnesota in 1912.

Life in America did not immediately change the fortunes of the Juran family. They exchanged the dirt floored house in Gurahumora for a tarpaper shack in the woods of Minneapolis. To make ends meet, the children went to work at whatever jobs they could find. Joe drove a team of horses and worked as a laborer, shoe salesman, bootblack, grocery clerk, and bookkeeper for the local icehouse.

Joe was a bright, even brilliant, boy. He so excelled in his school classes—math and physics, in particular—that he was repeatedly pushed upward through the grades and wound up three years ahead of his age group. In 1920, Joe enrolled at the University of Minnesota, the first in his family to attend college. Here he discovered an activity that profoundly changed his outlook on life: chess. His analytical mind reveled in the intricacies and complexities of the ancient game; he became the university champion and performed well in statewide competitions. For the first time, he felt the warmth of admiration and the pride of respect from others. This success at chess helped Joe revise his opinion of himself. Gradually, he shed the image of the skinny misfit and outsider; now he knew that his difference was in the nature of a gift, rather than a curse.

Discovering Quality

In 1924, Juran graduated with a BS in electrical engineering and took a job with Western Electric. He was assigned to the Inspection Department of the vast Hawthorne Works in Chicago, where 40,000 people worked, more than five thousand of them in inspection alone. Juran was intoxicated with this life characterized by steady work and steady pay, and—despite a complete ignorance of inspection or quality—plunged into his work with vigor. The Hawthorne plant spread out before him like a giant, three-dimensional chessboard, bristling with opportunities for investigation and learning. With his capacious brain and indefatigable memory, Juran soon developed what he calls "an encyclopedic knowledge of the place." It would have been impossible for Hawthorne's managers to miss Juran's intellectual and analytic gifts, and he quickly moved through a series of line management and staff jobs. In 1926, a team from Bell Laboratories made a visit to the Hawthorne factory. The team was made up of some of the pioneers of statistical quality control— including Donald Quarles, Walter Shewhart, and Harold Dodge—and their intention was to apply some of the tools and methods they had been developing in the laboratory to operations in the Hawthorne plant. Working in collaboration with Walter Bartky, an eminent professor from the University of Chicago, the team established a training program at the factory. Juran was selected as one of the twenty trainees, and then as one of two engineers for the nascent Inspection Statistical Department. It was one of the first such departments established in industry in this country. In retrospect, the greatest significance of this department may have been that it set Juran firmly on the path toward his life's work.

In 1928, Juran authored his first work on the subject of quality, a training pamphlet called *Statistical Methods Applied to Manufacturing Problems*, which explored the use of sampling in analyzing and controlling manufacturing quality. It became an input to the well-known AT&T *Statistical Quality Control Handbook*, still published today.

In 1937, Juran found himself as the head of industrial engineering at Western Electric's corporate headquarters in New York. During this period, he became a kind of in-house consultant, visiting and exchanging ideas about industrial engineering with many U.S. companies. It was on one such visit, to General Motors in Detroit, that he first conceptualized the Pareto Principle.

Launching a Canoe

In December 1941, Juran took a "temporary" leave of absence from Western Electric to serve in Washington as an assistant administrator with the Lend-Lease Administration, which managed the shipment of goods and material to friendly nations deemed crucial to the war effort. Here, Juran first experimented with what today might be called "business process re-engineering." He led a multiagency team that successfully eliminated the paper logjam that kept critical shipments stalled on the docks. The team redesigned the shipment process, reducing the number of documents required and significantly cutting costs. Juran's temporary assignment stretched to four years.

On September 1, 1945, Juran left Washington and, at the same time, disembarked what he called the "ocean liner" of Western Electric and launched his untested and unproven "canoe" as an independent. He would, he had decided, devote the rest of his life to the subject of quality management. His plan was to do it all: philosophize, write, lecture, and consult.

The seaworthiness of Juran's canoe was proven decisively in 1951, with the publication of his *Quality Control Handbook*. The *Handbook* established Juran's reputation as an authority on quality and became the standard reference work for quality managers throughout the world. On the strength of the book, Juran found himself in great demand as a lecturer and consultant, and its reputation extended well beyond the borders of the United States.

In 1954, the Union of Japanese Scientists and Engineers and Keidanren invited the celebrated author to Japan to deliver a series of lectures. These talks about managing for quality were delivered soon after another American, W. Edwards Deming, had delivered his lectures on statistical quality methods. Taken together, the visits represent the opening chapter of a story that every business manager in every country in the world knows by heart— Japan's remarkable ascent from its prewar position as a producer of poor quality, manufactured goods for export to its current reputation as a world paragon of manufacturing quality. Although Juran down plays the significance of his lectures there, the Japanese themselves do not. Nearly 30 years after his first visit, Emperor Hirohito awarded him Japan's highest award that can be given to a non-Japanese, the Order of the Sacred Treasure. It was bestowed in recognition of his contribution to "the development of quality control in Japan and the facilitation of U.S. and Japanese friendship."

A Final Contribution to Society

With the publication of *Managerial Breakthrough* in 1964, Juran's sphere of influence broadened further still and he became a trusted authority to general managers—in addition to quality managers—who came to rely on him as a source of knowledge and guidance. Gradually, Juran became recognized as an insightful analyst of developments and trends throughout the field of management theory and practice. As early as 1966, Juran warned Western business that "the Japanese are heading for world quality leadership, and will attain it in the next two decades." In 1969, he noted the growing dependence of the technological society on effective quality control. He has often referred to the "quality dikes" that serve as our best protection against such catastrophic breaches of quality as the Chernobyl and Bhopal disasters. In 1973, he argued that the "scientific management" model first espoused by Frederick Taylor in 1911 was antiquated and needed replacement. In the same year, he began to advocate that quality concepts are equally as applicable to service activities as they are to manufacturing.

In 1979, after 28 years of what Juran calls a "blissful life as an international author, lecturer and consultant," he changed course once again. Overcoming his reluctance to create an institution—which he feared would become his master rather his servant—he founded Juran Institute. The immediate purpose of the Institute was to provide a continuity of Juran's ideas through an emerging form—video programs.

The video series, *Juran on Quality Improvement*, met with great success, and the proceeds served to fund a host of other activities. Even with the responsibilities of this new role—which never ceased to be a burden to Juran, despite the Institute's success—he continued to write, lecture, and consult. In 1986, Juran expanded his analysis of the role managers must play in the quality process with publication of *The Quality Trilogy*. Also in that year, he helped with the creation of the Malcolm Baldrige National Quality Award (MBNQA), testifying before Congress and serving on the board of overseers of the MBNQA award management.

In 1987, Dr. Juran, with a sigh of relief, relinquished his leadership of Juran Institute. After a triumphant series of lectures in 1993–94, The Last Word tour, he ceased all public appearances in order to devote his time to writing projects and family obligations.

As a result of the power and clarity of Joseph Juran's thinking and the scope of his influence, business leaders, legions of managers, and his fellow theorists worldwide recognize Dr. Juran as one of "the vital few"—a seminal figure in the development of management theory. Juran has contributed more to the field—and over a longer period of time—than any other person, and yet, he feels that he has barely scratched the surface of his subject. "What I want to do has no end," he writes, "since I am on the endless frontier of a branch of knowledge. I can go on as long as the years are granted to me."

Today, Juran focuses his attention on a new mission: repaying the debt he feels he owes this country for providing him great opportunity and exceptional success. The sourness and the grudge he felt toward his life as a boy have long since been replaced with an abiding gratitude and affection. Juran has established The Juran Foundation to explore the "impact of quality on society" and make his contributions in the field—and those of others—available to serve society in a positive way. "My job of contributing to the welfare of my fellow man," writes Juran, "is the great unfinished business."

JURAN FELLOWSHIPS

The Juran Center for Leadership in Quality will annually select and honor as Juran Fellows PhD students who, upon graduation, are expected to contribute as new faculty members at leading institutions, fueling and broadening quality thinking in their chosen field. Juran Fellows will be expected to conduct rigorous and important research on the topic of quality. The research should meet the highest standards of scholarship and be focused on important problems that impact society. The research must have significant implications for both scholars and practitioners.

The Juran philosophy and the Malcolm Baldrige National Quality Award criteria are based on a number of concepts, including continual improvement, systems thinking, organizational learning, and prevention. These concepts are applicable to a broad variety of academic disciplines. A Call for Proposals is available to download in a PDF version of the 2004 Juran Fellows brochure on the website referenced earlier.

The purpose of the program is to support PhD students who upon graduation will contribute as scholars to broaden quality thinking in their chosen fields. The proposed research should meet the highest standards of scholarship and be focused on important problems that impact society. Any doctoral student can apply from any field of study. There are two levels of support: a $5,000 award to develop a thesis proposal and a $10,000 award for those who already have a thesis proposal. Applications are reviewed by a panel of academics and practitioners who provide feedback to all applicants, along with awards to the most deserving proposals. In 2003, Juran Fellows were made available at other leading research universities across the United States. These include Arizona State, Columbia, Penn State, Purdue, Harvard, Michigan State, North Carolina, Rutgers, University of California at Berkeley, and University of Wisconsin. In 2003, six Fellows were chosen. Of these, three were from Minnesota, plus one each from Purdue, Penn State, and North Carolina. This extension through other universities has been a success and will definitely be continued.

UNIVERSITY AND CORPORATE PARTNERS

The purpose of this program is to support the sustainability of quality concepts and ideas in corporations and universities. At the present time, many universities have only one or two faculty engaged in research and teaching in quality. When the faculty members leave or retire, the quality research and curriculum can easily suffer or die, since there is not a sufficient critical mass of faculty for sustainability. The Juran Center seeks to address this situation over the next several years by helping 10 partner universities build a cadre of about 10 faculty members each in the quality area.

Corporate partners will provide leadership, encouragement, knowledge, research sites, and financial support for this effort. The Juran Center seeks corporate partners that are leaders in the quality field with a strategy for sustainability of that leadership over time. Corporate partners will cooperate with other great organizations to spread leading practices and to support universities in their efforts to educate the next generation of quality leaders. The benefits to corporate partners will be access to students educated in quality principles, receipt of action research as it happens, and the opportunity to strengthen the quality field.

BODY OF KNOWLEDGE OVERVIEW

The body of knowledge on the Juran Center for Quality Leadership website is a database containing citations and abstracts of literature (journal articles and books) on the subject of quality and performance improvement. The database includes approximately 3,500 citations of materials published over the past 10 years, with some earlier "classic" citations. While we do not claim to have all of the relevant literature in the quality and performance improvement field, we do think we have the vast majority of it. Only citations and abstracts are contained in this database, but a source is suggested for full text when it is available on line. The database contains citations to both practitioner and academic articles.

The Criteria for Performance Excellence from the Malcolm Baldrige National Quality Award was used as a guide for deciding what to include in the database. We have used slightly modified versions of the categories, core values, and concepts from the Baldrige Criteria to guide our selections. The specific categories used were:

- Leadership for quality

- Strategic planning for quality

- Customer and market focus

- Information and analysis
- Human resource focus
- Process management
- Business and quality results
- Tools for quality improvement
- General approaches and philosophies
- Definitions of quality

We have developed reading lists for various users, depending on their interests and backgrounds. These reading lists are designed for those who are new to the quality field, while others may go directly to the search page and search for topics of interest to them. As this database is still in its infancy, we are open to suggestions for additions or corrections. As the reader might wish to browse the referenced website and associated database, and if ideas for additions occur, please submit them to juran@csom.umn.edu.

THE QUALITY SUMMIT

As referenced earlier, the Quality Summit is a critical forum for senior business leaders and leading researchers to examine problems related to Strategic Quality, Systems Thinking and Six Sigma. The Quality Summit is intended to provide a deep, rigorous examination of Quality Principles and Quality Leadership and an understanding of how these principles and leadership approaches may bear upon problems and opportunities across many fields of study.

In addition, the Quality Summit is designed to be an opportunity for America's leading quality thinkers, both academic and corporate, to gather, interact, instruct scholars, examine new research learnings, and provide guidance to the Juran Center. Through a partnering relationship with leading universities, we will help to select, invite, elevate, and educate some of the brightest U.S. faculty in quality principles and approaches. We will do so via the Quality Summit and a network of corporate and scholarly contacts.

As an example, in June 2002 the Juran Center for Leadership in Quality hosted a three-day summit, with Dr. Joseph M. Juran. Two keynote speeches were delivered, one by Secretary of the Treasury Paul O'Neill and one by Dr. Joseph Juran. Approximately one hundred of the nation's leading quality thinkers, executives, quality practitioners and leading faculty attended. The format was a mix of executive plenary presentations, academic comments and small group sessions for deeper topical analysis.

Day one of the summit began with a plenary session on leadership led by Treasury Secretary Paul O'Neill. Mr. O'Neill's talk dealt with systems thinking and the role of leaders. After Mr. O'Neill's remarks, Lloyd Barker, corporate division of quality of Alcoa, talked in brief about Alcoa's efforts for quality improvement. In the last piece of the first plenary session, Professor Peter Kolesar of Columbia University gave additional comments. The Summit attendees then dispersed into breakout sessions to discuss the challenges of various "systems disconnections."

The next plenary session began with a joint presentation by Dr. Michael Wood, CEO of Mayo Foundation, and Dr. Bill Rupp, former CEO of Luther Midelfort Hospital of Eau Claire, Wisconsin, a unit of Mayo Health System. Drs. Wood and Rupp laid out the history of Mayo as an organization steeped in quality and its current efforts to reduce medication error. Professor Jim Begun then provided an academic perspective that recapped major research findings regarding health care improvement.

The last speaker of day one was W. James McNerney, Jr., CEO of 3M Company. Mr. McNerney was introduced by outbound president of the University of Minnesota, Mark Yudof. Mr. McNerney described the necessary alignment between the business strategy, the improvement strategy and the long-term leadership transformation underway at 3M Company.

Day two of the summit began with a panel discussion moderated by author Clare Crawford-Mason (*Quality or Else: The Revolution in World Business* 1994). Panelists were Marilyn Carlson Nelson, CEO, Carlson Companies; Donald E. Petersen, chairman, retired, Ford Motor Company; and Edward Breen, (then) president, Motorola. Panelists tackled the knotty issues surrounding sustainability of a quality effort for a generation or more, and the role of board governance in the success or failure of sustaining the quality effort. Dr. Joseph Juran brought day two to a close. Dr. Juran outlined a proposal to break the quality sustainability impasse based on the mission of the Juran Center's executive advisory board.

The research session of the Summit on day three, addressed important research questions in the morning and the infrastructure needed to support research in the afternoon.

Call to Action

To break the quality impasse, Dr. Joseph M. Juran outlined a proposal based on the mission of the Juran Center's executive advisory board. This mission, Juran said, is pro bono publico (for the public good or welfare) and, coupled with the board's composition of senior executives from leading industrial and academic institutions, "confers a high degree of credibility."

Juran's proposal included the following measures:

- Significant research to discover and highlight the results of quality leadership and proven methods for attaining it. Juran envisioned using field teams to visit companies that had launched quality programs in the past two decades. The effort would require two to three years and several million dollars and be funded by nonprofit foundations.

- More involvement and coverage from business and mainstream media. Juran professed disappointment with the media's failure to recognize such major quality events of the 20th century as the Japanese quality revolution and the creation of national quality awards in the United States and Japan.

- Expansion of academia's role, including creating degree-granting curricula in quality management, preparing teachers well versed in the quality problems of industry, and establishing close partnerships with businesses.

- The evolution of all this academic expansion into a nationally recognized quality profession (similar to that of certified public accountants) and eventually into a science of managing for quality.

Dr. Juran's keynote address follows:

A CALL TO ACTION

Minneapolis, 26 June 2002

Thank you for inviting me to this historic event. To my recollection, yours is the most serious initiative ever undertaken to bring the United States to a position of world leadership in quality.

In my remarks, I will address several issues that are pertinent to leadership in quality.

My first point is rather obvious.

Leadership in Quality Is Attainable

We know that leadership in quality is attainable because some companies have already attained it. In Japan, enough companies have done so to bring that country to a state of world leadership in quality. Yet this was a country whose pre-World War II reputation was as a producer of shoddy exports.

Here in the United States we also have companies who became the acknowledged quality leaders in their industries, but those companies are relatively few in number. The great majority of our companies have yet to reach such a state. Our broad challenge is to bring all companies up to the level of the best.

Next, let me note that . . .

It Takes Years to Attain Leadership

I have estimated that by the mid-1970s, the Japanese had become competitive in quality with the West. A decade later, they had become generally acknowledged as world leaders. That suggests that it took them about 35 years, starting with one of the worst quality reputations. Yet their persistence paid off—their stunning performance in quality was the major reason for their becoming an economic superpower.

The U.S. quality leaders started with better quality reputations—they were generally competitive in their respective industries. Yet I know of none who took less than six years to become leaders; more usually it took closer to 10 years.

Why did it take so long? The chief reason is that most of the time was lost in exploring roads that led nowhere—*learning what not to do.*

One of our challenges is to provide the lagging companies with reliable information on which were the roads that led nowhere and which led to quality leadership. An example of such information is the presentations made by the Baldrige Award winners at the conferences organized by NIST, the National Institute for Standards and Technology.

Next let me point out . . .

We Know the Success Factors

I have studied the strategies used by the quality leaders, Japanese as well as those in the United States. I found that there was much commonality. The most frequent strategies included the following:

- The chief executives personally led the quality initiative.

- They trained the entire managerial hierarchy in managing for quality.

- They enlarged the business plan to include strategic quality goals.

- The goals included improving quality at a revolutionary rate, year after year.

- They set up means to measure progress against the quality goals.

- The senior managers reviewed progress regularly.

- They provided for participation by the workforce.

- They enlarged the system of recognition for superior performance in quality.

Let me here exemplify by way of the quality improvement process.

The Quality Improvement Process

Many of my early consulting engagements involved improving quality by improving the yields of manufacturing processes. Each company confided to me at the outset that "our business is different." From their perspective they were right; each did exhibit differences as to products, markets, technology, culture, and so on. Yet their quality problems exhibited commonality. To diagnose those problems, I employed common diagnostic tools. To provide remedies, I employed common remedial concepts and tools. To hold the gains, I employed common control concepts and tools. As I moved from one "different" company to another, I was going through the same cycle of events, over and over. The concepts, methods, and tools I used turned out to be applicable to any company.

I was intrigued by the existence of those commonalities, and I gradually identified the elements of that common cycle of events. In 1964, I devoted half of my book *Managerial Breakthrough* to the universal process for improving quality (or improving anything else). I then continued to refine that process, which became an integral part of my training manuals on managing for quality.

By the year 1964, I had unbounded confidence in the validity of that universal approach. I had field tested it in many client companies; it had repeatedly produced stunning results. I had witnessed the miracles and had thereby acquired the faith of the true believer.

We lack the time for me to go into the specifics of the quality improvement process. I must refer you to Chapter 5 of *Juran's Quality Handbook*, Fifth Edition, 1999. It uses 73 pages to set out the details.

Before leaving the quality improvement process, let me add some pertinent comments:

- Annual quality improvement is one of the essential success factors; without it there can be no quality leadership.

- It is a big advantage for companies to have available a field-tested, proven managerial process as an aid to annual quality improvement.

- Training is needed to enable company personnel to attain mastery of the quality improvement process.

- The training should include participating in actual improvement projects.

Next, let me note that some additional universal managerial processes have been evolved and field tested. Two of the more important are quality planning and quality control.

The Quality Planning Process

Figure 3.1 is a simplified input-output diagram showing the universal quality planning process as it progresses step-by-step.

There are many versions of this process in the quality manuals of companies. A highly, detailed version is available in *Juran's Quality Handbook,* Fifth Edition, pages 3.1–3.50.

The Quality Control Process

The quality control process exists to prevent adverse change. It is based on the universal feedback loop (Figure 3.2). A detailed explanation is in the *Handbook*, pages 4.1-4.29.

Those three processes are interrelated, as shown in the Juran Trilogy Diagram, (Figure 3.3).

Beyond those managerial processes, there is now available an extensive array of universal concepts, methods, and tools to help companies in their efforts to attain quality leadership.

That brings me to a logical and pertinent question . . .

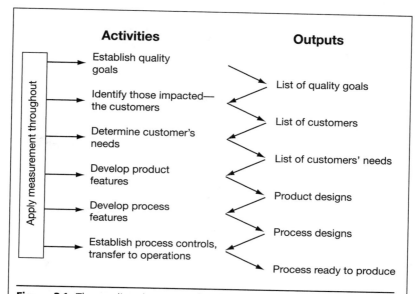

Figure 3.1 The quality planning road map.

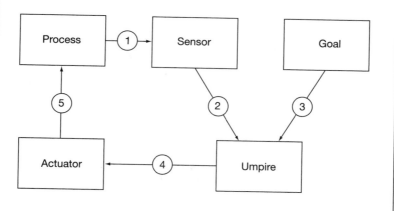

Figure 3.2 The feedback loop.

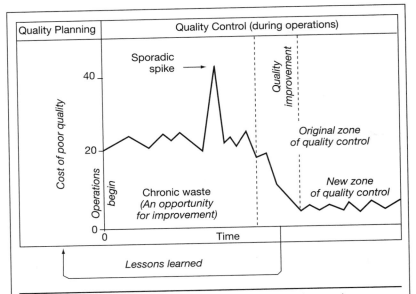

Figure 3.3 Interrelation of planning, improvement, and control.
(The Juran Trilogy® diagram).

Why Don't Our Companies Just Do It?

Given all that available know-how, why don't our companies make use of it to become quality leaders? We know some of the reasons:

- They are skeptical; many have tried and failed.

- They have learned not to trust the advocates, internal as well as external. They don't know whom to trust; there are many advocates and agendas.

- They cling to the mistaken belief that "our business is different."

- They believe that getting certified to ISO 9000 will solve their quality problems.

- The fact is that mediocre quality is still saleable.

- There is a confusion in language—the belief that "higher quality costs more."

- They believe the CEO can lead the company to quality leadership without personally becoming deeply involved.

While these and other reasons are all present, we don't know which reasons dominate; we lack solid research in this area. I respectfully suggest that such research is in order.

So We Are at an Impasse

Meanwhile, we are at an impasse. We know that quality leadership is attainable. We know which are the success factors and the managerial processes that have led to quality leadership. We have indications of the order of magnitude of the potential gains. Despite this array of knowledge, the bulk of our companies are not rushing to make use of it.

The challenge facing us is how to break that impasse.

Here I venture to offer a proposal that stems from the existence of the executive advisory board that is sponsoring this conference. The Board is composed of senior executives from leading institutions in industry and academia. Its mission is strictly *pro bono publico*. To my knowledge, such a mission, undertaken by so distinguished an array of high executives, is without precedent in the history of managing for quality. Such a mission confers a high degree of credibility, and that credibility opens the way for breaking the impasse.

A Proposal for Research

My proposal envisions a sizeable research to serve as the basis for a manifesto—a public declaration by the Board—setting out the results inherent in quality leadership, and the proven roads for getting there.

If we know all the things I set out earlier in my remarks, then why do we need a sizeable research effort? My reason is that some of the things we know may not be so. In any event, the Board's declaration should, in my view, not be based solely on assertions and claims by company managers and advocates like myself; they should be verified by independent research.

The research I envision would require teams to visit a sample of companies that had launched quality initiatives during the 1980s and 1990s. The visiting teams would reconstruct what had taken place and why. They would also evaluate the results achieved, along with the impact on the company cultures. The findings from those field studies would then be analyzed to draw the conclusions that would appear in the public declaration.

Such research would likely consume two to three years of calendar time and would require financing of several million dollars. Such financing should come solely from pro bono sources such as nonprofit foundations.

An example of such a research was the National Demonstration Project on Quality Improvement in Health Care. Its mission was to answer the question: Can the tools of modern quality improvement, with which other industries have achieved breakthroughs in performance, help in healthcare as well? That project was financed by the John A. Hartford Foundation. The findings were published in the book *Curing Health Care* by Berwick, Godfrey, and Roessner.

Contributions of the Media

I confess disappointment at the limited contribution made by our media during the massive changes undergone during the 20th century. With rare exceptions, they failed to recognize the major quality events of that century: the Japanese quality revolution; the associated emergence of Japan as an economic superpower; the creation of the Baldrige Award (in Japan the award of the Deming prizes is shown on national television); and the fact that market shares of the Baldrige winners greatly outperform the Dow Jones industrial averages. Similarly, the media failed to analyze the significance of such initiatives as the ISO 9000 series of standards or the more recent Six Sigma phenomenon.

During my years in the field, I have been interviewed by numerous business journalists. The subject of managing for quality was new to many of them, and I was embarrassed to watch them struggle—they had no idea of what questions to ask. There were exceptions—men such as Jeremy Main of *Fortune* magazine, Otis Port of *Business Week*, and Richard Spiegelberg, management editor of the *Times* of London. The first two had dug in and informed themselves about the subject; they then wrote some memorable articles. Jeremy Main went further. His book *Quality Wars* is a most useful analysis of the quality initiatives taken in many industries. Spiegelberg was a management generalist who was nevertheless fully at ease in the specialty of managing for quality.

In my view, the new importance of managing for quality justifies the designation of a few journalists to become well informed on the subject so that they can provide balanced interpretations to the electorate. There is no lack of such specialists in other fields—finance, sports, science, and so on. The media own the megaphones and thereby have the opportunity to be of great aid to useful initiatives.

The Role of Academia

Managing for quality grew enormously in importance during the 20th century. That growth has already impacted our economy considerably. Managing for quality has become a major element of competition, nationally and internationally. It provides a career path for huge numbers of specialists and managers. (The American Society for Quality has certified over 100,000 specialists in categories such as Quality Engineer.)

Academia took notice of that growth in managing for quality. The Bell Laboratories' invention of so-called statistical quality control (SQC) led to the creation of courses in the subject, first by the U.S. government during World War II and then by various U.S. universities. The leading textbook was by Professor Eugene L. Grant of Stanford University. Later still, some business schools and industrial engineering departments began to offer courses in managing for quality as a part of their curriculum. By the 1980s, formal alliances began to spring up between large companies and their favorite business and engineering schools, with a view of enlarging the role of the schools in preparing graduates for careers in managing for quality.

I suspect that during the 21st century, academia will greatly extend its participation in managing for quality. That extension will include creation of degree granting curricula in managing for quality. To present such courses will require teachers who are knowledgeable about the quality problems of industry. The schools will also need to establish close alliances with industry in order to keep up with the changing realities that face managers.

A byproduct of degree-granting curricula is the evolution of a recognized profession, along with national examinations such as are available for the title of Professional Engineer or Certified Public Accountant.

Toward a Science of Managing for Quality

A further role for academia relates to the evolution of a science of managing for quality.

Our ancient forebears were quite ingenious in developing ways to meet their quality needs. They invented quality specifications, measurement, warranties, inspection, quality audits, and more. They invented the village marketplace. They invented the concept of dividing work into recognized crafts—farmer, shoemaker, and so on. These were common-sense responses to the needs, but they were based largely on empiricism.

The passing centuries then brought massive changes. Villages grew into towns, cities, and nations. Competition grew and intensified. The Industrial Revolution and the factory system did extensive damage to the craft concept. Mass production and distribution brought with them large numbers of field failures along with problems of product safety and damage to the environment.

The response to those massive changes was at first largely empirical, and generally inadequate. The 20th century then witnessed a movement toward a more scientific approach. It began with the adoption of statistical quality control. The growth of measurement by variables then ushered in the concept of quantified process capability, with resulting great improvement in process planning. The evolution of models for reliability planning has greatly improved our approach to product design. (Amazingly, one of our most complex products, the commercial airplane, has a failure rate—a crash rate—of under one per million flights in the United States.) The discoveries that there are universal managerial processes for quality planning, control, and improvement—The Trilogy—has been of great aid to industry generally.

During the 20th century, academia contributed usefully to research in the field, but most came from industrial specialists and consultants. I expect that during the 21st century, academia will greatly enlarge its contribution.

That concludes my formal remarks. If time permits I'll be glad to join you in a question period.

REFERENCES

Berwick, D., M., A. B. Godfrey, and J. Roessner. 1999. *Curing health care.* San Francisco: Jossey-Bass.

Juran, J. M., and A. B.Godfrey, eds. 1999. *Quality handbook,* 5th ed. New York: McGraw-Hill.

Juran, J. M. 1995. *Managerial breakthrough.* 30th anniversary ed. New York: McGraw-Hill.

Main, J. 1994. *Quality wars, the triumphs and defeats of American business.* New York: The Free Press.

4

The Juran Medal and CEO Recipients

An Enduring Monument to Dr. Joseph M. Juran

Gregory H. Watson

Secretary-treasurer, International Academy for Quality; past-president, American Society for Quality; chairman, Business Systems Solutions International.

INTRODUCTION

The distinguished career of Dr. Joseph M. Juran is legendary throughout the global quality community. For most of his 100 years, Dr. Juran has been both a pioneer in the development of the core quality body of knowledge and an international ambassador extending the influence of quality thinking to the furthest parts of the globe. One area that Dr. Juran has emphasized is management's leadership role in propagation of quality within their organization. In recognition of both his long-term contribution to quality and the importance of this idea, in 2001 the board of directors of the American Society for Quality (ASQ) approved a senior medal named in his honor.

The ASQ Juran Medal recognizes leaders who accept the challenge of continuous improvement and who exhibit distinguished performance in a sustained role of organizational leader, personally practicing the key principles of quality and demonstrating "breakthrough management" by their exemplary service. This recognition has been reserved for members of the most senior executive level who operate by directing the strategic focus of a major organization. It is intended that this recognition be accorded only to those top leaders whose organizations have clearly and consistently demonstrated exceptional performance through quality methods and practices. Whereas awards like the Malcolm Baldrige National Quality Award provide recognition for the group effort, this medal is intended to provide specific concentration on recognition of the actions of the organization's leader.

CONTRIBUTIONS OF DR. JURAN
TO LEADERSHIP

The contributions of Dr. Joseph M. Juran and his service to the quality profession and the world are known broadly throughout the global quality community, and he has influenced almost every sector in the world's economic mosaic. Some of the most significant contributions of Dr. Juran that were singled out for recognition by the ASQ board of directors include:

- In 1928, Dr. Juran published the first textbook on statistical quality control for Western Electric. This book served as a foundation for the emerging quality movement and was a primary enabler for extension of this method in its initial propagation through the manufacturing sector (this book then evolved to become the *Western Electric Handbook on Statistical Quality Control*).

- In 1951, Dr. Juran published the first edition of the *Quality Control Handbook* and introduced the Pareto Principle as a means to explain the distinction in prioritization of decisions between the vital few and the trivial many. This principle has become a standard analytical approach used in a variety of problem solving and decision-making applications.

- As a result of the publication of his *Quality Control Handbook*, JUSE invited Dr. Juran to deliver a series of courses for executives and managers of Japanese companies beginning in 1954. Over 400 Japanese companies attended these lectures, with many of the participants drawn from the ranks of corporate chairmen and senior executives of their most important industrial companies. These course materials became the core of a management seminar series that was offered to several decades of Japanese managers.

- Dr. Juran's contribution to Japan's success has been frequently acknowledged as a critical success factor to the economic rebirth of Japanese industry. In 1981, the late Japanese Emperor Hirohito presented Dr. Juran with The Order of the Sacred Treasure (2nd class) in recognition of his personal contribution to "the development of quality control in Japan and the facilitation of U.S. and Japanese friendship."

- In 1964, Dr. Juran published his book *Managerial Breakthrough* as a way to define the distinction between the principles of creating beneficial change (which he called breakthrough improvement) and of preventing adverse change (the principle of control), which set the framework for a prevention-based approach to quality management.

- In 1986, Dr. Juran published a paper that introduced the "The Juran Quality Trilogy" to define a process for quality management—that is, the trilogy of processes for quality planning, quality control, and quality improvement—as the set of processes that constitute the generic approach to quality. His analogy between quality and financial management has provided many senior managers with a key to understand the role of quality management and to apply its concepts to enhance the competitiveness of their firms.

- In 1987, in recognition of his lifetime contribution to the improvement of commercial competitiveness through the development and application of quality principles and methods, the

Department of Commerce presented Dr. Juran with the National Technology Medal.

- Another significant influence of Dr. Juran was his thought leadership in the early days for creating the criteria for and oversight of the Malcolm Baldrige National Quality Award.

Throughout his extraordinary career, the writings and teachings of Dr. Juran have comprised original and valuable contributions that have helped to define the basic principles of modern management. Dr. Juran has distinguished himself with a consistent clarity of vision and breadth of analysis in economic, social, and political terms. To this date, he continues to be an influential leader, advisor, and shaper of the global quality community. He has continued to analyze emerging issues and infuse his personal perspectives to help shape the thinking of future business leaders and quality professionals.

ACKNOWLEDGEMENT OF ACHIEVEMENT

The ASQ Juran Medal was designed with a likeness of Dr. Juran on one side; on the obverse side of the medal is a Pareto chart that illustrates a major influence of his work, surrounded by the words summarizing the recognition: "For Distinguished Performance in Quality Leadership." One medal may be awarded on an annual basis to the individual who has distinguished him or herself as a quality leader and role model.

CRITERIA FOR THE AWARD

The ASQ Juran Medal is awarded to a "role model" leader who exhibits the following criteria—the ideal candidate:

1. Must be chief executive of a company that has received either national or international recognition for business improvement based on the body of knowledge of quality management.

2. Must have served continuously as the chief executive for a period of five or more years after establishing the quality direction or strategy.

3. Must demonstrate sustained excellence in business performance in his or her tenure as chief executive officer.

4. Must serve society as a public promoter of quality leadership with executive colleagues and through other public venues.

5. Must demonstrate a personal leadership role model that would be compelling to other chief executives for consideration of business strategies based on the chief cornerstone of quality improvement.

COMMENTS ON QUALITY LEADERSHIP FROM JURAN MEDAL RECIPIENTS

During the first four years of this award, the ASQ Juran Medal was presented to the following four executives: Robert Galvin (Motorola 2000), David T. Kearns (Xerox 2001), Roger Milliken (Milliken 2002), and John A. Young (Hewlett-Packard 2003). Here are some of the comments that these leaders have made about quality.

2000 Juran Medalist: Motorola's Robert Galvin

While Bob Galvin made informal comments at his acceptance speech for the Juran Medal, he made the following formal comments about quality at a leadership round table meeting held on June 26, 2002, at the Juran Center for Leadership in Quality of the Carlson Graduate School of Business in the University of Minnesota:

> *Each of our institutions has its natural culture and character. In Motorola's case, back in the 1970s, we had a couple of processes that were adding to our culture and character—participative management, quality circles, and things of that nature. We were investing, rather liberally, in what ultimately became "Motorola University." What is the significance of having factors like that at our institution? These are the tools and the mediums by which our people, who have the line-of-sight responsibility and who know what's right and what's good, augmented their skills so that they, as the root of the institution, can bring the real strength to a quality movement. Well, we taught our people particulars, things like mapping the job or the Pareto diagram, and so on. But it took the wisdom and the energy of our people to seed what became a quality movement in our company.*
>
> *The leaders have to do, among other things, the important job of role-modeling the act of listening. If there is any skill that I did possess, it was one of listening. I had so much to learn. It was well known in the organization that you could speak up in my presence,*

and that's why one of our officers challenged us one day in 1979 by stating that our quality stunk. From this point on, we started to build on the root factors that I've just described. Gradually we self-organized bits of a quality program until finally a pivotal idea came from one of our engineers who knew he could speak up. He called me one morning and said "I'd like to see you." I cleared the afternoon, and he came over and explained to me the theory of latent defects—the beginning of a statistical system. I didn't understand it enough the first time through; the second day I got it better. My associates caught on right away. And then they were able to weave these very salient ideas of Bill Smith into what ultimately became known as Six Sigma.

The role of leaders is to provide our wonderful associates, who are in the line-of-sight responsibility, an opportunity to bring to the table solutions to day-to-day and long-term issues. And then, if we listen, we can add our leverage. I think I did contribute one significant thing to our quality program, and each of us has to contribute to quality. I became impatient with the fact that my senior associates, who were doing a remarkable job as fine general managers, were focused all too much on budgets, forecast, and so on. These are essential. But quality was not being given the same amount of attention, and finally I became very impatient with that fact. Quality deserved equal status. So I proclaimed to our president and our executive vice president that from that point forward, quality would be the first subject on every agenda. At the board of directors meeting, the management meeting, the policy meeting, all of the operating meetings, every other meeting in the company, quality was to be the first subject on the agenda. I think that before nightfall, the people in Malaysia had heard that Bob said quality is first on the agenda.

2001 Juran Medalist: Xerox's David T. Kearns

The following comments by David Kearns were presented at the Annual Quality Congress in Denver, Colorado, on May 21, 2002.

It is a special honor to be awarded the Joseph M. Juran Medal by the American Society for Quality. I call it a special honor, because Dr. Juran played an important role in the development of the Leadership Through Quality program at Xerox and was recognized with a special award by our company for the thoughtful leadership he provided in the field of quality. Indeed, this award is in some ways very appropriate, because Dr. Juran was one of those who stimulated the Xerox quality journey.

I would like to make a few comments about the Xerox quality initiative—which I once called "the race without a finish line." During the late 1970s, the Japanese had attacked the Xerox product line, causing our profitability to drop precipitously. We had put in place employee involvement programs, and with the help of our Japanese connection through Fuji Xerox, developed the benchmarking methodology. By 1982, Xerox had dropped sufficiently to escalate our concern. In that same year, I witnessed first-hand lessons how quality can improve a business. The experience of Fuji Xerox as they pursued the Deming Prize helped to lead our entire corporation into a new era of management. This was a significant event for all of Team Xerox. It provided us with a concrete example of successful competitiveness and the fact that it was achieved in the heart of the Japanese market and in the face of the same competitors who were changing markets in the United States. We decided that all of Xerox would apply the principles and methods of "Leadership Through Quality" to increase our competitiveness.

Leaders are only as good as their followers—and I was blessed at Xerox with a strong team that took "Leadership Through Quality" into every corner of our organization.

While this medal is awarded to recognize business leaders for pursuing and then achieving a vision for quality, it is important to me that you recognize that this achievement belongs to all of team Xerox—and the special encouragement and personal examples of both Yotaro "Tony" Kobyashi, president of Fuji Xerox, who provided the initial example for applying quality principles to drive business competitiveness, and Norm Rickard, Xerox vice president of quality, who lead the day-to-day implementation of our global quality efforts. In addition, Team Xerox consisted of 100,000 people who learned the same methods for problem solving, meeting management and benchmarking. These people all shared the same spoken language of quality and followed the same processes to serve customers and improve the work they accomplished. The power of the team—participation and active involvement of all people at all levels—this was the secret that turned Xerox around. My job as the leader was to establish the direction and provide the spark that encouraged our people to do their best in pursuit of our goal. But the people of Xerox were its true power and the source of my energy and inspiration.

2002 Juran Medalist: Milliken's Roger Milliken

Roger Milliken made the following comments at his acceptance speech for the ASQ Juran Medal in Kansas City, Missouri:

> *Quality is a never-ending journey. Along the way, Milliken has explored many aspects of quality in all of its ramifications, and they are many! We have learned that all are important and must be continuously measured and reviewed if we are to reach our goals. If we are not measuring, we are only practicing! Milliken has conducted quarterly quality meetings for 40 years. And we have challenged ourselves for 23 years to go off-site, annually, in "pursuit of excellence" leadership get-togethers to stimulate ourselves to strive ever harder to reach the next level of total quality. And always, in my mind's eye, I see Joe Juran sitting up front at these meetings putting up a transparency, hoping to further inspire us. We owe him a great deal of thanks! I close by saying there is still much, much more to be done, because the largest room in the world is the room for improvement. That room cries for Milliken carpet.*

2003 Juran Medalist: Hewlett-Packard's John A. Young

The Juran Medal was presented to former Hewlett-Packard CEO, John Young, at the May 2004 Annual Quality Congress in Toronto. Some observations he has made over the years about quality, his role as a CEO, and Joe Juran's contributions include:

> *How do you grow an "excellent organization" that is already the recognized leader in its field? That was the challenge that faced me as I became president of Hewlett-Packard, following in the footsteps of two leadership giants, Bill Hewlett and Dave Packard. The strength of Hewlett-Packard rested on the values instilled in the organization by Bill and Dave, and we called this system of values the HP Way. Based on this solid core of values, my challenge was to establish a shared vision that would carry the company through the next decade.*
>
> *The role of the chief executive is to continuously deliver solid performance. The customer of leadership is not only the commercial customer, but also the organization's shareholders and the external world that affects its reputation and influences its brand value. This means that senior leaders must deliver the interests of*

these customers by providing both short-term and long-term value. However, there is no long-term without the short-term. The long-term is a sequence of connected short-terms. But short-term decisions affect long-term strength. So the eye of the executive must be focused not only on what is good today but on how today's strategies and decisions will drive organizational strength in the future.

The challenge that I set for HP at the beginning of my tenure was to achieve what has been called a stretch goal—achieving ten-fold improvement in the quality of our products over the decade of the 1980s. This represented a compound annual improvement of over 20 percent in the quality of our products. And we were already the leaders in product quality in almost all of our product lines. Why did I choose a ten-fold improvement? Well, the answer was not a very scientific one: I wanted the management team to focus on change, and I knew that most HP managers were smart and could finesse a five or even ten percent annual improvement. But at a constant twenty percent improvement, I knew that they would have to challenge their "same old way" of working and find innovative solutions to make quality improvement happen. This target became known as our 10X stretch goal and supported one of two dimensions of long-term strength for the company, a shared vision that defined direction for the organization.

The second dimension was to concentrate the entire company on increasing its speed to market for new products as a means to increase its competitiveness. Competitiveness is defined by the right technological choices and the agility to beat the competition into the market. Competitiveness has at its core both the development of technology and its innovation application. One way that speed-to-market can be increased is to create a robust architectural capability that can be leveraged across all product lines. HP invested heavily during the decade of the 1980s to create a technological vision of the future to develop reduced instruction set computing (RISC). Today this technology is found in almost all HP products, and it has provided the company with a differentiating technology that assured the company's long-term strength. The decision to invest in RISC technology was criticized at the time by many industry observers; however it illustrates the use of the HP core competence in technological innovation "to invent" new possibilities for its customers that also safeguard its future.

Practicing quality leadership at the executive level is one of the lessons taught by Dr. Juran—the imperative for identifying *and defining breakthroughs that take the organization to a higher level of competitive performance. Thank you, Dr. Juran."*

CONCLUDING REMARK

Dr. Juran made a comment during the process of finalizing the criteria for this medal that summarized his feelings about this award: "This medal is like a Baldrige Award for the chief executive officer—I like that."

The ASQ Juran Medal is an appropriate, enduring monument to the influence and life work of Dr. Joseph M. Juran.

5

Global Influence

Dr. Lennart Sandholm

Dr. Yoshio Kondo

Lennart Sandholm is a professor and president of Sandholm Associates, Djursholm, Sweden.
Yoshio Kondo is professor emeritus, Kyoto University, Kyoto, Japan.

Dr. Joseph M. Juran: A True Mentorship in Retrospect

by Lennart Sandholm

Dr. Joseph M. Juran's thoughts and writings have had a tremendous impact on where the science of quality is today. Professionals all over the world agree to this view. I have been fortunate to have had him as my mentor for almost 40 years. Juran has meant a great deal for me both professionally and personally. During the years I have had the privilege, as well as the pleasure, of working closely with him. New ideas have been tested and discussed, which has always been very inspiring. It is with great satisfaction that I have noticed that Juran has shown great confidence in my work and in me. For me, it is a great pleasure to look back and reflect.

FIRST MEETING, 1965

The first time I met Juran was at the European quality conference held in Rotterdam, Holland, in 1965. Having been the corporate quality manager for the Swedish household appliance manufacturer Electrolux since 1961, I had been invited to speak regarding the approach taken by Electrolux, which had become one of the pioneers in modern quality management. Supported by top management, I had the privilege of changing the prevailing inspection-oriented culture to a preventive- and improvement-oriented culture. In this work, I was very much stimulated and influenced by Juran's writings, mainly the second edition of his *Quality Control Handbook*, published in 1962, which became an important source of information and inspiration.

The late Carl A. Kofoed (at that time quality manager of the Danish manufacturing company Danfoss, a supplier to Electrolux) introduced me to Juran at the conference. This was certainly a great moment in the life of a young quality practitioner. I told Juran that I was supposed to go to the United States a month later to study for a period of seven months. Juran asked me to call him when I arrived there, which I did. This resulted in my visiting his home several times. This was a short journey, since Juran lived in New York City and I studied at Rutgers University in New Jersey. These visits to Juran's home laid the foundation for a long friendship and fruitful cooperation.

EUROPEAN CONFERENCE IN STOCKHOLM, 1966

As member of the board of the European quality conference to be held in Stockholm, Sweden, in 1966, I invited Juran to be a speaker, and he accepted. The conference was a success. It became an historical event, since it was the first time the growing Japanese development in quality was discussed outside Japan. Juran came more or less directly from a visit to Japan, highly impressed by the way the Japanese improved quality. In particular, improvement work done by workers in teams, that later were called quality circles attracted his interest. He described in detail how a group of young girls in an assembly department for car radios improved the attachment of knobs. Juran felt a great admiration for the achievements of these girls. Juran's experience of what he saw at this visit to Japan resulted in an article on quality circles.[1]

Juran's presentation at the conference received a lot of attention and it led to a special, extra session dealing solely with the quality circle story in Japan being set up. Among the contributors in this session, besides Juran, was Dr. Kaoru Ishikawa, Japan's quality pioneer. Juran made a prediction, still fresh in my memory: "The way the Japanese are working now, they will become the world leaders in quality twenty years from now, if we in the West are not doing anything." Juran's prediction was correct. Twenty years later, in the 1980s, the Japanese had become the world leaders in quality.

In connection with the conference, Juran visited the head offices of Electrolux, where he gave a highly praised seminar for top management. The seminar inspired in a tangible way the quality development in the company. Later in 1966, Juran came back to Sweden and conducted his one-week course, Management of Quality Control. This became a success, and the conference room was packed with enthusiastic quality professionals. This was probably the first time Juran gave this course in Europe.

MANY VISITS TO SWEDEN

Juran recalls in his memoirs published in 2003 that he paid 31 visits to Sweden.[2] The background was that in 1971 I left Electrolux to become a quality consultant. Inspired by Juran, I found this to be a challenging career. When I informed Juran about my plans, he immediately responded, "Good. Then I will come to Sweden to give my courses and seminars. You organize them!" It turned out in that way.

After 1973, Juran came to Sweden every year. To start with, he presented the one-week course, Management of Quality Control. Later, as a consequence of the development of the quality profession, the title was changed to Management of Quality. As interest for the course increased, it was decided to hold it twice each year. Those who attended the course were mainly quality professionals from industrial companies. Very seldom did any top managers or representatives from the service sector show up. Quality in the 1970s and for that matter even in the first part of the 1980s, was something for manufacturing companies mainly and dealt with by a separate department labeled inspection, quality assurance, or quality control.

When it later became clear to more and more company executives in the West that customers preferred Japanese products due to better quality (see the following), even top management started to attend Juran's lectures. In order to meet the needs of these managers, Juran developed a top management seminar, Upper Management and Quality. This seminar was given at the end of the 1980s as a complement to the course, Management of Quality.

Juran's visits to Sweden came to an end in 1991, as he had then decided not to travel internationally any longer. I recall Juran saying, "At my age I have to prioritize what I am doing. I have 50 years of work in front of me. Travelling takes too much time, I have to stop it." His "Farewell Tour to Europe" in 1991 included top management seminars in London, Paris, and Stockholm.

Juran's lecturing in Sweden for over 20 years had a great impact on the quality development of Swedish industry. He inspired thousands of managers and quality practitioners to work in a better way to improve quality and increase profitability. Juran's visits were not limited to public courses and seminars; however, they also included visits to major Swedish companies for consultation and lecturing. When meeting with top managers, Juran frequently asked them about the three most serious quality problems for the company. This was his advice to me as a consultant in order to find out how much the managers really know about their company.

Juran had the talent to captivate an audience. Everybody attending a course or a seminar listened with great interest, even if the course lasted for a full week. Juran's lectures were well structured, starting very often with examples from his own consulting work and thereafter generalizing a conclusion on the topic in question. This was an approach that was very much appreciated by an audience involved in practical work. The attendees could easily relate Juran's teaching to their own work situation and find useful ideas for development. Juran did not need to use any conspicuous means for catching the interest of the audience. He just sat next to the overhead projector for the whole session talking and writing on a roll of transparent film, occasionally supplementing it by showing a transparency. Juran was a firm believer that the attendees should have good documentation at hand. This documentation should also serve as a useful reference after returning from the training. In the longer programs, the *Quality Control Handbook* and *Managerial Breakthrough* (Juran's pioneering book on quality improvement) were always included in the documentation.

Juran had a wish that my partner, Dr. Olle Björklund, and I do some of the lecturing in his course. He prepared us for this for some of the topics. It was not an easy task for us, however, since the course contents were very much based on Juran's own practical experience, and the audiences wanted to listen to Juran.

JURAN IN EUROPE ON VISITS

Juran made many trips to Europe, often attending the annual quality conferences organized by the European Organization for Quality Control, (EOQC), later called the European Organization for Quality (EOQ). At many of these conferences he gave highly appreciated contributions as keynote speaker, many of which turned out to be pioneering. Besides lecturing in Sweden, Juran conducted courses and seminars in other European countries, visiting France, Holland, and Great Britain for that purpose.

JURAN AND DEVELOPING COUNTRIES

Early in my carrier as consultant, I got interested in the quality situation of industrial companies in developing countries. In order to get support for my idea of offering training in quality for these countries, I approached the United Nations Industrial Development Organization (UNIDO), as well as the Swedish governmental agency providing aid to developing countries. The response from the two organizations was positive, which resulted in financial support being granted. This was the starting point for many training programs conducted for managers and engineers in developing countries. The programs ranged from one-day top management seminars to 10-week courses for quality managers. Over the years, more than 10,000 people from about 100 countries attended these programs.

When I informed Juran about my plans for these training efforts, he got very interested and offered to come to Stockholm free of charge to meet and have discussions with the first group of young quality practitioners who came from different countries in Africa, Asia, the Caribbean and South America. Juran enjoyed these discussions very much, which meant that he returned to present future courses.

The national organizations for standardization started to play an important role in the development of quality in developing countries. However, Juran had some doubts about the role of national standardization in the context of quality control in companies. After having presented the phases of industrial development, from subsistence economy to production of sophisticated products for the international market, Juran got, as he stated it, a "flash of illumination" from a young gentleman from the Jamaican Bureau of Standardization. In a graphical way, this gentleman started to discuss the changing role of the standards organizations in the different phases of development. In the following discussion, the chart was refined further. The discussion led to a pioneering article about standardization and quality.[3]

Based on my own experience, I found Juran's writings very useful to practitioners. For this reason, I included Juran's *Quality Control Handbook*, as well as the book, *Quality Planning and Analysis*, by Juran and Frank M. Gryna, in the literature of the international training programs. In this way, Juran's ideas were disseminated in developing countries.

JURAN'S IMPACT ON THE QUALITY MOVEMENT IN JAPAN

Juran was impressed by the Japanese development in quality. The training programs conducted by him in the 1950s were attended by executives, who, according to Juran, started a "quality revolution." This revolution and its impact on companies in the West were dealt with in a paper presented by Juran at the European conference held in Paris in 1981.[4]

A question Juran was frequently asked at the training sessions in Sweden dealt with his importance to the Japanese development in quality. Juran's response was, "I have not been the important factor, nor has Deming. The most important factor was the Japanese executives. They listened to us and acted accordingly. We have lectured for many American executives, but they didn't do anything." This very modest comment from Juran has to be placed in contrast to the self-centered views given by Dr. W. Edwards Deming in NBC's feature "If Japan Can, Why Can't We?" in 1980. The feature got a lot of attention among American business leaders facing very severe competition from the Japanese. They saw in Deming the solution to their problems.

NBC's feature created the myth that Deming was the one the Japanese had to be grateful to for their astonishing achievements in quality. This myth became widely established. Robert E. Cole describes in plain terms the background of this myth.[5] Deming's training conducted in Japan was limited to statistical quality control and this training was given very early in the 1950s. After that, Deming never come back to Japan to conduct training courses.

A contributing factor to the development of the myth about Deming is that JUSE in 1950 created two national quality prizes (one for companies, one for individuals) named after him; the funding of the prizes was based on Deming's payment. The Deming prizes later became well known, and in this way, Deming became a name. In 1966, JUSE created a new quality prize to be given to companies that had won the Deming Prize for the second time. They wanted to name it the Juran Prize. Because of miscommunication between the Japanese and Juran, this name did not come through.[6]

The late Junji Noguchi, once executive director of JUSE, is quoted in an article in *Business Week*: "Juran was more important to Japan than Deming," and, "Juran applied quality to everybody, from managers to clerical staff."[7]

JURAN'S CONTRIBUTION TO THE SCIENCE OF QUALITY

In his long life devoted to quality, Juran's influence on the progress of quality has been immense. His clear thinking, analytical talent, and eminent way of communicating (orally, as well as in writing) help to explain his great influence on the existing body of knowledge in the field of quality science. Here are some major contributions.

Meaning of Quality

The meaning of quality has changed, and this has influenced the development of the quality profession. Juran broadened the definition of quality from conformance to specification to "fitness for use."[8] He also considered two aspects of product quality. One is "freedom from deficiencies" and the other is "product features."[9] Quality improvement was earlier primarily focused on reducing deficiencies but has developed to include even adding product features that meet the needs of the customers in a wider way. This has become more and more important. Later Juran added a new quality dimension when he introduced the concept of "Big Q" to distinguish from the concept of "Little Q."[10] The meaning that Juran gave "Big Q" was much more than product quality (meaning "Little Q"). In addition to product quality, "Big Q" also included quality of services such as accounting, invoicing, communication, and so on. The concept of "Big Q" contributed essentially to the concept of total quality management.

The Spiral of Progress in Quality

Early on, Juran moved quality thinking from inspection and testing to all functions affecting product quality. This he did by introducing "The Spiral of Progress in Quality."[11] The Spiral shows all specialized departments that contribute to product quality. For me, when I had just started my career in quality, the Spiral was an important eye-opener.

The Pareto Principle

Early in his consulting work, Juran found that a few factors contributed more than all other factors.[12] He discussed this as "the vital few and the trivial many." Having been exposed to the work of Vilfredo Pareto, an Italian engineer and economist, at a visit in 1941 to General Motors Headquarters,[13] Juran named this state the Pareto Principle. Juran found later that he had credited the Pareto Principle to the wrong man.[14] When Juran later found that "the trivial many" also had to be dealt with in improvement work, he renamed them to "the useful many." He then started to talk about "the vital few and the useful many."

Breakthrough and Control

In his book, *Managerial Breakthrough*,[15] Juran introduced as a complement to the concept of control the concept of breakthrough. Breakthrough was a means by which a decisive movement to a new, higher level of performance was achieved. Control is to "keep the status quo," while breakthrough is to "change the status quo." Related to improvement work, control is to deal with sporadic problems, breakthrough to deal with chronic problems.[16] Juran developed a distinct sequence of events for dealing with chronic problems project by project.

The Juran Trilogy

Juran later added another dimension to control and breakthrough: planning. According to him, there are three processes in quality management: quality planning, quality control, and quality improvement (which means breakthrough). He named this concept the Juran Trilogy.[17]

Poor Quality Costs

Already in the first edition of his *Handbook,* published in 1951, Juran has a comprehensive discussion on what much later became known as costs of poor quality.[18] The great importance that Juran gives this subject is reflected by it being the first chapter of the book. The title of the chapter is "The Economics of Quality," which shows that the contents go beyond merely cost aspects. Juran uses the term avoidable costs or "gold in the mine" for the costs of poor quality. In the training material, *Management of Quality Control*, Juran refers also to the "hidden plant" when discussing costs of poor quality: "Every plant has a hidden plant, producing waste goods."[19]

Controllability

There has been a tendency for managers to blame operators for defects. Juran clarified responsibility by making a distinction between management-controllable and operator-controllable defects.[20] According to his experience, about 20 percent of all errors are operator-controllable. Far more are then management-controllable. The Zero Defects movement in the 1960s was based on blaming the operators. Juran gave a critical and clear analysis of this trendy movement.[21]

Video-Based Training

Around 1980, when more and more top managers realized that Japanese competition was forcing them to do something to improve quality, I remember Juran saying that he got so many requests for lecturing that he was unable to cope with them. The solution Juran found was to "lecture by electronic means." His course, Management of Quality, became a test site for the first videotape. Juran received useful feedback from the course participants. The product was improved, and Juran then launched his video program, *Juran on Quality Improvement*. This became a success, used, for instance, by Motorola in its improvement work, later called Six Sigma. Electrolux translated the program into Swedish, and it contributed considerably to the success of the company's extensive improvement program carried out from 1981 to 1984. Two other video-based training programs were developed: *Juran on Planning for Quality* and *Juran on Quality Leadership*.

History of Managing for Quality

A project Juran gave high priority to after having stopped travelling early in the 1990s was to publish a book on the history of managing for quality. This project was completed with the publication of the book *A History of Managing for Quality in 1995*.[22] The book includes a series of chapters describing how quality was managed under different circumstances (time spans, geographical areas, products, and political systems). Several authors have contributed under the editorship of Juran. In the final chapter of this unique presentation on the history of quality management, Juran gives a summary, trends, and prognosis.

Juran's Quality Handbook

In 1951, Juran published the first edition of his handbook, titled *Quality Control Handbook*. Four editions have followed, with Juran being the editor-in-chief. The latest, published in 1999 and also with A. Blanton Godfrey as editor-in-chief, has the title *Juran's Quality Handbook*.[23] The different editions of the handbook include contributions from many specialists. It was with great pride that I accepted Juran's request for my contribution in the three latest editions. I am sure that the other contributing authors felt the same way. The handbook has become the international reference book on quality and as such has served as a useful source of inspiration for thousands of quality practitioners all around the world.

Six Sigma

Many companies have considerably improved their profitability by means of Six Sigma, which originated at Motorola. Due to the tough competition from Japanese manufacturers, the head of the company, Robert W. Galvin launched an extensive improvement program early in the 1980s. Juran was called in to assist in the improvement work. He gave three important pieces of advice: (1) work on chronic problems; (2) institute project oriented improvement work; and (3) organize a steering arm (management's leadership of the improvement work) and a diagnostic arm (which meant setting up project teams). Together with his colleague Frank M. Gryna, Juran gave training to management on how to perform effective improvement work. The project teams were trained by means of the video-based training program, *Juran on Quality Improvement*. Motorola later gave the name Six Sigma to the improvement program. Without the support from Juran, Motorola would probably not have been so successful with its Six Sigma program.

Dr. Joseph M. Juran
and the Quality Revolution
in Japan

by Yoshio Kondo

Japanese industries were almost completely destroyed during World War II. Prior to the war, Japanese research and the application of modern quality control were limited, and Japanese product quality was poor relative to international levels. Although these products of poor quality were sold at ridiculously low prices, it was difficult to secure repeat sales.

At the end of the war, the former Japanese military and political leaders were no longer in power, having been replaced in large part by relatively young industrialists who wanted Japan to advance as an industrialized country and not to fall back into the old agricultural economy of the type prevalent in some parts of old Asia. After this decision was made, they faced a difficult road. Poor product quality was a principle obstacle; as mentioned above, no one wanted to repeatedly buy such low-quality goods. For a country so lacking in raw materials as Japan, the inability to sell finished goods for export also meant an inability to earn foreign exchange and hence an inability to buy the materials needed to create an upward spiral of industrial development. Thus, a revolution in product quality became essential for Japanese industries (Juran 1981).

This quality revolution has been taking place in Japan since the early 1950s as the result of efforts to apply the concept and techniques of statistical quality control on a companywide scale. It may be said that the Japanese cultural environment is rather favorable to the adoption and development of modern quality control. This can be summarized as follows.

1. The adaptability of Japanese people to foreign culture is fairly high.

2. Japan's population density is virtually the highest in the world, and the competition among companies has been intense in both domestic and international markets.

3. Japanese society is rather homogeneous, with the same race and language, and the mobility of workers among companies is relatively low as compared with the United States. In these

circumstances, Japanese companies are very enthusiastic about the education and training of employees.

4. The labor market in Japanese industries became increasingly tight in the late 1960s and early 1970s. Rising educational levels in Japan led to an increasing proportion of new labor force entrants who were unwilling to accept the least demanding jobs. Instead, the workers wanted jobs that would allow them to develop their abilities and talents. The introduction of modern quality control and the creation of participative work structures appeared to management to be one reasonable strategy (Cole and Walder 1981).

5. The kind of professionalism prevalent in the western countries has not yet been fully established in Japan. Japanese companies needed to promote "companywide quality control," in which all employees participate, rather than providing a large, central quality department with numerous centralized functions of quality planning, coordination, and auditing (Juran 1978).

JUSE was founded in 1946, and its activities gradually became focused on collecting and investigating information relating to modern QC activities. In 1949, the QC Research Group, composed of people from industry, academic institutions, and government, was formed within JUSE. The same year, the Basic QC Course lasting six months was inaugurated with the aim of reporting the QC Research Group's findings back to industry.

Japanese industry thus introduced the concepts and techniques of modern QC eagerly. This occurred not only because statistical methods were very suited to the Japanese, who love novelty, but also because they succeeded in improving quality, driving down costs, raising productivity, and shortening lead time by reducing defects and rework. In this way, QC made a major contribution to recovery and reconstruction of Japanese industry, which had been virtually annihilated during the war.

Two famous Americans, W. Edwards Deming and Joseph M. Juran, visited Japan since 1950 and 1954, respectively, at the JUSE's invitation to give some short-term QC courses for engineers and for top managers. Deming's lectures were also greatly helpful for the course participants to understand the importance of statistical concepts and methods in the manufacturing industry. They were also extremely useful for preparing for Juran's courses, which were started a few years later.

In 1954, JUSE invited Juran to hold QC courses for top and middle managers. These courses had an immeasurably large impact on Japanese

QC in the sense that they extended the QC philosophy (which had previously tended to be restricted to the narrower fields of production and inspection) to almost every area of corporate activities and clearly positioned QC as a management tool. (Juran advised JUSE to use the term of companywide quality control (CWQC) in order to distinguish this activity from total quality control, or TQC, proposed by Feigenbaum.) Taking its lead from these courses, JUSE initiated the Middle-Management QC Course in 1955 and the Special QC Course for Executives in 1957. These courses are improved and are still held today.

Two examples of Deming Application Prize winning companies are Teijin (a synthetic fiber manufacturer), which won the prize in 1961, and Sumitomo Electric Industries, a prize-winning company in 1962. At these two companies, QC activities were broadly defined to include suppliers' activities as well as in-company activities such as market research, design, purchasing, production, inspection, sales, and administration. The top management internal assessment in the form of "hoshin kanri" (policy management) is one of the most important companywide activities. The CWQC campaigns conducted by these companies produced revolutionary results, and the successes posted by these two companies stimulated QC campaigns being conducted by many other Japanese enterprises. They also acted as an extremely powerful incentive for other organizations, including American, Indian, and Thai companies that won the Deming Application Prize to broaden their definition of QC activities and extend their QC activities to every link in the production chain.

The First International Conference on Quality Control (ICQC) was held in 1969 in Tokyo. At this conference Juran delivered the following message:

> *It is the Japanese who have demonstrated to the world that determined people can revolutionize their quality performance, even out of ashes of war, and can do so within the life span of a single generation. The Japanese are to be congratulated on having created their first worldwide QC Conference. By any measures, it reaches a new level of QC attainment. Never before has so distinguished an assemblage of QC experts been drawn from so many national origins to discuss so vitally a range of QC subject matters. Those of us who have the good fortune to attend this historic conference are most grateful to our Japanese hosts. ICQC '69 is a monument to their vision and courage in undertaking so bold a concept, and to their competence and dedication in bringing this concept to fruition (Chapman 1969).*

Later, in 1981, Juran summarized the following three features of quality control activities in Japanese industries that created the revolution in quality:

1. A massive, quality-related education and training program

2. Annual programs of quality improvement

3. Upper management leadership of the quality function

Juran visited Japan many times and conducted various kinds of QC seminars and discussions. After the seminar in Tokyo in October, 1974, I was given the opportunity to enjoy one day of sightseeing with him in Kyoto. One of the spots was Ryoan-ji temple of which the garden is so simple: it consists of only white sand and a few rocks. It is called the "stone garden." Juran sat on the corridor of the temple in silence for about twenty minutes, just watching the garden. He said, "This is a good place for meditation." I understand that he is a distinguished philosopher.

ENDNOTES

1. Juran, J. M. 1967. The QC Circle phenomenon. *Industrial Quality Control* (January): 329–336.
2. Juran, J. M. 2004. *Architect of quality*. New York: McGraw-Hill: 309.
3. Juran, J. M. 1975. Standardization and quality. *Quality Progress* (February): 4–5.
4. Juran, J. M. 1981. Product quality: A prescription for the West. 25th EOQC Conference, Paris.
5. Cole, R. E. 1999. *Managing Quality Fads*. Oxford: Oxford University Press: 72–74.
6. Juran, J. M. 2004. *Architect of quality*. New York: McGraw-Hill: 292, 293.
7. Port, O. 1991. Duelling pioneers. *Business Week* (December 2): 24.
8. Juran, J. M. 1974. *Quality control handbook*, 3rd ed. New York: McGraw-Hill: 2.3, 2.4.
9. Juran, J. M. 1988. *Juran's quality control handbook*, 4th ed. New York: McGraw-Hill: 2-2 and 2-3.
10. Juran, J. M. 1989. *Juran on leadership for quality*. New York: The Free Press: 47, 48.
11. Juran, J. M. 1974. *Quality control handbook*, 3rd ed. New York: McGraw-Hill: 2–10.
12. Juran, J. M. 1951. *Quality control handbook*, New York: McGraw-Hill: 37–41.
13. Juran, J. M. 2004. *Architect of quality*. New York: McGraw-Hill: 157–158.

14. Juran, J. M. 1975. The Non-Pareto principle—Mea culpa. *Quality Progress* (May): 8, 9.

15. Juran, J. M. 1964. *Managerial breakthrough.* New York: McGraw-Hill.

16. Juran, J. M. 1962. *Quality control handbook.* 2nd ed. New York: McGraw-Hill: 1-35, 1-36.

17. Juran, J. M. 1986. The quality trilogy—A universal approach to managing for quality. *Quality Progress* (August):19–24.

18. Juran, J. M. 1951. *Quality control handbook.* New York: McGraw-Hill: 34–41.

19. Juran, J. M. 1971. "Management of quality control," training materials. Wilton CT.: Juran Institute: 165n.

20. Juran, J. M. 1968 Operator errors—Time for a new look, *Quality Progress* (February): 9–10, 54.

21. Juran, J. M. 1966. Quality problems, remedies and nostrums, *Industrial Quality Control* (June): 647–653.

22. Juran, J. M. 1995. *A history of managing for quality.* Milwaukee: Quality Press.

23. Juran, J. M., A. B. Godfrey. 1999. *Juran's quality handbook.* 5th ed., New York: McGraw-Hill.

REFERENCES

Chapman, M. K. 1969. The world prosperity through quality. *Quality Assurance* (December): 28–31.

Cole R. E., and A.G. Walder. 1981. Structural diffusion: The policies of participative work structures in China, Japan, Sweden, and the United States. CRSO working paper no. 226, University of Michigan, February.

Juran, J. M. 1978. Japanese and Western quality—A contrast. *Quality Progress* (December): 10–18.

——— 1981. Product quality—A prescription for the West. Proceedings of the 25th Conference EOQC. Paris.

——— 1992. A look back: 10 years of IMPRO. Proceedings of IMPRO92, Chicago. November 11–13.

Section II

Selected Works of Dr. Joseph M. Juran

Dr. Joseph M. Juran

6

The Two Worlds of Quality Control

INTRODUCTION

For some years now, the world of industry has exhibited a division of thought and action respecting the performance of the quality function. This division has resulted in the existence of two worlds of "quality control":

1. The world of the top management of industrial companies

2. The world of the quality control specialists

The cleavage between these two worlds has given rise to troubles for both. Top management is faced with some very important quality problems for which present solutions are inadequate. At the same time, quality control specialists are groping for a more distinguished role in the company and in society. Neither group is satisfied with the present situation.

It is the purpose of this article to examine the causes of this cleavage and to propose a program for action.

THE QUALITY FUNCTION

We commence with the viewpoint of society and of the heads of the institutions of society—the company presidents, the government administrators, and so on. The views here are unanimous. Quality of product or service must meet business, defense, and other social purposes, and it is someone's job to see that these social purposes are identified and met.

Editor's Note: The paper appearing here in Chapter 6 was published in 1964 in *Industrial Quality Control* (November) 21(5): 238–9.

In the language of the industrial leader, *quality is primarily a business problem, not a technical problem*. The survival of the industrial company depends on its ability to meet the quality needs of society. (The company can perish for a variety of reasons, but it cannot possibly survive without meeting the quality needs of society.)

In broad terms, the quality function is the collection of activities through which we discover and meet the quality needs of society. Applied to an industrial company, the definition narrows; the quality function becomes the means through which the company discovers and meets the quality needs of its customers.

"Quality function" is thus a shorthand label for a collection of activities. The specific activities within this collection likewise have names: market research, product development, product design, process development, production, inspection, sale, usage, and so on. Each of these activities includes a subactivity devoted to quality, that is, market research includes (among other things) the discovery of the quality needs of customers.

We will shortly examine, in more detail, the nature of the list of quality activities or specialties which, collectively, make up the quality function. But let us notice in passing that a major difference between the "two worlds" is that: top management is primarily concerned with performance of the quality *function*, the specialists are primarily concerned with the *specialties* within the quality function.

MANAGERIAL AND TECHNICAL QUALITY ACTIVITIES

We can simplify matters greatly by distinguishing at the outset between two very different kinds of quality activity:

1. The broad planning and controlling of quality. Here we are dealing mainly with the business, economic, and, especially, the management activities associated with quality:

   - Setting quality policy

   - Establishing quality objectives

   - Developing plans to meet the quality objectives

   - Defining responsibilities as to quality

- Selecting, training, and motivating the human beings to carry out their responsibilities respecting quality

- Measuring results achieved against the quality objectives

- Taking action when results fall short of quality objectives

2. The execution of the broad quality plan. Here we are dealing mainly with the *technical* activities associated with quality:

  - Designing the quality aspects of materials and products

  - Preparing quality specifications

  - Developing the quality aspects of processes

  - Designing measuring instruments and test procedures

  - Building the quality capability aspects of machines and processes

  - Fabricating the quality aspects of the product itself

  - Inspecting and testing the product for its quality characteristics

  - Marketing the qualities of the product

  - Determining the quality performance of the product during use

  - And (to go through a full turn of the upward spiral) redesigning the quality aspects of materials and products

The technical activities associated with quality are timeless. All species of life carry on some forms of these technical activities.[1] However, the managerial activities associated with quality are unique to man.

ORIGIN OF THE MODERN QUALITY FUNCTION

Today the activities that constitute the quality function are dispersed over numerous departments in a company, numerous departments in its vendor companies, numerous links in the distribution chain, and numerous consumers. This wide dispersion is the source of so much difficulty that it becomes informative to look back to see how the quality function was handled in earlier centuries before such wide dispersion set in.

In earlier centuries, goods and services were provided largely by men acting as individuals (hunters, farmers, weavers, smiths), by men working together in small teams (families, shops). The individual craftsman carried out both the managerial and technical quality activities, but with unequal effectiveness: his conduct of the managerial activities (of planning and controlling of quality) was superb. As a one-man enterprise he learned of the customers' needs, planned to meet them, and took the brunt of the feedback from the customers. He, was party to all transactions, to all happenings. Above all, he was naturally gifted with the marvelous self-coordination provided by the human nervous system. His conduct of the technical activities (of executing quality plans) was generally poor, because of the low state of technology and because of his own limited knowledge of such technology as was then possessed by human beings.

On a long leg of good management and a short leg of poor technology, our village craftsman carried on. In doing so, he was performing, in microcosm, the entire quality function.

At a later time the quality function was carried out by early team efforts. Through such team efforts, construction projects were undertaken, requiring a grand design and a conformity to that design. Other collective forms (stores, shops, and so on.) emerged to provide services and manufactured products.

These collective endeavors, no less than those of individuals, had quality problems. They required the managerial activities of quality planning and control, and they required the technical activities of execution. But now this quality function was no longer neatly housed within one marvelous human organism. Instead, the quality function was now dispersed over a number of human beings. Such dispersion required a new invention—a means of unifying the efforts of these human beings.

This invention took the form of a plan of division of work. The master (owner, boss, overseer, and so on.) reserved to himself the role of setting the key standards, sensing the key happenings, analyzing and interpreting the key results, deciding what should be done, and stimulating action. The subordinates were left with a role of executing the decisions of the master, plus performing such sensing analyzing and so on., as the master had not reserved to himself.[2]

Despite the division of work, the master was able to remain in full command. He was able to do so because of two favorable circumstances:

1. The enterprise was small. It employed few people, processed a modest amount of product, and sold it to a limited number of customers.

2. The master was physically present where he could see and hear all that transpired in this small enterprise. He had the authority of

command. And he could still make use of his natural gift of the human nervous system to achieve self-coordination.

Actually, the one-man shop and the master of the small shop enjoyed still another favorable circumstance—"company" performance and personal interests were identical. As we shall see, retaining this identity becomes increasingly difficult as the quality function is dispersed over many men.

EFFECT OF THE INDUSTRIAL REVOLUTION

This explosion (by whose forces we are still being blown about) had an enormous impact on the importance of the quality function, and on the technical and managerial activities through which this function is performed.

As the benefits of technology became widespread, men began to reorganize human affairs around these benefits. One result has been to make society increasingly dependent on the successful performance of the quality function. An electrical circuit breaker is defective, and the resulting power failure paralyzes a community. A short-lived product is marketed under a five-year guarantee, and the company loses millions. A highly publicized missile fails to launch, and a nation is humiliated. A monstrous defect in a drug escapes detection, and thousands of infants are doomed to tragic lives. No longer is the industrial company alone vulnerable to quality failures; the well-being of society itself is increasingly bound up with proper quality performance. Small wonder that today we see the heads of great governments discussing publicly the need for improving quality performance, not only of weapon systems, but of goods and services.

The Industrial Revolution also spurred another growth. Industrial companies grew to great, even huge proportions. These companies were faced with carrying out the technical and managerial activities of a quality function that was becoming increasingly important and critical. The companies' response on the technical side was masterly; on the managerial side, it was chaotic.

The companies met the technical challenge by creating technical specialists. These specialists, with tools, instruments and increasing expertness over narrowing specialties, have greatly outperformed the craftsman and the master as to technology. The technical quality activities of today make the work of our predecessors seem primitive.

How the companies met the managerial challenge is quite a different tale. Because of specialization and indeed just sheer growth, no longer was the entire collection of quality activities housed in close proximity, under the watchful eye of one master. Instead, the quality activities were widely dispersed among various divisions, departments, and subdepartments. In addition to wide organizational dispersion, there was wide physical dispersion. Any idea that the company president, the industrial descendant of the master, could personally plan and control such widely dispersed quality activities became simply fantastic. The needs for the managerial quality activities now had to be met in some other way.

At the risk of over-simplification, Table 6.1 depicts how the technical and the managerial activities of the quality function have been carried out to date. The question mark in Table 6.1 is still with us, and is, in my experience and judgment, the overshadowing unsolved quality problem of all industrialized nations.

EVOLUTION OF THE MANAGERIAL QUALITY ACTIVITIES

We can only speculate on the details of the confusion that resulted when the growth of industrial companies forced a widespread loosening of the masters' firm grip on the managerial quality activities. But in broad terms, the results are clear:

- Departmental quality goals and controls replaced company quality planning and controlling interdepartmental coordination became generally lax and fortuitous

- Failures (resulting from inadequate quality planning and controls) led to mutual recriminations and to local defensive measures

A major consequence of all this was that the focal point of internal quality activities shifted from the company's broad quality objective of meeting the quality needs of its customers to the much narrower objective of meeting the quality specification. We have since become increasingly

Table 6.1 Evolution of responsibilities in the quality function.

Type of enterprise	Performance of technical quality activities is by	Performance of managerial quality activities is by
One craftsman	The craftsman	The craftsman
The small shop	The workmen	The master
The large company	The specialized department	?

aware that these two objectives can differ remarkably. However, our predecessors were often forced in desperation to focus on the specification when
the real focal center became too elusive to grasp.

A defensive measure of great significance was the stationing of full-
time inspectors in strategic departments to watch the movement of product
and to separate the good from the bad, meaning the conforming from the
nonconforming. The activity of "inspection" was a technical activity of
observing, measuring, and testing. (The idea of using inspection as an
important aid to managerial quality control came later.) But the appointment of inspectors became the first step along a long road which may lead
to reestablishment of adequate managerial activities for planning and controlling quality.

The building of defenses through inspection resulted in the appointment of large numbers of full-time inspectors. Now, for the first time in the
history of manufacture, there were large numbers of men whose principal,
even fulltime activities, were bound up with quality of goods (or services).
A new industrial species had evolved. Up to that time, such men had been
found only on construction projects, and then in small numbers.

A rule of life is that like seeks out like, for mutual benefit. The inspectors were no exception. Through evolution and revolution, the inspection
department emerged as a separate, central organization unit of the company.
This was again a first—an important department devoted full time to quality.

A study of industrial history discloses that the main reason for the formation of these centralized inspection departments was technical in nature.
There was a pressing need to safeguard the integrity of measurement, of
test, and of decisions on acceptance. The scattered inspectors were being
rather trampled on by production supervisors. Under a chief inspector,
much of this could be eliminated.

The idea that the inspection department might, in time, become a base
for managing the entire quality function was not much in evidence. In any
event, such an idea was, in the early 20th century, largely academic. The
main problem of the new chief inspectors was how to perform their narrow
role of making and enforcing their decisions on conformance to specification. Their infant departments had been born in a climate that was nothing
short of hostile. They faced severe obstacles in recruiting qualified men, in
training them, in providing them with space and facilities, in establishing a
status for them. These were problems of sheer survival. There was no time
for grand strategy.

By the early 1940s, the concept of a central inspection department was
no longer in danger. Meanwhile, some inspection departments had in fact
pushed salients into other quality activities—defect prevention, standardization, complaint analysis. In some companies efforts to unify quality

activities took the form of committees: new product committees, quality committees, and so on. In isolated instances, full systems of quality planning and control were designed and effected. But these were the exceptions. The general progress was still at a pedestrian pace.

Suddenly there was no more time. The slow evolution was shattered by the intrusion of swift-moving events—the statistical quality control movement; the reliability movement; the creation of the American Society for Quality Control; the general movement by companies to raise the stature of the quality function. One result of all this ferment is that quality managers have been presented with an unprecedented opportunity to create, in their companies, a broad conceptual approach for unifying the quality function.

Our mission, in the remainder of this article, is to examine how quality managers might make the most of this opportunity. To detach ourselves from our own reflexes, it is well first to look sideways at how some other function has achieved unity.

THE FINANCE FUNCTION: A CASE HISTORY

The finance function is a good case in point. The function is as old as commerce. The ancient traders, high priests, kings, and others all faced the problems of balancing income with outgo. The finance function, with its tools of accounting, credit, insurance, and so on, was the means by which this balance was struck.

As enterprises grew very large, the problems of balancing income with outgo proliferated remarkably. Numerous departments received "income" in money, in goods, in machines, in services, in promises to pay. All departments participated in "outgo," again in a variety of forms. Yet the very life of the enterprise depended on maintaining a balance between income and outgo.

The solution of the managers was to develop a conceptual approach under which there would be brought together a unified portrayal of financial activity for the whole company. Under this conceptual approach:

1. All income, no matter where collected, would be identified and evaluated.

2. All outgo, no matter where spent, would be identified and evaluated.

3. For the main financial activities, there would be established:

   • Standards of performance

- Measures of actual performance

- Review of actual versus standard

The financial specialists have in fact executed such a concept. They have invented a common language through which all matters, money, goods, time and even intangibles are evaluated in money. They have promulgated the use of this common language in all departments of the company. They have invented the necessary techniques for summarizing assets and liabilities, incomes and expenses, profits and losses, and still other compilations. They have invented tools such as budgets and standard costs for establishing standards of performance. They have invented techniques such as depreciation and accruals to facilitate the manipulation of the more complex variables.

Clearly all this activity has required much technique that is special, if not unique, to the finance function. The financial specialists have supplied this technique. But this is not all. The finance specialists have also provided the managerial coordination of all financial activity within the company. This coordination must be understood fully.

Consider the annual budget. It is a plan under which all company departments anticipate and list the deeds they expect to perform for the year ahead. These are "priced out" and summarized by the finance specialists. The summaries are reviewed, modified, and approved by the upper management. The approved budget not only becomes the official operating and financial plan for the year ahead, it provides financial standards for all departments as well as for the company as a whole.

It is seen that the financial specialists have made contributions to all this in two major ways:

1. The managerial activities of:

   - Setting financial policy and objectives

   - Financial planning and defining responsibilities

   - Selecting, training and motivating people

   - Measuring financial results

   - Acting on deficiencies

2. The technical activities of inventing a common language:

   - Invention of tools (chart of accounts, burden centers, depreciation formulas, accrual methods, and so on)

   - Design of specific systems, and so on

NEEDS FOR UNIFYING THE QUALITY FUNCTION

We return now to the quality function. As we do, we observe some remarkable parallels to the financial function: the quality function is vital—the company can live only so long as the quality of its product or service is acceptable to its clientele.

The quality function is all-pervasive; every department in the company influences the company's quality performance, and optimizing the company's efforts in the quality function requires a conceptual approach somewhat as follows:

1. All effort for achieving quality, no matter where expended, should be identified and evaluated.

2. All benefits through achieving quality, no matter where collected, should be identified and evaluated.

3. For the main quality activities, no matter where conducted— in the various company departments, at the vendors' plants, at the customers' points of use—there should be established:

    - Standards of performance (objectives, targets, goals)

    - Measures of actual performance

    - Review of actual performance versus standard

Execution of such a concept requires:

1. The managerial activities of:

    - Setting quality policy and establishing quality objectives

    - Quality planning

    - Defining quality responsibilities

    - Selecting, training, and motivating people

    - Measuring quality results

    - Acting on quality deficiencies

2. The technical activities of:

    - Inventing a common language

- Inventing tools (process capability, sampling, control charts, design of experiments, analysis of variance, and so on)
- Design of specific systems, and so on

NO NEED FOR COMMAND

It is also essential to note that unifying the company's quality activities does not require that one man be given command over all such activities.

The finance officer does, through his role as coordinator, contribute much to coordinating the company's financial activities. But the finance officer does not command the various operating departments. They make the operating decisions of what to spend and what not to spend. In like manner, a quality manager can coordinate the quality function without commanding the product designers, the manufacturing planners, the purchasing agents, the sales servicemen, and so on.

This point—that unification can be achieved without command—has been missed in many companies. In part it has been missed because of human drives for power. But in part it is the result of failure to consider the process by which unification is carried out. This process consists of:

1. A plan for unification

2. Execution of the plan

3. Audit to see that the plan is carried out

The question of command becomes controversial only with point 2. If execution can be left to the operating departments, the problems of command largely disappear. This can generally be accomplished as in Table 6.2.

The approach shown in Table 6.2 is precisely the means used by the finance officer in achieving coordination without command. The same approach is available to the quality manager.

Table 6.2 Unification through separation of planning, execution, and audit.

Activity	Operating departments	Coordinating department
Design of the plan for coordination	X	X
Execution of the plan	X	
Audit to see that execution is carried out per plant	X	

HOW ARE WE DOING NOW ON THE TECHNICAL QUALITY ACTIVITIES?

We are doing rather well. The proliferation of tools and techniques is all about us. We see the evidence in the companies, in the conventions, in the journals. Our engineers and specialists are responding handsomely, to the point of overflow.

If anything, one might conclude that preoccupation with technique has diverted attention from the managerial needs. Certainly there has been much terrier-like burrowing into unproductive channels. In our finance analogy, the cost accountants who go into great detail in measuring tiny costs while the company executives do without the balance sheet, the profit statement, and other essentials of managerial control would be paralleled by the excesses of the quality enthusiasts who pour out myriads of uneconomic control charts.

Undue preoccupation with technique is itself a problem in management. Moreover, the need in management is not merely the negative need to moderate the enthusiasts and fanatics. Even more important is the positive need to do the full managerial job.

HOW ARE WE DOING ON THE MANAGERIAL QUALITY ACTIVITIES?

We are doing rather badly. At this writing, few companies have grasped the concept of a quality function as well as they have grasped the concept of other functions.[3] Moreover, few quality managers have grasped the concept clearly. However, there has been a trend among the quality managers toward rebuilding their staff specialties to repair the damage done by the overemphasis on statistical methods and broadening the base of technique to include other technical tools and managerial tools

This rebuilding and broadening is bringing the quality manager into greater participation in customer relations, new product development, vendor relations, and still other matters. In some industries, for example, military and space systems, these changes have been dramatic.

From the managerial view, one of the more significant of the recent "movements" is that of "reliability." This managerial significance is not due to the mathematical techniques associated with reliability. The significance lies in the realization, by the leaders of the movement, that the interdepartmental effort needed to plan and achieve product reliability should not be put on the conventional basis of every department for itself.

The parallel to financial management are again illuminating. There is a reliability prediction (equivalent to the sales forecast). Reliability goals or objectives are established, and subobjectives set for various components and departments. (This is analogous to the financial budget pyramid.) Measures are set up to determine actual reliability against target, and so on. All this is managerial planning and control applied to an important segment of the company's quality mission.

THE ROLE TO BE PLAYED

What we lack is a unified approach to the broad planning and controlling of quality. More specifically, we lack a unified approach to:

Forming *quality policy*. Shall we go for quality leadership, or for a respectable grade, or for what can get by? Shall we use precision, reliability, and other quality features as a major element in our grand business strategy? Shall we go for building a well-known image around our quality performance? Only as we crystallize our views on such matters can we establish objectives and plans to make these dreams come true.

Establishing broad *quality objectives*. Objectives are specific, attainable goals, such as extending our product guarantee to five years; reducing our guarantee charges by 50 percent; cutting our scrap and rework losses by 25 percent; converting our situation of unrealistic tolerances, loosely enforced, to a situation of unrealistic tolerances, rigidly enforced; putting our vendor relations on a surveillance basis; and launching our new designs with confidence that they can be executed, sold, and used successfully. Lacking clear objectives, we lack unity of purpose, and are driven to the confusion of "every man for himself."

Planning to meet these quality objectives. Broad objectives cannot be carried out unless there is wide participation in the planning. Materials, facilities, manpower, the time-table, and still other ingredients can best be provided through such participation. The chaotic evidences of lack of unified planning are all about us, and we are unhappy with the spectacle.

Organizing is that part of planning that is of special importance to managers. It demands clear definition of responsibility for the various quality activities to be performed in the numerous departments, in vendor companies, and in the distribution chain. It requires establishment of positions, lines of command, lines of communication, means for coordination, and the rest. Until we study these responsibilities and relationships, it is utter folly to say, "You do your job and I'll do mine." It is folly because the job is joint.

Only through careful organization study can we establish who is to do what. Even then, there remains a substantial residue of joint activity.

Manning is the selection, training, and motivating the human beings who are to carry out the quality responsibilities. The various department heads are certainly "responsible" for manning of their departments. But much remains to be done in training and motivation on quality matters. Getting this done is commonly beyond the scope of the unaided department head.

Measuring results against objectives. This is the feedback to departmental and upper management. It conveys to all how we are doing on quality. Lacking such broad feedback, we are limited to feedback on a few narrow departmental objectives, and we are readily stampeded by sporadic and minor troubles. Yet all the time, the larger needs are there waiting to be met.

It is evident that, as in the finance function, the missing role is one of broad planning and control, not one of command. These matters of quality policy, quality objectives, quality planning, and so on, are all-pervasive. They affect all departments and top management as well. It becomes nonsense to think that we can solve the problems of unity through some command formula, through changing the solid lines on the organization chart. As we have been in Table 6.2, unity of command of the entire quality function is unnecessary. There are other ways of achieving unity of purpose.

It is also evident that broad quality planning and control collectively add up to a vital role. As we advance further into industrialization, the role must grow in importance. It now seems likely that such a role will bring, to the quality function, a seat in the president's cabinet. This has, in fact, begun to happen.

A ROLE IN SEARCH OF AN ACTOR

In human affairs, important changes do not happen naturally—they happen because determined men decide that they should happen. In this role of unifying the two worlds of quality control, who is to become the leading actor?

In isolated cases, it may be the upper management. Through some fortuitous combination of circumstances, the man at the top recognizes a need and sets the wheels in motion. However, in most companies, this will not happen. To be sure, top management is fully aware that product quality is essential to the life of the business. Moreover, top management understands something that has to date escaped the quality manager:

Quality is a business problem primarily and a technical problem secondarily. But while top management understands these business truths, it is unaware of the nature of the quality function.

Is the quality manager a logical candidate for the role?

I happen to believe that the *position* of quality manager is a natural base on which this role might be built. The position is devoted full time to quality affairs.

Whatever its shortcomings in its present efforts to unify the two worlds of quality control, the quality manager position still comes closer than any other organization unit. Here again we can learn from the finance function. When the time came to choose an actor for the role of unifying the finance function, most companies built on the base of the position of chief accountant. That position had long been full-time devoted to financial affairs. Its members possessed many skills in financial matters. It was a natural base on which to build the role of unifying the finance function.

However, it is also my observation that the great majority of quality managers, as *persons,* are still oriented mainly to technical problems and techniques rather than to business problems and the nature of the quality function. The failure of quality managers to "sell" their wares to top management are commonly the result of efforts to sell techniques, in technical language (variation, sampling, probability, and the rest). The need as seen by top management is for proposals to solve business problems and to state these proposals in the language of top management (marketability, return on investment, organization, and so on.)[4] The lesson of the reliability movement is again in point.

A PROGRAM FOR THE CHIEF EXECUTIVE

When a chief executive puts to me the question, "All right, how do I go about it?," I advise him to create an interdepartmental team and to give the team a charter to:

1. Discover and state the company's needs for broad quality planning and control.

2. Identify and evaluate the company's present means for meeting these needs.

3. Recommend what the company should do about the deficiencies.

I also point out to the chief executive that the team must be provided with the necessary assistance for putting together data, analyses, and proposals. Commonly, the quality manager serves as secretary for such a team, and does much of the data collection and analysis.

A PROGRAM FOR THE QUALITY MANAGER

The foregoing suggests the road to be followed by any quality manager who is motivated to achieve, in his company, a unity of the two worlds of quality control:

1. He should brief himself thoroughly on the nature of the quality function in industry. Unless he understands this, in its broadest implications, he will be unable to supply responsible leadership for the steps that are to follow. His efforts and his proposals may well (to others) seem to be proposals for self-aggrandizement rather than proposals for improving the company's effectiveness.

2. He should enlist the aid of his peers in the various departments to do, informally, the very things that a formal team would do:

   • Discover and state the company's needs for broad quality planning and control.

   • Identify and evaluate the company's present means for meeting these needs.

   • Recommend what the company should do about the deficiencies.

3. He should then make formal proposals on how the company should go about unifying the two worlds of quality control.

Whether these proposals lead to a program of action depends mainly on whether they meet two essential tests:

1. Are they stated as business needs of the company, in the language of upper management?

2. Are they essentially acceptable to the various interested departments (whose collective opinion is a decided factor in upper management's decision)?

A particularly sensitive area is the matter of proposals for change in organization. Normally some changes in organization form will be needed to unify the activities of quality planning and control. It is important to draw these organizational proposals in a way that generates confidence that their primary purpose is to improve company effectiveness rather than to enlarge the scope of some person or department.

In this sensitive area, the quality manager again must brief himself thoroughly. There are many ways to organize for coordination or unification. Interdepartmental coordination can be set up through use of:

- *The common boss.* In very small companies or small divisions of a large company, this may be the logical way. In cases where the common boss was formerly closely associated with the quality function, this form would have added attraction.

- *A standing committee.* This impersonal organization device has much merit as an interim organization form until a more permanent structure suggests itself.

- *An "assistant to."* Coordination may, temporarily, be achieved through a staff assistant who stands in lieu of the common boss.

- *Creation of a new department.* This approach has been used often, whether for broad planning alone (that is, the budget office, and manufacturing engineering), or for both combined planning and control (that is, financial control and production control). Many of the new reliability departments have been of this planning and control combination (as applied to reliability).

- *Broadening the role of an existing department.* This was done, for example, in the personnel function in the years following the explosive growth of industrial unionism.

These organization forms do not exhaust the list. There is also opportunity to invent some new forms. But the list is already broad enough to provide a wide range of choice, enough to meet most situations.

It is well to repeat the admonitions about the needs for the quality manager to:

1. Brief himself thoroughly on the nature of the quality function in industry.

2. Understand the variety of ways in which we can organize to unify a function.

Industry has learned from experience that a technique-oriented specialist is unlikely to solve a management problem. Again, we can look sideways at the finance function.

The proper conduct of accounting requires much technique. The accountant properly regards his job as requiring much special training plus a continuing development of new techniques. In its highest form, accounting qualifies as a profession, as the licenses of Certified Public Accountant will attest.

When top management first recognized the existence of a finance function, they tended to look to the chief accountant to perform the function. However, many of the accountants were technicians and professionals, not managers. It became necessary to create a new office, that of controller, to perform the managerial duties of the finance function. (It was convenient, in addition, to give the controller command over the chief accountant, but it was not really necessary.)

L'ENVOI

This article commenced with the argument that there are two worlds of quality control, that these worlds are not adequately joined, and that they should be.

Few men or companies embark on a new road solely based on logical reasoning. Most of us take new roads only after the venturesome few have tried them and found them good.

Our need is for venturesome men to set out on their own approaches to unify these two worlds in their own company. It is their experiences, their stories of success and failure that become the essential feedback on that the conservative many will then base their unifying action.

ENDNOTES

1. All living things are concerned with quality. Living organisms must decide whether to accept, reject, or modify the qualities of their environment and their internal well-being. Organisms seek or avoid light, reject or accept food, choose activity or hibernation. Such decisions require that the organisms establish standards for various qualities; use sensors for detecting these qualities; employ systems for analyzing and interpreting these sensory data; and stimulate effectors to take action based on the decisions reached through such analysis and interpretation. Man, as one species of living organism, has been no exception to the universal rule of concern with the qualities of his environment and his internal well-being. Mastery over these forces has

required solution of the problems of shelter, food, clothing, hygiene, weapons, transport, communication, and so on. Every single one of these solutions has included quality components.

2. We must note that this division of work was essentially along the cleavage line that divides managerial from technical activities. The master reserved to himself the key managerial responsibilities of quality planning and control.

3. An important exception is seen in the service orientation of some of our public utilities, the telephone companies for example. In such companies, the planning and control of quality of service is closely observed and coordinated by top management itself.

4. It comes as a surprise to an audience of quality managers to be told that my reports to presidents (on the status of the quality function in their company) commence with "What is the effect of our quality on marketability of the product, that is, is our quality of product an asset or a liability to the sales force?"

Presented before the San Francisco Section of ASQC, January 23, 1964

7

Quality Problems, Remedies, and Nostrums

The current "movement" of motivational programs of the "Zero Defects" (ZD) type is receiving widespread publicity as an all purpose remedy for industry's quality problems. The author contends that: in all essential respects, the effectiveness of the ZD movement is grossly exaggerated; the unsuccessful programs have been more numerous than the successful: motivational programs have a narrow, not a broad range of application: the premises underlying the ZD programs are suspect; the main purpose behind the movement has probably been customer relations, not quality improvement.

The author lists the essential prerequisites to conducting a motivational program at all, and proposes modifications for using the ZD programs wherever these prerequisites are met.

Once again the world of quality control is in the midst of a "movement." This movement goes by a dozen names and acronyms. I will use the name *Zero Defects* which appears to have spawned them all, and will also adopt the ZD initials for shorthand purposes.

The symptoms of a "movement" are all there: an outpouring of enthusiastic papers: published assertions of excellent results, speeches by industry and government officials, moving pictures in sound and color, a laudatory press, and a new, "hot" seminar subject.

Over the last 25 years, the quality function has been exposed to two major movements, statistical quality control and reliability, along with a whole host of minor movements and would-be movements. The record of

---

Editor's Note: The paper appearing here in Chapter 7 was published in 1966, *Industrial Quality Control* (June) 22(12): 647–653.

results attained versus the energy required to make these movements effective has been questionable, to say the least. (I prefer the word "bleak".)

There is now every indication that the ZD movement is blowing up into a major movement. It is, therefore, timely to examine it and to see where it is taking us. Such is the purpose of this paper.

I will conduct this examination by considering:

- What do the ZD programs consist of?

- Who is conducting them?

- Why are they doing it?

- What results have they gotten?

- What are the implications for companies that have not yet tried ZD programs?

THE INGREDIENTS OF THE PROGRAMS

Despite some variation among companies, there is a discernible pattern to the ZD programs. They embody two main ingredients, (1) a motivational package and (2) a prevention package.

The *motivational package* is aimed at persuading employees, especially production operators, to make fewer errors. The outward evidences of this package are loud and clear. There is an advance publicity campaign: posters, loudspeaker announcements, the bulletin board, the company newspaper. Then there is a dramatic kick-off in a circus atmosphere, with participation by top management and visiting dignitaries of all sorts: political leaders, community leaders, industry leaders, the press, key customers.

The *prevention package* is aimed at the removal of causes of defects. The programs do not seem to distinguish between sporadic and chronic defects, but the methods adopted are mainly aimed at sporadic defects. (I will elaborate on this later.)

These packages are delivered through a well-organized approach. Prior to the kick-off day there has been:

- A top management decision on going ahead with a program

- Participation by top management in defining the general approach

- Creation of a broad-based committee to plan the program, work up a budget, time-table, and so on

- Appointment of a ZD coordinator to do the leg work

- A pre-selling to the supervisors and to the union

Following the kick-off day, there is an organized follow-up consisting of:

- A regular scoreboard on results achieved

- An organized means for securing employee ideas on causes of defects

- Assignment of staff assistance to investigate ideas for defect reduction

Behind this well organized approach are some very dubious assumptions or premises. I will return to these.

WHO HAS BEEN CONDUCTING ZD PROGRAMS?

So far, these programs have been conducted mainly by companies that are under contract to the government military and space agencies. This has certainly been the general belief, and there are now two sets of data to support this belief:

1. During the last few months of 1965, the journal *Quality Assurance* encouraged readers to report on plans to undertake ZD programs or on results achieved. During the period September–December 1965, the journal received responses identifying 46 users of these programs. Of these respondents, 44 were industrial companies or divisions thereof; 2 were government departments. The 44 industrial units break down as follows:

   - 29 are engaged in military or aerospace contracts.

   - 8 are part of a company that is engaged in military or aerospace contracts.

   - 7 are not clearly identified as to participation in such contracts.

2. In October 1965, at a seminar of quality managers at the University of Connecticut I took a poll of the 57 men present as to the prevalence of ZD programs in their companies, and their relation to government contracts. The following data emerged:

- Of 28 companies having some extent of government contracts, 9 were conducting ZD programs. This is about 1 in 3.

- Of 29 companies having no government contract, 3 were conducting ZD programs. This is about 1 in 10.

The disproportion of the number of ZD programs in "the government sector" versus "the civilian sector" is far greater than these ratios would suggest. Defense and space account for only about 10 percent of our economy. Since the ZD publicity has been widespread, the bulk of the programs should, under uniform adoptions, be in the largest sector of the economy. The facts are the precise opposite. It becomes important to understand why this disproportion exists.

WHERE LIES THE COMPANY INITIATIVE?

Of the 12 ZD programs being conducted (among the 57 companies represented at the above seminar):

- 8 had been initiated by top management.

- 4 had been initiated by quality control management.

Not only do these programs seem to be mainly the result of top management initiative, there is evidence that some of these programs are being instituted over the opposition of quality control management.[1]

Discussions of why it is that the initiative is so largely coming from top management has brought out numerous theories, of which the most plausible seem to be:

1. Government officials have become strong advocates of the ZD programs, and top management's are responding to this pressure as a matter of good customer relations.

2. The published assertions of the results of ZD programs are accepted as valid, and it is decreed that a similar program be adopted on the basis that "if others can get such results, why can't we?"

3. The top managements are not satisfied with things as they are or with the lack of initiative of the quality control people in doing something about it. Hence, any reasonable-sounding program is adopted as a possible change for the better. (A form of stirring up the animals.)

In my opinion, the signs all point to government advocacy of these programs as the main force, both for their adoption in the defense and space industries, and for the fact that the company initiative comes from top management.

Whatever the explanation, there is a "new" lesson to be learned: assurance to customers may have to take the form of putting on a program that they urge. In a competitive society, the customer has the decisive economic power. The basic quality mission in selling products and services is "fitness for use." However, the means used by some customers to judge this fitness include the management practices of the manufacturer. These practices cover a wide spectrum and, as we now see clearly, can suddenly put great emphasis on the manufacturer's approach to motivation.

The quality manager may not agree with this reasoning of the customer. He may resent bitterly the loss of the initiative to the "Madison Avenue Boys" whose "measure of progress is the size of the press clipping file."

But all quality managers should take the lesson to heart. Assurance to customers has taken many forms since the days of the simple village market. The ZD programs are a new form. Nor will the matter end there. Still other forms are right now coming over the horizon. If the quality manager is to have the initiative in these matters, he must be the first to identify these new forms and to give leadership to company deliberations on what to do about them.

THE GOVERNMENT PRESSURES

The support of government officials for the ZD programs goes beyond anything in my experience. I have seen a lot of government advocacy for results as well as awards for results, such as the Army-Navy E. The ZD advocacy is different, since it is an advocacy for a particular technique. There has been previous advocacy for SQC, for PERT, and for still other techniques. But the advocacy for ZD is in a class by itself.

It is instructive to look at the nature of this pressure in order to understand better why the industrial companies act as they do. For example, at a 1965 joint industry-government conference, one of the government officials put it this way:

> *I have taken this opportunity to tell you about a program that has served a vital national interest—our ability to defend our country. It is a program discovered, designed, and executed by an industry in serious trouble. It is a program concerned with perfection in the manufacturing of products that will take human life if defective. It*

is a program I have observed closely and to which I have con-
tributed. I have seen it work. In my present position . . . I cannot
help but ask the question: Can the Zero Defects concept—by some
other name perhaps—serve our nation through its adoption by
those industries whose products must be error-free? I will not try
to answer the question, but will leave it with you for whatever con-
sideration you believe it merits." (At this point a movie on the
Martin Company's ZD program was shown.)

The closing session of the same conference featured a speech by the
commissioner of the government agency that had wide regulatory powers
over this industry. Referring back to the earlier remarks of his assistant, the
commissioner said:

In this morning's session, Mr . . . presented you with a challenge
—the challenge of Zero Defects. He has described a motivational
program that has worked successfully in the missile and other
defense industries. We do not offer Zero Defects as the final
answer to the problems discussed here this week, but it certainly
merits your and your company's serious consideration.

Generally the government officials properly leave it to the companies
to give the programs their serious consideration. Some officials have more
trouble restraining themselves. Here is how one Defense Department official puts it:

I strongly urge that you seriously consider the advantages of insti-
tuting a Zero Defects program and, more important, consider ways
and means of keeping the program alive. Zero Defects concerns
both your private interests and the interests of our country, and it
helps, oh, how it helps, to keep your organization competitive.

In the case of the ZD programs, the advocacy by government officials
has gone beyond speeches. There are now such things as ZD participation
awards; I have seen company statements which point out that they were the
first to receive this award in their region. (This statement is made at the
time of launching the program. It would be months before they could know
whether any good came of it.)

It must be self-evident that in the face of such government advocacy, the
company's decision to go ahead may have little to do with the likelihood of
improving quality. The company may well conclude that the ZD program is
only a gamble for improving quality, but that is a sure thing for better customer and public relations.

THE RESULTS, PUBLISHED
AND UNPUBLISHED

Most of the published papers and speeches give no quantitative data on the results of ZD programs in terms of quality improvement. The few that do give such data would make any good manager fairly drool: 72 percent reduction in defects, specific employees working weeks and even months on end without a single defect, a 70 percent acceptance rate on suggestions turned in, and an 80 percent positive disposition of "error cause removals."

No data have been published on the customer relations or public relation benefits of the programs. But we can safely assume that the companies that pioneered in the movement, and are identified with such pioneering, have benefited considerably from the favorable publicity. For the non-pioneers, the act of putting on a ZD program (which may include participation by the very government officials who are the advocates) does get "results" in terms of customer relations, though not as stunning as was the case with the pioneers.

In spite of the published accounts of results obtained in specific companies, the results of the ZD movement are not very impressive. Since this statement is certain to be questioned and contested, I will elaborate.

In the first place, there is unpublished evidence that the failures exceed the successes. At the recent seminar on quality control management (October 1965, at the University of Connecticut) 12 of the 57 men present had ZD programs going on in their plants. Of the 12 men only 2 felt that their company was better off as a result of the program.

Secondly, the published results are suspect. I have had occasion to question several companies that have published papers on their programs but that gave only qualitative data as to the results obtained. I found that their asserted results did not exist; they had published the story of their programs as an aid to customer relations. In two instances, where I visited the premises, I found that the published qualitative statements of results were highly colored versions of the actual results.

If, as I believe, the failures have greatly outnumbered the successes, then it is understandable how conscientious men can become advocates for ZD programs despite the fact the movement as a whole may be a dud. The simple fact is that people speak boldly of their successes and speak quietly or not at all of their failures. Through this bias, only success stories get to be published. The man who would like to publish a failure story will have quite a time getting through the clearance procedure, whether in industry or government. The men who exchanged failure stories at the University of

Connecticut seminar were doing so in an atmosphere of academic freedom, and not for publication.

It is this same bias that has fooled the industrial press. In consequence, this press has only thrown gasoline on the fire. Here are two examples of their conclusions. One journal, under the heading "Zero Defects, Countdown to Perfection" goes on to state, in key sentences:

> *Zero Defects gives you a big return on a modest investment— immediately Zero Defects gives you the same fast payoff reported by these plants . . .*

A second journal, in a question-and-answer box, includes this exchange:

> *Q. Does Zero Defects really work?*

> *A. You bet it does! Without exception, every participating company has profited from the plan. Some of the results border on the phenomenal. Besides, the concept seems to breed increased enthusiasm as it is put into practice.*

To give the journalists the benefit of the doubt. their conclusions (stripped of editorial flamboyance) may well be logical when related to the sources they contacted. To get their stories, they go to the people who have published the articles. But as we have seen, these same people are in no position of academic freedom when speaking for publication. Under the GIGO[2] principle, the journalists started with a biased sample and were bound to end up with a biased story.

This gives the journalists the benefit of the doubt. Some readers might resent this. They could, with validity, point out that when a "movement" seems to show signs of becoming important, some program makers, magazine editors, and other media come a-running for stories. If they can't find a hot one, they warm up a cold one.[3]

None of the foregoing is meant to question the validity of the published quantitative results in specific companies. Over the years, I have been personally involved in too many defect-prevention programs to regard such results as "amazing." When the problems are there, and when a program is tailor-made to fit those specific problems, good results are usually forthcoming. What is decisive is whether the problems are known before the remedy is chosen or whether the remedy is chosen without regard for what the problems are.

This brings us back to the matter of the premises underlying these ZD programs.

THE CAUSATION PREMISES

Defects do not just happen; they are caused. However, there is a long list of causation patterns: marginal product designs, incomplete process engineering, poor vendor quality, lack of employee training, inadequate tool maintenance, employee carelessness, insufficient feedback of inspection data, sale for the wrong applications, and so on. Each of these families of causes of defects has its own pattern of remedy, and no other remedy will do. Nothing except design changes will remedy a poor product design.

Defect patterns vary remarkably from one industry to another. They also vary, though less remarkably, from one company to another in the same industry. They also vary from year to year in the same company.

Because of these variations in defect patterns and because of the highly specific relation of remedy to cause, it is essential, before launching any program, to know what defects are we fighting. Given this knowledge, we can choose the appropriate remedies and build our program around them. Lacking this knowledge, we are guessing as to remedies. Likewise, if we start with a prefabricated remedy and build our program around it, the program will be successful only if the defect pattern happens to fit the prefabricated remedy.

With respect to defect causation, the ZD programs are indulging in three basic premises:

1. Most errors are employee-controllable.

2. Human fallibility is a myth.

3. The management-controllable errors are mainly sporadic in nature.

In my experience, every single one of these premises is defective.

THE PREMISE OF EMPLOYEE-CONTROLLABILITY

The major premise of the ZD programs is that of employee-controllability. Under this premise it is assumed that defects are mainly caused by carelessness, forgetfulness, blunder, indifference, and other factors that are under the control of the employees, especially the factory operators. By implication, the company has provided these employees with the essential information, tools, and methods, so that the rest is up to the employees. Hence, runs this premise, adequate motivation is *all* that stands between the employee and a reduction in errors.

In my experience, taking industry as a whole, only about 20 percent of our defects are employee-controllable. The remaining 80 percent are caused by failure of the company to provide the employee with all three of the indispensable means for "self-control:"

1. Means for knowing just what it is he is supposed to do.

2. Means for knowing just what it is he is actually doing.

3. Means for closing the loop, that is, how to change what he is doing in order to conform to what he is supposed to be doing.

These essentials must all be provided, by management, before an employee can do a good job. (Once they have been provided, motivation enters in to decide whether he or she *will* do a good job.) If any one of these indispensables has not been provided by the company, the defects resulting from such omission must be regarded as management-controllable.

The figure of 20 percent is derived not merely from my own experience in a wide assortment of companies in the United States. It has been widely confirmed by other practitioners, both here and abroad. However, the degree of employee-controllability varies widely between companies, and even more widely within departments of the same company. In departments such as assembly, wiring, or soldering, the employee-controllable defects are often in the majority.

The pioneering ZD programs were mainly in the missile and space business, and were, in fact, directed mainly at factory departments such as assembly, wiring, or soldering. For such departments, the premise of operator-controllability has a good deal of validity.

However, there have been other programs in which the premise of employee-controllability was not valid. Yet these companies could readily have checked this. It is fairly simple to analyze the defect pattern to see whether the premise of employee-controllability is valid. In my experience, no company should embark on a motivational program without knowing in advance what proportion of the defects are employee-controllable. If the proportion turns out to be low, this fact alone may be decisive in deferring a motivational program.

Anyone who has seen the final disintegration of a misdirected motivational program will not soon forget it. The employees sense that the program is aiming at a minor part of the problem, but they can't prove it. So they decorate the posters and charts with short and vulgar slogans of their own. This led one harassed quality manager to observe, "Thank God this month is the end of our quality campaign. Then we can get back to quality."

THE PREMISE OF HUMAN INFALLIBILITY

Here the ZD programs make a bold departure from traditional thinking. They assert that the old belief in the fallibility of human beings is unsound. They cite instances in which human beings assertedly attain perfection, for example, human beings never forget to eat at meal time, never ram their cars through the rear of their garages, never let themselves be short-changed at the bank. Since (under this assertion) human beings can exhibit infallibility outside the company, it should be possible to motivate them into infallibility inside the company. It is this premise of human infallibility that leads the proponents of the ZD programs to put the zero in zero defects and to urge that there be no compromise with zero.

As it happens, I am unable to accept this premise. The instances of asserted human infallibility are not convincing as applied to conditions in an industrial company. Moreover, the idea that through motivation we could create errorless employees brings up visions of errorless baseball players, chess players, and so on, which sounds fantastic, since the motivations of many of these players are already as intense as anything in human experience.

However, I doubt that the philosophic debate (of whether humans can be motivated into infallibility) is worth the time. The more practical considerations are that:

1. On the record, we have reduced human error mainly through better methods and through foolproofing than through motivation. This has been the case with safety matches, jigs, and fixtures; prelaunch count-down procedures for missiles and rockets; and myriad of other technological developments. It has also been the case with the human being's use of his own body as a machine for work. Few human beings are as intensely motivated as our athletes. Yet after generations of a plateau, we still get breakthroughs in athletics. This is achieved not only through new technology, for example, the fiberglass pole for the pole vault; it is achieved also through new discoveries on how to use senses and muscles. The four-minute mile had eluded generations of athletes until the recent breakthrough. The breakthrough was not the result of more intense motivation of the runners; it was the result of a more fundamental study of how runners could get the most out of their energies. The coach who worked it out did not just exhort his men to greater exertion and leave it up to them; he

supplied the answer to their proper question, "What do you want me to do different than I have been doing?"

2. The talk about infallibility obscures the same proper question when asked by the employees. "What do you want me to do different than I have been doing?" This question is practical and sensible, and the company that evades it is only dumping the problems into the lap of the employee body. Often the solutions are already in the house. Analysis of data of individual performances can be used to identify which employees are consistently low in errors, which consistently high. Study of the actual work techniques of these employees can then discover what is the difference in technique that accounts for the difference in performance. This discovery can then be used to bring all employees up to the level of the best.

3. Finally, in most of industry there is no compelling need to reach zero. The need arises primarily when human life and health are at stake. As to all else, we apply the standard of economic balance, not the standard of perfection. If, through advanced technology, perfection also becomes economic, we can rest assured that the interest in perfection will broaden considerably.

THE PREMISE OF SPORADIC CAUSES

Some defects are the result of a sudden, "sporadic" flare-up of a process that is normally well behaved. Other defects are "chronic" in nature: they go on and on because there is a permanent cause that we have not yet remedied (or even discovered). The prevention activity of the ZD programs is aimed primarily at the "sporadic" causes of defects. Yet for most industrial situations, this prevention activity is misdirected; it should be directed at the chronic causes of defects.

My overwhelming experience is that defect patterns follow the principle of the "vital few and trivial many." A few dominant defects account for the bulk of the total defectiveness, *and these few dominant defects are chronic*. They go on and on until some fundamental analysis discovers their real cause and sets the stage for remedy. The reason the defects have been chronic is that while the symptoms become evident in one department, the causes remain hidden amid conflicting theories.

The ZD programs put the emphasis on the sporadic defects in which the cause-and-effect relationship is relatively simple. For such defects, the employees can be an invaluable source of ideas, and the ZD programs do provide for this participation.

However, for chronic defects the analysis must mainly be conducted by the technical staff. In my experience, a company that aims to improve its quality performance should, by all means, analyze the defect patterns to identify the few chronic defects which account for the bulk of the defectiveness. These few chronic defects then become projects for solution through a team set up for the purpose.

Here again, there is no need to debate or theorize. The question of whether the defects are mainly sporadic or chronic can be settled by analysis of the data. I would certainly advise any company to get this analysis made before embarking on a program, since the roads to diagnosis and remedy differ remarkably for sporadic defects and for chronic defects.

Finally, let me note that in these ZD programs, the companies tend to be carried away by their own propaganda about craftsmanship, pride of workmanship, and the rest. It is obviously a good thing to reach a state of such pride of workmanship. But this should not confuse the distinction between the building of quality and the improvement of quality. The employee does have a major role to play in the building of quality and in the associated control procedures. Given the specifications, the machines and the tools, it is the employee, and no one else, who builds in the quality. But when it comes to improvement of quality through eliminating chronic defects, the employee's role is usually limited by the complexity of the cause-and-effect relationships inherent in modern industry. These chronic defects can, in the main, be removed only through the combined action of the supervisory body and the technical specialists. Such is the inherent situation, and no amount of motivation of employees is going to change it.

With the sporadic defects it is otherwise. Here the cause-and-effect relationship is often simple and localized, and the employee is often in the very best situation to point out the solutions.

WHAT IS REALLY NEW?

Motivational programs have been around for a long time.[4] In fact, it is the enduring nature of motivation as a timeless tool that should create the strongest presumption in favor of any "new" program based on motivation. Long before defect prevention, there was error prevention. In earlier millennia, the kings cut off the ears, noses, hands, or heads of thieves, or for that matter, of fallible waiters who merely spilled the soup. On the positive side, the exhortations of ancient kings and generals to their troops still make stimulating reading, thousands of years later.

What Then Is New About ZD?

Organically, ZD is not really new. The organized approach is well thought out but is not really new either.[5] The idea of human infallibility is new (and may have caused the publicity breakthrough), but it is of dubious validity.

Yet there is something "new" and it is important. The ZD program is the first of many, many similar programs to achieve wide publicity, and favorable publicity at that. Because it enjoys a good press, it has become a good banner under which to launch a motivation program—a form of innocence by association.

Old slogans and names wear out (as will ZD in its turn). When a program or movement acquires a bad reputation, just putting it under new management may not be enough. The old name becomes so intertwined with the bad reputation that keeping the old name is a kiss of death. In such cases, an essential step in revitalizing the movement is to give it a new, sexy name. The performance of past motivation programs has been so shockingly poor that a fresh, clean banner-like ZD is most welcome.

There is another new element. The ZD type programs have been the first error reduction programs to "go companywide." They have addressed themselves to errors in purchasing, marketing, engineering design, and other functions, as well as to production errors. This broadened approach has been overdue, but to my knowledge, the ZD type programs were first to face the needs squarely.

SOME NEGATIVES

It is tempting to dismiss the ZD-type programs as a new form of hokum, cooked up by publicity-seeking quacks to build up their public image, to sell their services and books, to become the high priests for a new religion, to become kings of a newly created hill. There may well have been some of this. If the movement snowballs further, we may be sure there will be plenty of it. But aside from the emotional rejection of these programs generally, there are some dubious specifics.

1. The program has a narrow range of application, no matter what the proponents say to the contrary. It fits only those company situations that meet the criteria I have set out in the following summary.

2. The programs will have a limited, not a continuing life. Like statistical quality control, total quality control, and so on, ZD

will wear out as a "good" name and will be replaced by the next well-publicized name.

3. The concept of human infallibility through motivation is very likely a pipe dream.

4. The 100 percent "voluntary" signing of pledge cards is a fabrication. The whole pledge card idea is a risky business. Where operator-controllable defects are a small minority of the total, many employees will regard the pledge as an insult. It probably serves no practical purpose in any case.

5. The proponents and enthusiasts may be working up a stampede. There are some clear storm warnings: inflated claims, both as to results and as to breadth of application; blindness to other useful programs and tools; biased presentations through omitting the negatives inherent in such programs; failure to define the conditions for application; ignorance of the number of programs that have failed.

Collectively it is a severe indictment. The indictment should be directed not so much against those who present an objective account of individual company experiences as against those who purport to generalize from a cross-section of other people's experiences: company zealots, government overenthusiasts, irresponsible journalists.

Mine is only one man's experience, but from that experience I have developed some beliefs as to what usually distinguishes the successes from the failures in these movements:

- The failures start with a prefabricated remedy, a panacea, an answer to all problems. The successes start by asking, "What are the problems?"

- The failures build a program to fit the prefabricated remedy. The successes defer choice of remedy until the problems are identified.

- The failures are energized by devoted salesmanship on the part of the advocates of the prefabricated remedy. The successes are energized by the spirit of teamwork among people faced with a common problem.

- The failures measure progress by the degree of adoption of the remedy (how many charts are on the machines, how many pledge cards were signed, and so on). The successes measure progress by the effect on the problems.

FOR CUSTOMER RELATIONS ONLY?

A program undertaken to score points in customer and public relations, but in the absence of real motivational need, carries with it a hidden price of serious proportions. That price is the damming done by the insincerity of the motivational approach and by the undermining of the leadership of the regular supervisors and the quality control department.

Actually, the big payoffs in customer relations are collected by the pioneers and leaders of such movements, not by the followers. The followers should realize that their customer relations gains will be minimal, while their internal stresses will be substantial. The urge to put on a show for customers may well divert attention from the real quality problems. The incidental resentment of supervisors and technical people (to a takeover by the promotional people) can be long lasting.

Despite all this, upper management may still decide that the show should be put on: too much potential business is at stake. The decision may be correct. But the price to be paid should be known in advance.

SUMMARY

In concluding this paper, we may well emphasize that the ZD programs, as practiced, are a narrow application remedy applicable to a closely restricted set of company problems and conditions. I would list these conditions as follows:

1. There exists an actual quality problem, so that the program is to be aimed at that problem and is not intended solely as window dressing for customers and outsiders, or just to keep up with the industrial Joneses.

2. The company has already done a respectable job of reducing manager-controllable defects to a point near the practical limit, and hence is coming to the employee body with clean hands.

3. The employee-controllable defects are substantial enough, for economic or usage reasons, to warrant a serious motivation effort.

4. There is a relationship, between the company and the employees of sufficient mutual confidence that employee participation in a motivational program is likely to be genuine.

5. There is a sufficient open-mindedness among the supervisors that they will seriously study employee ideas for improvement. It is a

fact that the motivation programs include an effort to secure ideas and suggestions from the bottom of the company. Ideas for improvement that no one has bothered to bring up or that have previously been brought up but not acted on now must be looked at seriously. Over and above this is a new atmosphere for creative thinking. This is all to the good, but it does require a genuine acceptance by the supervisors.

6. There is a willingness by top management to show a personal interest, and especially, to set an example of changing the priority of emphasis on quality in relation to other elements of company performance (delivery schedule, cost, and so on.). It is a fact that the motivational programs can bring the upper management into quality problems to a degree not previously encountered. Top management is necessarily involved in decisions to create a circus atmosphere and to invite numerous dignitaries. This same involvement exposes top management to some new facts of life as they pertain to quality. As a consequence, there may be a realignment of the priorities of attention, since top management for the first time has become aware that the priorities they have set are not compatible with the new quality goals.

7. There is a reservoir of adequate technical staff to keep up with the ideas for error cause removal that will emerge in the early stages of the program. The programs as conducted seem to me to understress this point (presumably because they proceed on the theory of employee-controllable defects as the main contributing source of defects).

Given a set of conditions that meet the foregoing criteria, a motivational program of the ZD type should be all to the good. The company can, in conscience, put it up to the employees:

- Good quality is important to you as well as to us.
- Both of us can contribute to good quality.
- We can provide you with the information, tools, and methods that we believe you need.
- You can tell us what else you need.
- You can also tell us what you think we could do to help remove causes of errors.

- You can also help by changing some things you have been doing, and here is what we want you to do that is different from what you have been doing.

The likelihood is that the ZD banner will be in good standing for several more years. It will, of course, then fade and be replaced by something else. In being replaced, it will leave a permanent residue by having dramatized, more indelibly than any prior program, an organized approach to employee motivation for quality. It will also leave with all quality managers a new dimension for thought: the forms of customer assurance are ever changing, and the ability to detect and act on these new forms is essential to keeping the initiative.

ENDNOTES

1. In this connection, the author encountered a hilarious instance at the 1965 Annual ASQC Convention (Los Angeles). He was poised to enter the session on Quality Motivation (three papers on ZD type programs), when he was stopped by two well-known executives. One was a military officer with important responsibilities in the defense program. The other was the director of quality for a major industrial company. We will call them A and B.

   "Long time no see. How about joining us in the bar?" They asked the author (a total abstainer), "I was planning to sit in on this session. To this date, I haven't made up my mind as to whether these programs are getting results or are just hogwash."

   A: "Don't waste your time. I can tell you right now they are just hogwash."

   B: "I can tell you the same thing. But right after this convention I have to put on such a program because my top management has ordered me to."

2. A well-known principle in data processing. An acronym for Garbage In, Garbage Out.

3. The tout sheet for an "institute" starts off: "Research indicated "zero defects" will do more than any other methodology to bring about higher quality at lower cost."

4. For some quality control instances, see Juran, J. M. 1962. *Quality Control Handbook*, 2nd ed. New York: McGraw-Hill: 11-55 – 11-69.

5. See, for example, Juran, J. M. 1954. Nine Steps to Better Quality. *Factory Management and Maintenance* (March): 112–3.

8

The QC Circle Phenomenon

The QC Circle is a small group of departmental work leaders and line operators who have volunteered to spent time outside of their regular hours to help solve departmental quality problems. Since the QC Circle movement originated in Japan about four years ago, a phenomenal rate of growth has taken place. The effect of the movement on the Japanese drive toward quality leadership may well be dramatic.

On the afternoon of Wednesday, April 20, 1966, a Westerner visiting the Daiichi Seimei Hall in central Tokyo would have witnessed a remarkable sight. The meeting in progress in this historic auditorium (General Douglas MacArthur staged his large conferences here) was billed as the 14th QC Circle Conference. It had started at 1:00 p.m., and, after some ceremonial addresses, the technical program got under way. Seven Japanese companies presented reports on improvements they had made on a variety of company problems. For example, the first report, by Takenosuke Kakegawa of the Stereophonic plant of Tokyo Sanyo Electric Company, was on "Finding a Solution to Trouble about Solder." The seventh report was by a trio, Shoko Yazawa, Reiko Yamada, and Mitsuko Yamazaki, from the car radio division of Matsushita Communication Industrial Company, who reported on "Decrease of car radio defects in final assembly." Each report was allowed 15 minutes, with 7 added minutes for discussion from the floor.

To understand what was so remarkable about the conference, let us look in detail at the presentation made by the trio from Matsushita. They had taken on a project to reduce final assembly defects in the radios which

Editor's Note: The paper appearing here in Chapter 8 was published in 1967 in *Quality Progress* (January) 23(7): 329–336.

Matsushita makes for sale and export to automobile companies. From information of assembly rejections and customer troubles, the trio prepared a Pareto analysis,"[1] and established that the number one defect was loose control knobs. This "public enemy number one" accounted for 80 percent of all final assembly defects. The number two defect, missing mounting brackets, comprised 13 percent of all defects. The remaining 7 percent were assorted minor defects. Collectively, all defects ran at a level of 2.2 percent of the product.

Next, the trio considered each of the two principal defects (loose control knobs and missing mounting brackets) as a project requiring a breakthrough to a new level. The control knob is designed with a blind hole to mate with the control shaft. To provide enough friction to hold the knob tight, the shaft is slotted to create two springy sides that are then spread with a screwdriver during the final assembly operation.

However, there was a difference of opinion as to the cause of loose control knobs—was it parts, operators, tools, or methods? The trio mapped out the variables on an Ishikawa diagram, as shown in Figure 8.1.[2]

From analysis and from some experimentation, it was established that the two main causes were:

1. Variation in slot size when enlarged by different operators

2. Screwdriver not well suited for the operation

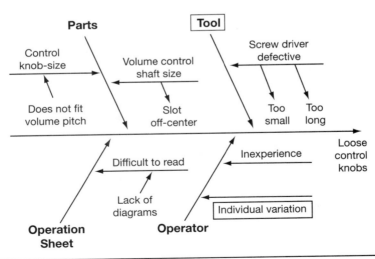

Figure 8.1 Ishikawa diagram showing factors resulting in loose control knobs.

A solution was found by providing screwdrivers with a parallel-sided blade instead of a tapered blade.

The missing mounting brackets were the second project. (These brackets are used in the car factory to mount the radio to the automobile dashboard.) The cause of missing brackets was "operator error." Radio assemblers in a prior stage of manufacture have a wide range of operations to perform, and sometimes omit one or both mounting brackets.

The solution was to foolproof the final assembly operation. An assembly jig had been needed anyway as a holding device during final assembly. Now the job was built, and built in such a way that the mounting brackets were the means of supporting the radios in the jig. This simplified handling the radio during final assembly and also eliminated shipment of radios with missing mounting brackets. These two quality breakthroughs lowered the final assembly defect rate from 2.2 percent to 0.6 percent.

The trio had divided up their 15-minute presentation into three sections of five minutes each. Shoko led off, followed by Reiko and Mitsuko, respectively. In the manner of such Japanese conferences, the visual aids were large painted sheets of paper hung from a long, horizontal, wooden two-by-four, like wash on the line. These sheets showed sketches of the parts, the flow of the process, the methods of analysis, and charts of the results obtained. The trio made their presentation with a sure-footed grasp of their subject. Even to this author, whose knowledge of Japanese is minimal, the explanation was clear. The well-prepared visual aids helped quite a bit. During the seven minute question period, Mitsuko, being the final speaker, also fielded the questions from the floor. This was likewise a virtuoso performance, for Mitsuko was alert and ready with the answers before the questions were half finished.

What was remarkable about all this was the fact that the presentation of the seven reports at this conference involved not a single manager, supervisor, engineer, or other management specialist, nobody from what an American calls the "exempt payroll." Instead, the speakers were mostly what we call "working foremen" or "work leaders." (The usual Japanese word is *Gemba-cho.*) Some speakers were production operators off the assembly floor. All were either leaders or members of QC Circles. *Shoko, Reiko and Mitsuko were young women off the assembly line.* Their full time job is to assemble car radios. Shoko and Reiko were 21 and 23 years old, respectively. *Mitsuko was 18!*

Each of these seven reports represented the work of a QC Circle, QC meaning quality control. This QC Circle movement, which began in 1962, has been snowballing into something massive. As of April 1966, there were already over 10,000 such circles in Japan, and every one of them exhibited the following characteristics:

- The membership consists solely of people at the bottom of the company organization—nonsupervisors and working supervisors.

- Membership is voluntary.

- The work of the circles is mostly conducted outside of regular hours.

- Compensation for this out-of-hours work varies from full time down to nothing.

To understand how a QC Circle, such as the three young girls off the assembly line, could take on and complete a project like improving the assembly quality of car radios, it is necessary to go back a few years, and in some respects, a few centuries. We will shortly return to this.

RESULTS TO DATE

There is a good measure of results achieved by the QC Circle movement because a measuring stick has been built in. Each Circle is required, as part of each project undertaken, to evaluate the results. From these evaluations, the editors of *Quality Control for the Foreman* (*Gemba to QC*) have determined that:

- The Circles have averaged savings of about $3000 each.

- The 10,000 Circles have collectively achieved $30 million in improvements.

This is astounding for a movement that is still only a few years old. No less significant is the fact that this has been done without preempting the time of the managers and engineers, who remain free to devote themselves to interdepartmental and upper level projects. The idea that these Japanese companies have found a way of going through all operations with a fine tooth comb, and without adding to the burdens of the managers and engineers, is something to ponder on.

The main effect has been in control, this being inherently the basic role that can be played by the QC Circle. There has been much analysis of sporadic troubles, and much done to reduce variation and to prevent recurrence. More and sharper control tools have been made available to the factory floor: clearer interpretation of standards, more complete instrumentation, better data feedback, control charts, and so on.

Part of the improvement in control has been an increased awareness of the sequence of steps in the control cycle. As quality improvements are worked out, action is taken to incorporate the improvement into revised, standardized methods. Further steps are then taken to set up the foolproofing, the feedback, and the alarms that will hold the gains. Beyond improvement of control, a gratifying proportion of the projects are of a breakthrough nature—by systematic study they take the department to better levels of performance, levels not previously attained.

The intangible byproducts of the foregoing results are evident but not measurable:

- The foreman's ability to control and lead his department is increased. His job of promulgating instructions is noticeably eased.

- The operators have greater interest in their job, and higher morale. This extends to people formerly indifferent, and to the older age group as well.

- The relationship between the staff people and the line workers has improved noticeably.

- There is being developed, on the factory floor, a generation of workers with successful experience in use of what have to date been regarded as management tools. The potential of these workers to become the managers of tomorrow is simply breathtaking.

HOW THE QC CIRCLES STARTED

The QC Circles are not some isolated invention; they are a very logical outcome of the Japanese drive for training and accomplishment in quality control. It is easy to trace this evolution.

The authoritative Japanese narratives (by Koyanagi, Ishikawa, and others) all trace formal training in modern quality control methods to the early 1950s. The seed courses were Deming's lectures in statistical methodology (1950) and Juran's courses on Management of Quality Control (1954). The Japanese zeal for learning and for self-sufficiency brought out a follow-up of numerous courses, by local experts, for engineers and managers at all levels.

The Japanese were not content to conduct this training for engineers and the supervisory levels. Japanese concepts of organizing work do not follow the strict Taylor concept of division of work, that is, planning to be done by the engineers and execution to be done by the foremen and workers. Instead, the Japanese leave a good deal of planning and creativity to be carried out by the production force.

These same concepts of organizing work have carried over into the quality function. The broad based quality control department, with its arrays of quality control engineers, reliability engineers, and still other specialist categories, so commonly found in America, is a minority organization form in Japan. The Japanese approach has been to teach quality control methodology to managers in *all* functions—research, development, design, production, purchasing, sales, accounting, and so on. With such a broad base of training, the need for a broadly-based quality control department is diminished, as is the need for specialist engineers. (Japanese engineers are seldom specialized as quality control engineers.) As a consequence, the quality control department in Japan has mainly an advisory, consulting, and promotional role. A minority of these departments do conduct quality planning. More usually the various line departments have the responsibility for achieving quality by utilizing modern quality control methods while the quality audit is done by a specialized staff department.

Under this Japanese system of organizing work, it became logical to extend training in quality control to the category of *Gemba-cho*. The *Gemba-cho* is a sort of "working foreman," that is, he is partly a work leader and teacher, and sometimes a production worker. Since this category of *Gemba-cho* consists of many thousands of people, it was necessary to resort to mass media of training. Japanese ingenuity rose to the occasion by creating new training forms as well as by adapting conventional forms.

The conventional forms consisted of textbooks and manuals, such as Professor Ishikawa's textbook, *Introduction to Quality Control*. First published in 1952, the Third Edition (1964 and 1966) has grown to 350 pages and to two volumes, and now includes much on management of quality control. The more recent (1959-1960) *Quality Control Text Book for Foremen* runs to 234 pages and provides cookbook information on quality improvement as well as quality control. This manual is edited by Professor Ishikawa's group of consultants in the JUSE and is published by JUSE Press Co.

Turning now to the unconventional training forms, the first of these was the radio broadcast courses in quality control. The pioneering course was a series of 91 lessons of 15 minutes each, broadcast daily from June through September 1956 and repeated later in the year. This course was repeated annually through 1962. The radio text for these courses sold over 100,000 copies!

A television lecture series was next. The first of these ran from April 1960 to March 1961 and consisted of a series of weekly lectures, each 30 minutes long.

The journal *Gemba to QC* was launched in 1962 on a quarterly basis. Now on a monthly basis, it has a lively, practical content, and a circulation of over 28,000 copies.

Annual Foremen's QC Conferences started in November 1962. (November is designated as quality month in all of Japan, and the Q flags really fly all over.) These conferences are staged in various industrial cities, with a burgeoning attendance.

With such a background, the logic of extending training to the rank and file becomes more evident. Given an extensive training of the *Gemba-cho*, his ability to put this training to use is in proportion to the use he can make of the resources around him, especially the human resources. It remained to find a mechanism for using these human resources, and this mechanism turned out to be the QC Circle.

Evidently the initiative for the QC Circle concept came from the editors of *Gemba to QC*, who saw in the nonsupervisors an immense potential for contribution through training and motivation. The QC Circle idea was born in about 1962. By August 1966, there were about 8,000 registered circles, with a membership of over 120,000 employees. The unregistered circles probably involve an even greater number of employees.

The regional and national organization for QC Circles followed as a matter of course. The journal *Gemba to QC* became, naturally, a national journal for the QC Circles as well. The first regional conference was held in May 1963. A little over three years later, the 20th conference was in session.

HOW THE QC CIRCLE MOVEMENT SPREADS

Now that these circles already number in the thousands, the pattern for creating new ones has become well established. The concept makes its way into a company through awareness of successful results in other companies. This awareness comes from the numerous success stories in *Gemba to QC*, from attendance at the annual foremen's QC conferences, from attendance at QC Circle conferences, and from visiting companies that have active programs going. Further stimulus comes from the internal QC staff people or from the external consultants who are on the staff of *Gemba to QC*, or of the Japanese Union of Scientists and Engineers.

As the gathering awareness creates a favorable atmosphere, various *Gemba* encourage the formation of QC Circles in their departments. Each circle is trained, mainly off the job, by a combination of three training methods.

1. Training by the book. This is a course, of 10 to 20 hours duration, in specific techniques, mainly:

    - The Pareto analysis to find the "vital few" problems

    - The cause-and-effect diagram (The Ishikawa diagram)

- Histograms

- Graphs

- Control charts

- Stratification

- Binomial probability paper

2. Discussion of cases worked out in other companies, as reported in *Gemba to QC*

3. Discussion of internal quality problems, solved and unsolved

With the training behind them, the Circle identifies a problem to be solved, tackles it and solves it. It then tackles another, and another. (Some have solved over 60 problems.) The record of successful internal solutions breeds other QC Circles within the same company, and the movement spreads. As the number of Circles in one company grows, there arise new opportunities for stimulating interest and action. Companies organize in-house conferences of their QC Circles, providing opportunity for publicizing results and for giving recognition to the Circles who achieved the results.

At the Matsushita Training Center near Osaka, I saw a large training facility devoted to QC Circle activities. The walls of this large room were literally papered with the record of projects successfully carried out at various plants—projects on transformers, tuners, speakers, resistors, and so on. An example is shown in Figure 8.2. In addition to the reports, there were pictures of the members of the Circles which had achieved the results, along with other forms of recognition.

In the Toyota Motor Company plant in Nagoya, I saw use made of a most interesting information center in each shop department. The information center consists mainly of a large bulletin board, plus satellite boards for exhibiting samples of defects and such. The bulletin boards commonly exhibit:

- A diagram of the flow of the process, including location of control stations as well as control points and control levels at each station

- The Pareto analysis for key defects

- The Ishikawa cause-and-effect diagram for these key defects

- Data on current quality performance, usually in the form of control charts, the bulletin boards also carry some nonquality information such as departmental cost trends, the safety record, and so on

An interesting diagram on one board was a matrix listing on one axis the operations performed in the department and on the other axis the names

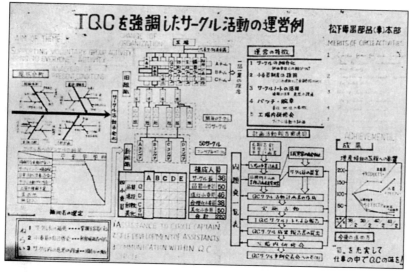

Figure 8.2 Example of QC Circle activities for TQC.

of the operators. The chart showed which operators had qualified to perform which operations, and was displayed for information and motivation.

The most successful QC Circles have the opportunity to get their projects published in *Gemba to QC*, and to attend the QC Circle conferences. These are important forms of recognition to the foremen and workers involved, many of whom are astonishingly young. One of the interesting projects reported on the walls of the Matsushita Training Center was by a QC Circle of four men and three women whose ages ranged from 16 to 23, with an average of 20.3 (Matsushita's car radio assembly line has several QC Circles in addition to that of Shoko, Reiko, and Mitsuko. The ages of these circle members range from 15 to 26, the average being 19.)

The published reports of projects completed are remarkably well documented. The typical report relies heavily on graphic presentation to tell the story. It is the rule, not the exception, for these reports to show:

- Sketches of the product under study

- The flow diagram of the process

- The Pareto analysis identifying the vital few troubles

- The Ishikawa cause-and-effect diagram mapping out the variables which might be causing the trouble

- Histograms, frequency tables, control charts, and other statistical analyses of data

- Charts showing the reductions in defects resulting from the project

- A computation of the yen of cost improvement. In companies with a firm history of use of QC Circles, the collective results have begun to show up in the company planning and budgeting as something substantial and predictable—a form of budgeted cost reduction

THE ROLE OF THE HIERARCHY

While participation in the QC Circles is voluntary, the existence of such Circles raises practical questions of how to coordinate the work of the Circles with that of the hierarchy. When the company is large, and the QC Circles number in the hundreds, this coordination can become complex, since the grain of the two structures runs in different directions. To date, the experience gained has already identified some helpful principles of coordination. One of these is a dual approach to selection of projects. Projects for the QC Circles are proposed in two ways:

1. By the Circle itself, based on its job knowledge plus the collective creativity of the members.

2. By the management hierarchy. For example, the company goal may be to cut rejects from 5 percent to 2 percent. Breaking this goal down into subobjectives can result in projects for QC Circles.

From the nature of things, the first projects taken on by a QC Circle are those of control—improved control of the local process, reduction of operator controllable defects. As a firmer grip is secured on these control problems, more elaborate projects are chosen, involving breakthrough into new levels of performance. Here the Circle finds itself conducting more sophisticated analyses, setting up experiments and otherwise walking boldly into the unknown.

As these more elaborate projects are tackled, the QC Circle may find itself faced with causes and influences that are outside of its own department. Commonly such matters are beyond the scope of the Circle, which is necessarily limited to intradepartmental problems. Except for the *Gemba-cho*, the members of the Circle are limited in their knowledge of, and access to, the happenings in other departments. For example, Kanto Auto-Works Company has found it useful to set up a two-way feedback of findings of the QC Circles and of the field service mechanics to promote the Circle

Table 8.1 Comparison of QC Circle and QC team.

Aspect	The QC Circle	The QC Team
Creation	Voluntary	By management order, hierarchical
Identification of projects	Mostly by the Circle	Mostly through management planning
Scope of activities	Intradepartmental	Interdepartmental
Membership	*Gemba-cho* and his nonsupervisors	*Gemba-cho* and supervisors and engineers
Life	Can be continuous, for project after project	For this project only

leader's quality and cost consciousness, and to provide special guidance in predelivery inspection and maintenance work. Such communications can be made only through the hierarchy.

When problems of an interdepartmental nature are encountered, the approach is to broaden the communication through a QC Circle leaders' meeting or a QC Circle joint meeting. If a project of an interdepartmental nature needs to be taken on, it is assigned to a QC team. The QC team is quite different from the QC Circle, as is seen in Table 8.1.

An added problem facing the hierarchy is that of providing the training facilities, the budgets, the support for aiding the Circles in their work, the follow-through to make remedies effective, and the means for giving recognition. In a large company like Nippon Kokan K.K., or Kobe Steel (which has about 1000 QC Circles), this requires positive organization machinery. To date, the companies have gladly paid the price, since the return on investment has been eminently satisfactory.

There is also evidence to suggest that the QC Circle concept may be broadened considerably, in two respects.

1. To deal with nonquality problems as well as with quality problems, that is, a universal way of using nonsupervisors for projects of all sorts—for improvements in cost, safety, productivity, and so on. Some of this has happened. Matsushita's QC Circles are in fact involved with some non-QC matters. Even the company chauffeurs have a QC Circle. However, for the QC Circle movement to broaden out into an all-purpose movement will require, as a prerequisite, that additional tool kits be developed, one for each area of subject matter. The success of the Circle movement as applied to quality control has, to an important degree, been due to the existence of a kit of tools that simplify greatly the attack on quality problems. Some of the tools in this kit, for example, the

Pareto Principle, are universals—they are helpful in solving any problem. However, as applied to other subject matter, the kit is incomplete, and would need to be supplemented.

2. As a leading device for strengthening relations between the company and the employee body. During my April 1966 seminars in Japan, several company directors made this point. In Nippon Kayaku K.K., the managers stimulated a QC Circle movement as part of a defensive program to prevent leadership of the workforce from being taken over by radical agitators. The resulting QC Circles played a significant role as part of a total program of "turning around" the performance of a sick plant.

THE MOTIVATIONAL BASE

To a Westerner, the most astonishing aspect of the QC Circles has nothing to do with quality control. What is astonishing is the degree to which the Japanese have succeeded in harnessing the energy, ingenuity and enthusiasm of the workforce to the unsolved problems of the company. In the West (on both sides of Churchill's Iron Curtain), it is difficult enough to do this during working hours. The Japanese have gone beyond this—they have done it outside of working hours as well. It is of the utmost importance to understand *how* it is that the Japanese have been able to bring this off.

First of all, it must be recognized that the Japanese manager has, for the most part, retained the leadership of the workforce, and has not lost it to the Union, the politician, or the intellectual. In Japan the usual, traditional relationship of companies to employees has been one of lifelong employment, with the company voluntarily assuming important social responsibilities: sick benefits, unemployment benefits, old age benefits, and so on. In the non-Communist West, the tradition has been otherwise. Companies generally did not voluntarily provide these benefits. (Even those which did, usually did it badly—they were guilty of paternalism.) In consequence, the workforce was driven to find elsewhere the solutions to the problems of unemployment, sickness, old age. New leadership sprang up to propose collective solutions, and the political power of the many made these proposals effective over the resistance of the managers. In the process, the leadership of the men passed from the managers to someone else, and still rests there. The Western manager may look askance at the high fringe benefit percentages of Japanese companies (as do some Japanese managers). But the Western company has paid the price both ways—it is taxed to pay the benefits, and has lost the leadership to boot. To regain this leadership is a long journey, and the present generation of managers will not make it (in my opinion).

Secondly, the Japanese concept of organization of work differs markedly from that followed in the West, especially that followed in the United States. American companies, under the Taylor influence, have gone far down the road of separating manufacturing planning from execution. The engineers play the dominant, if not the exclusive, role in planning, leaving to the production supervision the execution of the plan. The Western European countries tend to give the top managers the main role in the planning, really a dual role of directing and engineering. However, the Japanese evolution resulted in less formal planning, either by the engineers or the top managers. There remained a considerable residue of planning to be done by someone else, that is, the production supervision. This evolution has, of course, enlarged the responsibility of the *Gemba-cho*. In turn, the carrying out of these broader responsibilities has broadened the skills and effectiveness of the *Gemba-cho*. (We have some of this in America in some job shops and in some service departments where there has been no tradition of extensive use of engineers for planning.)

Finally, the priority of industrial motivational incentives in the Japanese culture is quite different from that prevailing in the West. However illogical this priority may seem to the Westerner, it is very logical to the Japanese. As well as I was able to determine, here is the order of importance:

1. *Improving the company's performance.* Under a tradition of lifetime association with one company, and with enlightened company practices as to employee welfare problems, the employee has a stake in the company's health, and responds to opportunities to do something about it. This loyalty to the company is evidently not limited to the company as an abstraction. There are loyalties to the particular shop and to the local work group that can contribute further to the overall relationship between the company and the workforce.

2. *Self-improvement.* The Japanese zeal for learning and for doing attaches itself to opportunities for training and for creativity. This self-improvement is also one of the tools for bypassing seniority as the basis for promotion.

3. *Recognition.* The QC Circle movement has enlarged the social standing of the *Gemba-cho*, who previously had not participated fully in social recognition. Opportunities now exist for the *Gemba-cho* to get out to conferences, to visit other companies, and even to become a member of a team to go abroad to study

foreign practice. The journal *Gemba to QC* is itself a recognition of a status of importance. Collectively it all adds up to quite a rise in social stature.

4. *Creativity amid boredom.* Particularly among nonsupervisors, and to a degree among all who work on the factory floor, the day-to-day job can be monotonous and boresome to an oppressive degree. If essential human needs (ego needs, social needs, creativity, self-fulfillment) are not met on the job the employee must find them elsewhere—in his hobbies, in sports, in noncompany associations. By providing a group opportunity for creativity with respect to the job (although out of regular hours) the company has provided a new opportunity to neutralize the problems of boredom and monotony.

5. *Money incentives.* It may come as a surprise to a Westerner that this incentive (for joining a QC Circle) has the lowest priority. Yet such seems to be the case. There is wide variation in practice so far as paying for time spent is concerned. Some companies make no payment at all. At Kobe Steel Company, one hour a month is paid for, the rest is not. The Matsushita women were paid at rates equal to half of their regular pay (not time-and-one-half) plus tea and cake. Some companies pay at full-time rates for the out-of-hours work of the QC Circles. The above relates to payment for *time* spent out-of-hours. In the case of *results* achieved, there is no payment as a direct consequence of such results. There is however, an indirect effect. The results of a successful project improve the company's profit, and thereby the employee bonuses, which are commonly geared to company profits by one formula for all employees.

As it happens, Matsushita has recently conducted a morale survey among QC Circle members. All workers mentioned the benefit of learning through the studies. In addition, they pointed out the following advantages:

1. By attending the QC Circle meetings, they acquired the ability to speak in public.

2. They made more friends and this contributed to a more cheerful atmosphere in the workshop.

3. They became more conscious of the importance of their jobs and their responsibility, and through the awareness of this importance, now have more pride in their jobs.

4. They improved their personality and acquired the ability to concentrate on solution of problems. These experiences with the QC Circle they apply in their home life.

COMPARISON WITH OTHER MOTIVATIONAL PROGRAMS

Inevitably the QC Circle concept must be compared with other motivational forms. What is different about it? In what respects is it limited in application to the Japanese culture, and in what respects is it based on universals?

To make this comparison, we might look at a wide assortment of motivational schemes as practiced in the West: the long-standing systems of piecework; the familiar suggestion systems in force in many companies; the system of Stakhanovism and its derivatives as practiced in Eastern Europe; the Scanlon plan of joint committees for improving productivity; and, because of current interest, the ZD family of programs.

We may look at these various plans from a number of standpoints:

1. *Voluntary or compulsory?* Joining the QC Circle is voluntary, and this characterizes most motivational schemes. Piecework is an exception. So also is the "voluntary" signing of ZD pledge cards, which can hardly be considered voluntary, although most of the rest of the ZD activity is left to voluntary action.

2. *Out-of-hours or on the job?* Here the out-of-hours QC Circle is virtually unique. This feature may be unique to Japan as well. In Western countries, it is common for employees to take training courses on "their own time." However, in no Western country known to me would there be any significant response by the workforce to studying projects on their own time, unless this were negotiated through the unions, and paid for at acceptable rates of pay. In the Eastern European countries there may be some of this, but I am not clear on this aspect of their practice.

3. *Premises as to need for analysis.* The QC Circle concept starts with the assumption that the causes of poor quality performance are not known, and that there is need for analysis to discover what actually causes the poor performance. Except for the Scanlon plan, the other programs largely assume, as an axiomatic belief, that the workforce could do better but is holding back for no good reason. While in all companies there are instances that can support this assumption, on a broad basis, the assumption is

defective, and is misleading to many, many managers and companies all over the world.

4. *Need for prior training in use of the tools of analysis.* The QC Circle concept is unique in accepting this need. This is, of course, consistent with the belief that the causes of poor performance are not really known. Other motivational systems, founded mainly on the prior assumption that the workforce "can but won't," see no need for training in how to analyze, that is, what is there to analyze if we know the causes at the outset? It is a tribute to the Japanese that they have recognized this need for prior training (see Table 8.2).

5. *Group or individual analysis?* The QC Circle is designed for group study. Except for the Scanlon plan, all the rest look to individuals for contribution.

6. *Identification of projects.* The QC Circle concept provides for projects to be proposed by the company hierarchy as well as by the QC Circle itself. Again, except for the Scanlon plan, other motivational plans look mainly to the individual to identify "his own" project.

7. *Conduct of the analysis.* The QC Circle conducts its own analysis, although with access to the hierarchy if needed. To a degree, all systems provide for self-analysis, but for the most part the analysis, if any, is left for someone else, for example, a suggestion blank is filled out and dropped into a box. Here again, the prior training has served a vital purpose, by making the QC Circle largely self-sufficient as to analysis.

8. *The reward.* The QC Circle emphasis is mostly on nonfinancial rewards, featuring improvement (company improvement, self-improvement) as a goal in its own right. The system of Stakhanovism also has this feature, although emphasizing the abstraction of communism, or its derivative of building a better Socialist world. The ZD schemes stress pride of workmanship. The piecework and the suggestion systems rely on money incentives, the amount being related to the value of the work or the suggestion.

9. *Follow-through to make changes effective and set up controls.* Here the QC Circles play a larger role than is found in other motivational systems, again because of being trained in how to play this role.

Table 8.2 Comparison of training plans.

Elements of the plan	As practiced in:	
	Conventional motivational plans	QC Circles
Choice of projects	Left up to employee to identify his own project	Some projects identified by management; others identified by the QC Circle
Training in how to analyze a project	None provided	Formal training program provided out-of-hours; voluntary
Analysis of the project	By employee himself or with such aid as he can muster; otherwise, by formal suggestion that is analyzed by someone else	Analysis is by the QC Circle, out-of-hours, using training tools previously provided
Payment for time spent	None	Varies from no pay to full pay for hours spent
Payment for successful idea	Definite payment varying with value of idea	No payment. Indirect effect on company profit and resulting bonus that uses one formula for all employees
Nonfinancial incentives	Opportunity of creativity and recognition; pride of workmanship	Opportunity for training; opportunity for creativity and recognition; membership in a group; response to company leadership

It is evident that the QC Circle is different enough to be regarded as a new industrial form. The Scanlon plans have some of the features but are not really based on the workforce—they involve joint committees of managers, union officials, and the workforce. (Union officials are debarred from membership in the QC Circles.)

Table 8.2 summarizes the foregoing comparison as applied to creative projects.

MORE THAN MOTIVATION

Of the utmost importance is the fact that, through the QC Circles, the Japanese have made a clean break with a tired, outworn theory that plagues the West. This is the theory that the company's quality troubles are due to operator indifference, blunder, and even sabotage. Under this theory, the operators could solve the company's quality problems if only the right motivational lever could be found and thrown.

The QC Circle concept starts with a different set of beliefs:

- We don't really know the cause of our quality troubles; we don't even know which are the main troubles.

- We must teach people *how* to analyze the trouble pattern to identify the main troubles.

- We must teach people how to list the suspected causes of the main troubles, and how to discover which are the real causes.

- We must help people to secure remedies for these real causes.

- We must teach people how to hold the gains through modern control.

All this is in refreshing contrast to the painted, noisy spectacles that characterize all too many of our motivational programs.[3] The speeches are made, the posters go up, the pledge cards are signed, the hot potato is thrown into the lap of the operators. Yet, except as a show for customer relations, what good is it if the basic assumptions are defective? Have these assumptions been checked? Are the main troubles really operator-controllable? Can the operators, by themselves, discover what to do differently from what they have been doing ? If these assumptions are not sound, the structure built on them cannot be sound either.

CONCLUSION

The QC Circle movement, standing by itself, must be characterized as a brilliant achievement—a *tour de force* in management leadership. Nowhere else have I seen industrial companies succeed in so constructively harnessing the interest, the time, and the ingenuity of the workforce to the myriad's of intradepartmental problems—not only problems of control, but problems of breakthrough as well.

Whether the QC Circle concept can be adapted to other cultures is at present open to serious doubt. At the June 1966 Conference of the European Organization for Quality Control (in Stockholm, Sweden), I related the QC Circle story from the lecture platform. It turned out to be the high point of the conference. The questions from the audience required that a special, added session be set up, devoted solely to the QC Circle story. At this special session, and in the corridor discussions thereafter, it became evident that no one envisioned readily how to make the QC Circle concept effective in any other culture. It is amazing that such should be the universal reaction.

Finally, it is well to note the broader setting of which the QC Circles are a part. That broader setting is the revolution that the Japanese have created in their approach to quality. Here I venture to publish, for the first time, the prediction I have made in my 1966 lectures (in America, Japan, Sweden, and Yugoslavia). This prediction is based on seeing, at first hand, the trend of events in Japan and in a good many other countries over the last two decades. During those decades, the Japanese, through a revolution in quality control practices, have already attained a world competitive position, despite starting with the worst quality reputation among the industrial nations. Now there is evidence that the energy that created this revolution, far from being spent, is still in full vigor.

In my observation, no other nation is so completely unified on the importance of good quality achievement, so eager to discover and adopt the best practices being followed in other countries, so avid in training all company levels and functions in modern methods of controlling quality, so vigilant in regulating the quality of exported goods. To be sure there is progress along these fronts in all countries, but nowhere else is there the broad-based sense of devotion and, especially, the *sense of urgency* that is so evident among the Japanese. Witnessing their accelerated pace, and comparing this with the pedestrian progress of other countries, the conclusion is inescapable:

The Japanese are headed for world-quality leadership, and will attain it in the next two decades, because no one else is moving there at the same pace.

ENDNOTES

1. Juran, J. M. 1964. *Managerial breakthrough.* New York: McGraw-Hill, Chapter 4: The Pareto Principle.
2. Juran, J. M. ed.,1962 *Quality control handbook.* 2nd ed., New York: McGraw-Hill: 11–13.
3. Juran, J. M. 1966. Quality problems, remedies and nostrums. *Industrial Quality Control,* (June) 22:647–653.

9

Operator Errors—Time for a New Look

There are good grounds for asserting that our managerial convictions about "operator error" are derived mainly from unsupported beliefs that, over the years, have acquired an aura of mystery, superstition, and dogma. It further appears that these beliefs have become deeply rooted in the managerial culture to a point that they are stubbornly resistant to challenge, whether by competitive theory or by contradictory facts.

My grounds for these assertions are broader than just one man's experience. In recent years, in my courses on Management of Quality Control, I have been taking soundings from the attending managers through assignment of group projects for discussion and solution. Some of these projects deal with the subject of operator error. Tallying up the results of the polls, discussions, and conclusions of these and related soundings taken in these courses, it is my conviction that despite all the programs, posters, pledge cards, pep talks, and the rest, many companies have been fighting a war without knowing clearly who is the enemy. This is no way to fight a war.

What is lacking is clear, quantitative knowledge about the nature of errors. Only through such knowledge can the superstition and dogma be challenged successfully. However, since we lack this knowledge, there persists a widespread confusion about the nature and extent of operator errors. Amid such confusion, it should not be surprising if managers appear to grasp at straws, at panaceas, at the lure of the demagogue. To many of these managers, such programs are squarely in line with their axiomatic beliefs, and, hence, completely logical.

Editor's Note: The paper appearing here in Chapter 9 was published in 1968 in *Quality Progress* (February) 1(2): 9–11, 54.

It is high time for our theoreticians and practitioners to wade into this subject, to think it through, and to put together the factual data needed to identify and quantify the elements that make up what we so glibly call *operator error*. What follows here is one man's contribution.

CONCEPT OF SELF-CONTROL

One most useful step we could take is to talk about first things first. There has been too much talk about operator motivation as if it were the starting point in dealing with errors. In modern industry, the starting point is not operator motivation but rather the concept of self-control. Under this concept, we set up a job so as to make the job holder self-sufficient. We provide him with the means needed to carry out his assigned job, and we then hold him responsible for getting results. We have been rather clear about insisting that the job holder produce results, but we have been less than clear about defining the "means needed" to carry out the job, that is, the *criteria for self-control*. These consist of the following essentials:

1. Means for knowing what he is supposed to do

2. Means for knowing whether he is doing what he is supposed to do

3. Means for changing what he is doing if it does not conform with what he is supposed to do

If we have failed to provide any of these essentials, the resulting errors should be classed as management-controllable. If we have provided every one of these essentials, the resulting errors should be classed as operator-controllable, and it then becomes timely to talk about motivation.

It is most important that we understand clearly, in any specific situation, whether we are dealing with management-controllable or operator-controllable errors. These two species differ remarkably as to methods of diagnosis, and, especially, as to methods for remedy. The one species requires that we look mainly to the designs, processes, methods, instruments, and other features of the "situation," using the tools of science, engineering, and management. The other species requires that we look mainly to the operator, using the tools of the behavioral sciences.

In the majority of companies, there has been little study to determine what proportion of errors is operator-controllable and what proportion is management-controllable. Such is the feedback from my courses. However, enough of such studies have been conducted to tell us a great deal about these proportions. By and large, about 20 percent of all errors are operator-controllable, although this varies greatly among companies, and, especially, from process to process. Accordingly, each company should know its own situation, *in toto*, and the important subdivisions. Lacking this knowledge, the grand strategy of error reduction is blind—the managers don't really know what they are fighting.

MANAGERIAL THEORY OF OPERATOR ERROR

The feedback from the courses on Management of Quality Control has been rather illuminating in discovering managers' beliefs about operator error. The polls (originally by a show of hands and more recently by secret ballot) have been in response to two questions relating to managers' beliefs about worker motivation:

1. On a by-and-large basis, do your fellow managers back at home subscribe to the indifference theory of industrial behavior (that is, workers exhibit no enthusiasm for good work because people are no damn good), or do they subscribe to the craftsmanship theory (that is, workers exhibit no enthusiasm because the managers haven't designed industrial jobs in a way which makes them very interesting). In 12 such polls conducted during courses held in the United States (1964–1967), out of 522 attending managers polled:

   - 209, or 40 percent felt that the managers back home adhere to the indifference theory.

   - 313, or 60 percent felt that the managers back home adhere to the craftsmanship theory.

   (The polls taken in the courses I have conducted abroad reveal some very interesting differences in managerial attitude internationally, but that is another story.)[1]

2. If you (the managers attending the courses) were given charge of a brand-new plant, would you run it under the indifference theory or the craftsmanship theory?

   Out of 129 attendees polled:

   - 121, or 94 percent would choose to operate under the craftsmanship theory.

   - 8, or 6 percent would choose to operate under the indifference theory.

As to this question, there seem to be no differences internationally. In no country has such a poll shown less than 80 percent of the attendees favoring the craftsmanship theory. From these polls it is my conclusion that:

1. Company managements differ widely in their beliefs as to what causes industrial behavior adverse to company interests.

2. To an astonishing degree, managers attending the courses do not concur with these beliefs as presently held by their companies' management.

Under such a state of affairs, it seems evident (to me) that an essential prerequisite of a motivational program is an understanding of (1) what is the prevailing company attitude toward worker motivation, and (2) to what extent is this attitude really supported by the managers. This is important, since the managers do not merely theorize; they act on the theories. The decisions about whether to trust operators or not, whether to use many or few inspectors, whether to rely on system versus people, are all related to the managers' beliefs about motivation. The character of the motivational program is likewise affected by these beliefs.

Subspecies of Operator Error

Beyond the need for understanding the state of managerial theory about operator motivation, there is a need to look deeper than ever before into the nature of operator error itself. Right now there exists a widespread belief among managers that once we have met the criteria for operator self-control, the manager's job is done, and the rest is up to the operator. In terms of organization theory, this belief is wellfounded. However, in terms of getting results, the belief is a gross oversimplification, since it ignores the wide differences in the kinds of operator error.

Some years ago this editor undertook to categorize the subspecies of inspector error. It turned out that these subspecies were so different from one another that knowledge of these differences was an essential prerequisite to reduction of inspector error.[2]

In the light of this experience, and with the clear need for a deeper understanding of the nature of operator error, it is timely to propose that we classify operator error into its subspecies. There are at least three of these:

1. *Willful errors.* The operator is *deliberately* failing to comply. He could comply, but he has no intention of doing so, for reasons that are good enough for him.

2. *Lack of skill.* The operator is *unintentionally* failing to comply. He is aware of the errors as he makes them, but he is *unable* to eliminate the errors—he isn't skillful enough.

3. *Inadvertence.* Not only is the error unintentional, the operator is even unaware he has made the error.

We have very little data on what is the industrywide breakdown of operator errors among these subspecies. (This editor would welcome such data.) Since, as we shall see shortly, each of these subspecies has its own problems of diagnosis and remedy, the lack of this breakdown is again a handicap to grand strategy. Lacking data on the breakdown of operator errors by these subspecies, it is all too easy for managers to conclude that the errors are all willful, and all too many managers actually believe this.

Willful Errors

Willful errors result from a wide variety of personal reasons: a shortcut to make it easier to meet some other standard (cost, schedule, and so on), a belief that the quality standard is nonsense, a way of getting even with the boss, and so on. Some, perhaps most, of the reasons are the result of "good" intentions rather than malice. However, the logic behind all of these reasons is based on the premises of the operator. The manager who tries to understand these willful errors by logical reasoning from his own premises ends up in a state of frustration or in a state of unwavering belief in the X (indifference) theory of operator motivation.

The missing ingredient is the understanding of what is on the worker's mind when he makes and continues to make willful errors. Seldom can this understanding be arrived at solely by discussion among managers. They are trapped by their own premises within their own self-sealing thought system, including the fact that they (the managers) are also a part of the problem. To get objective answers, the managers would need to sample employee thinking. In turn, since most managers are but amateur psychologists, such a study would require that they enlist the aid of the personnel specialists and behavior scientists. To bring these people into the act has complications of another sort. Such a project is difficult to organize, and it carries the risk that at the end of it the manager will get answers not in the form of meaningful data but in the form of the gibberish of the of psychology.

Lack of Skill

In studying processes that are highly operator-controllable, it is common to find that some operators make fewer errors than others. This is a *consistent* phenomenon—it goes on month after month.

What causes this consistent difference? There is a wide variety of theories: the better operators come from an ancestry with a tradition of good work; they are naturally better motivated; they have a knack; they have a natural aptitude (how do you explain Bill Tilden?), and so on.

This editor takes a dim view of these armchair explanations. In my experience, when there is a consistent difference in operator performance, the place to discover the reason for the difference is the factory floor, not the office. The technique is to study, in detail, the operations as performed by both the "good" operators and the "bad" operators. Most of the time these studies are rewarding; they disclose what it is that the one does which the other does not. In this way the "secret" is made known to the managers who then possess the key for bringing all operators up to the level of the best.

The foregoing technique is not limited to quality improvement; it has universal application in other industrial functions and outside of industry as well. In its generalized form, the technique consists of:

1. Measuring the performance of multiple performers to discover who are consistently the best and who are consistently the worst.

2. Observation of the actual practice of the performers, both best and worst, to discover the differences in their practice.

3. Experimental verification to identify which of these differences of practice bring about the differences in results.

4. Extension of the best practices to all performers through retraining, redesign of the process, or other appropriate means.

The main significance of such studies lies in the fact that a solution is already in the house, that is, the "best" operators are in fact solving the problem somehow. However, the nature of this "somehow" is not known to the management or to the "worst" operators. (I have seen plenty of instances where it wasn't known to the "best" operators, either.) The problem in lack of skill is more usually one of finding this secret solution than one of inventing a new solution.

The successful end of such studies is to bring everyone up to the level of the best, to make a champion out of every duffer.

Inadvertent Errors

The distinguishing feature of this subspecies is that at the time of the error, the operator is not even aware of its existence until it is called to his attention, either by someone else or by some evident consequence of the error. Such errors are inherent in the fallible nature of the human animal (or at least such is the experience and hence the belief of some of us).

Recently we have seen an attempt to solve this problem by denying its existence, that is, by asserting that human fallibility doesn't exist once the right motivational lever is thrown. In due course, the experimental evidence will have the last word as to this new theory. Meanwhile, the record is of another sort: Historically, human beings have been fallible, including the champions. Historically also, we have reduced inadvertent errors not by motivation but by fool proofing operations. Our factories exhibit masterpieces of error-free processes. The managers properly take pride in them and exhibit them as works of art, which indeed they are. (See Table 9.1)

The concept of foolproofing is not limited to solution of inadvertent errors; it can deal with any subspecies of error, whether due to lack of skill, willfulness, or still other causes.

Table 9.1 Possible role of operator

Activities in sequence	Management		Operator controllable errors	
	Controllable errors	Willful	Lack of skill	Inadvertent
Observe errors	x	xx	x	–
Theorize as to causes of errors	x	xx	x	–
Analyze to discover true causes	x	xx	x	–
Theorize as to remedies for causes	x	xx	x	–
Analyze to discover optimum remedy	–	xx	–	–
Apply chosen remedy	–	xx	x	–

Legend: xx operator's possible role is significant, even decisive
x   operator's possible role can be useful
–   operator's possible role is dubious

Role of the Operator

Elimination of errors, whether operator-controllable or management-controllable, requires that we go through an invariable sequence of activities:

1. Observe errors by their symptoms.

2. Theorize as to causes of symptoms.

3. Analyze to discover the true causes.

4. Theorize as to remedies for these causes.

5. Analyze to discover the optimum remedy.

6. Apply the chosen remedy.

Table 9.1 depicts the usual extent to which the operator can play a useful role in the foregoing sequence.

I have structured the table (published here for the first time) to reflect conditions as commonly found in American practice. Obviously, the table would differ depending on conditions in different plants. In a radically different culture, such as the Japanese QC Circles, the table would be remarkably different, since the operators are trained in the use of the tools of analysis and are motivated to take on projects of discovering causes and remedies for all types of errors.

Table 9.1 offers a do-it-yourself matrix for any company. (If the table doesn't reflect the conditions in your company, tailor the table to fit.) The point is that it is feasible for any company to judge the useful role of the operator as to the various permutations of subspecies of error and of activities needed to convert symptoms into remedies.

It is significant that the operator can make a useful contribution not only as to operator-controllable errors but also as to management-controllable errors. However, in the case of the latter species, his contribution is concerned with identifying the shortcomings in the system of self-control. The operator is commonly in a good position to discover these shortcomings, since he meets them at every turn: information incomplete, machines in need of maintenance, instruments out of calibration, and so on .

Not only is the operator often aware of these shortcomings, he often brings the matter to the attention of the supervisor. Sometimes this is done by the operator taking the initiative in response to suggestion schemes and the like. More usually the operator does it defensively, to avoid being blamed for something beyond his control.

Some of the worst quality morale situations are found in plants where these findings of the operators are not acted on by the supervisors. These inactions tell the operators that the management has no interest in quality, no matter what the posters say. In fact, one of the very real benefits of the motivational campaigns is that the supervision is now forced to take action on these same shortcomings in the system of self-control.

CONCLUSION

The foregoing is necessarily a limited analysis. Some of the assertions are backed up by ample data; mostly they are not. But they are assertions that can be tested by any practitioner who has a living laboratory in which to conduct a do-it-yourself study.

The main burden of this paper is to urge practicing managers to dig out the facts as to:

- The state of self-control

- The proportions of management-controllable versus operator-controllable errors

- The proportions of the various subspecies of operator errors

Any one conducting such a study not only stands to clarify the factual situation in his own company, he stands to make a contribution to his fellow practitioners as well. His factual data will certainly be studied with interest. But more than this, our experience is that when new data are collected, fresh challenges can be put to long-standing beliefs. We can make good use of a few such challenges.

ENDNOTES

1. Juran, J. M. 1982. *Quality control handbook,* 2nd ed. New York: McGraw-Hill: 10-15 to 10-17.
2. Ibid. 8-25 to 8-35.

REFERENCE

Juran, J. M. 1967. The QC Circle phenomenon. *Industrial Quality Control* (January) 23(7):329–336.

10

Mobilizing
for the 1970s

W e approach the 1970s with the apprehension that we are about to
encounter some very uncomfortable experiences with respect to
quality of products and services. It is strange that such should be
the case when we look back on what has been a lot of genuine progress.

During the last quarter century, we have seen several useful revolutions in our approach to achieving quality. The most brilliant of these revolutions has been in technology: new machines, tools, instruments,
materials, products. A second revolution has taken place in management of
the quality function, and has brought us new forms of organization, quality
planning methods, and tools (some of which have been less than brilliant).
A third revolution has been in manpower, through creation of a new category of highly trained quality specialists.

It would be pleasant indeed if we could pick up our newspapers and
journals and read that all this progress has brought us to a golden age of
quality control. Instead, we read that our automobiles are being recalled by
the millions, that our appliance repair services are both dishonest and
incompetent, our advertising is deceitful, our product warranties are
watered down, and our shockingly costly defense system is something less
than reliable.

As it happens, most of the newspaper stories are well founded. Yet I,
for one, do not feel that our quality has been going downhill. Within any
one product line, we have been getting better and better, decade by decade.
Our food keeps getting more nourishing and tasty, our homes more comfortable, our drugs more efficacious, our transport swifter, our weapons

---

Editor's Note: The paper appearing here in Chapter 10 was published in 1969 in *Quality Progress* (August) 11(8): 8–17.

more deadly, and our canned music more like the real thing. Why, then, is there so much public clamor? I believe there are two major reasons.

One reason is that the total visible extent of user trouble due to quality failures is actually rising. The rise is not because products are getting worse. Rather, it is the result of usage rates rising more than enough to off-set continuing quality improvements.

The second reason for public clamor is more subtle, but is also much more important, since it consists of a major historical event. Ours is the century in which, for the first time in human history, great masses of human beings have placed their safety, their health, and even their daily well-being behind numerous protective dikes of quality control. Just look at a few of these dikes:

- National defense and prestige are today precariously balanced on the quality and reliability of complex hardware.

- The daily safety and health of the common man now depend absolutely on the quality of manufactured products: drugs, food, aircraft, automobiles, elevators, tunnels, bridges, and so on.

- The ability of our industrial plant to produce goods and services now depends heavily on the reliability of the automated process, which is, in turn, dependent on the quality and reliability of the systems of power, communication, transport, computers, and so on.

- The ability of this same industrial plant to sell its goods and services now depends heavily on their quality and reliability, both domestically and internationally.

- The very continuity of our daily lives is built around the continuity of numerous vital services: power, transport, communication, water, waste removal, and many others. We have structured our society on the premise that these services will continue without interruption. A major power failure paralyzes the lives of millions of people.

We can paint a pleasant picture of the good life, provided that the dikes of quality hold fast. We are also aware of what a monumental mess is created when a dike breaks. What we have not grasped adequately is that life behind all those dikes is a form of living dangerously. Under such a form of life, we have no peace merely because our own dike holds fast. If our neighbor's dike breaks, all dikes become suspect, including our own. As with John Donne's tolling bell, the news of someone else's quality failure multiplies our own apprehensions. The facts of these failures (and their skillful exploitation by the professionals) raises a crescendo of publicity that reaches the lawmakers and to which they contribute fully.

What is new is the decision of the human being to risk his safety, health, and daily well-being on the integrity of the dikes of quality control. (This decision has already gone past the point of no return.) Having made the decision and now experiencing life behind those dikes, the human being has discovered that the dikes are suspect. He is in no mood to be told that we have always had failures. Instead, he is taking the position that the failures had jolly well better stop, and he is enlisting quite an array of support to make his point.

It is time to recognize that the user has a very real problem and that industry is not supplying much of the leadership for solving it. Into this vacuum of leadership there is rushing a wild assortment of candidates: sincere reformers and politicians, consumer cooperatives, independent test laboratories, labor unions, government agencies, insurance companies, and still others, including plenty of the dregs—the political demagogue, the professional muckraker, the unscrupulous lawyer. The industries which fail to supply leadership to the user will find themselves in the position of followers, with policies and goals being set by some combination of this wild assortment. It is hardly a rosy outlook.

The foregoing is the central theme for the 1970s. The user has made his decision to live behind those dikes of quality control, and the dike builders are in a new ballgame. The stakes are simply enormous. It is not merely that huge sums are at stake in product failures, in down time, in recalls, in law suits. The biggest stakes are in share of market, in the very existence of the companies who produce the goods and services in question.

The saving feature is that the user has enough money to pay for good dikes. In this sense what we face is a marketing problem of: discovering what it is the user wants or needs, creating the products and services that will fill these needs, and convincing the user that he should pay the bill.

If industry takes the leadership in doing these things, the threat of the 1970s will become an opportunity. If industry fails to supply the leadership, the threat will become a nightmare.

THE INGREDIENT OF RESPONSE

It is elementary that a revolutionary need requires a revolutionary response. No amount of refining of controls or of patching up the details of planning are of avail when the revolution makes obsolete the long-standing policies and goals. Nothing short of a revision of policies and goals will suffice.

I believe that our present quality policies and goals are seriously out of date. They evolved out of centuries of experience during which quality of product had little effect on the lives of great masses of humanity. We have reached a state where quality of product greatly affects the lives of great masses of people. We must now revise our policies and goals to be responsive to this new state. The ingredients of this response may be listed as follows:

- We have been emphasizing conformance to specification. We need to emphasize fitness for use.

- We have been optimizing the costs of the manufacturer, merchant, and service shop. We need instead to optimize the costs of the user.

- We have studied in depth the effect of quality on our costs. We need to study in depth the greater effect of quality on our income.

- We are tolerating a creeping perfectionism. It is time to set the brakes.

- We are badly confused on the matter of motivation for quality. It is time to get straightened out.

- We have done a lopsided job of training for quality. It is time to balance this.

- Our organizational forms are unlikely to keep us in the race for world quality leadership. We should take a hard look at these forms.

- We have not yet given our vendors full membership on the team. It is high time we did so.

- We have been lax in our approach to launching new products. This should be tightened up.

- We have been designing products. We should give more attention to designing systems.

- A huge wave of new government regulation of quality is coming at us, and we should try to head it off.

- Another wave, that of product liability, may be building up to huge proportions. We can do a good deal to cut this one down to size.

- Our top management's provide inadequate leadership for the quality function. It is time to forge the tools that will enable top management to provide this leadership.

- Finally, there are some interesting roles looking for actors.

Let me now elaborate on all this.

FITNESS FOR USE

The most fundamental need is the revision of our concept of the company's quality mission. We commonly state this mission as one of making a *product* that conforms to specification. What is needed is a concept of supplying a *service* that meets the needs of the user—"fitness for use."

Fitness for use comprises four main elements:

1. Quality of design, that is, the collection of characteristics of the product as intended by the designer.

2. Quality of conformance, that is, the extent to which the product adheres to the design.

3. Availability, that is, the extent to which the product performs its functions when called upon by the user to do so.

4. Customer service, that is, the extent to which the manufacturer and the marketing chain provide prompt and fair action on product failures, complaints, guarantees, and so on.

The user has no interest in buying products as such. Instead, he has a keen interest in securing various services he needs: transport, comfort, recreation. To secure these services, he may be forced to buy a product: the car, the air conditioner and the television set, respectively. But that is today. Tomorrow someone will offer him a way to secure the service without buying a product—by lease of the product, by sale of the service only, by some system redesign that renders the service unnecessary

Two hairnet manufacturers were in competition. They devoted much energy to improving the qualities of the product and to strengthening their marketing techniques. They were both made extinct when someone developed a hair spray that gave the user a better way of holding her hair in place.

It doesn't need to be as dramatic as the extinction of a product. During my recent seminars in Spain, a quality manager related how his company had ordered steel, by specification, from a Japanese steel company. Back came a cable: "What use will you make of this steel? Could you send us a picture of what you are planning to make?"

I was discussing this same problem with executives of an East Coast company. One of them observed, "We spend a lot of time arguing about standards for the finish plating on our products. We don't even know whether the users would prefer paint."

It may be protested that all this is merely an exercise in semantics. Don't we try to write our specifications so as to achieve fitness for use? Certainly we do. However, just compare our approach for discovering what is fitness for use with our approach for assuring conformance to specifications.

In the matter of assuring conformance to specification, it is the rule, not the exception, in the civilian as well as in the defense industries, for us to prepare a comprehensive quality plan, drafted by trained specialists, spelled out in a written quality manual, and approved by the cognizant managers. We then review the action taken, again by trained specialists to whom we give authority to stop the proceedings in case of failure to conform to specifications.

Our approach to discovering and assuring fitness for use is, by comparison, a rambling, loosely organized affair, in which hunch, guesswork, and just honest ignorance play important, if not vital, roles. We act as though the user's interest is in buying a product, so we stress that product and its definition through specification. We are weak in studying the user's basic needs—the very situation that stirs up his interest in products. We are weak in understanding the user's problems, his environment and, especially, his economics. It is the exception, not the rule, for us to go after understanding the user's needs with the same thoroughness, formality, and professional skills as we go after conformance to specification.

Discovery of fitness for use cannot be made in the manufacturers' offices or laboratories: it can be made only on the user's premises. Only by seeing the user in action can we discover what are his quality problems—his costs, his down time, his discomfort, his market.

As we learn these things, we discover, of course, that we can eliminate some of his troubles by refining the product—beef up the bolt that keeps breaking. However, we discover also some problems of the user which require a different answer—a contract revision for selling on a service basis rather than on a unit of hardware basis, that is, so much for an hour of service. In other cases we can, through a system redesign, relieve the user of a disagreeable chore, as in self-lubricating bearings or soluble coffee. In a word, we must learn to sell performance, not products.

In fitness for use, we are at our worst when we know the facts but ignore them because we have a vested interest in perpetuating some evil. A shocking example of this prevails in the spare parts business. It is worth examining this in some detail.

Our original equipment manufacturers (OEM) buy many of their components from vendors. Usually a few large OEM companies dominate the industry, and these companies make very large purchases. To a vendor, the gain or loss of one of these purchase contracts is a matter of great significance—it may represent 10 to 50 percent of the sales in that product line.

OEM companies are very much aware of their overwhelming economic power, and they insist that their purchasing agents use this power. These purchasing agents are skilled specialists who are supported by competent engineers and well-equipped laboratories. Collectively, they use these skills, backed up by the OEM economic power, to force vendors to compete sharply against each other, in price, in quality, and in service.

So far, it sounds like a normal competitive situation that brings out the best in all concerned. However, OEM companies do not stop there. They drive the vendors' prices down to a point such that there is little or no profit in selling to OEM companies. OEM companies know this, but they keep up the practice just the same.

The vendors also know there is little or no profit in selling to OEM companies, and many would just walk away from such customers if it were not for the spare parts business. Here the market is completely different.

The vendors sell spare parts to numerous wholesalers, distributors, and other merchants. These, in turn, sell to retail service shops who use the spare parts in making repairs to failed hardware. In contrast to the few OEM customers, there are many merchants who buy the spare parts.

With some exceptions, the purchases of any one merchant are not a matter of great significance to the vendor. Hence, the merchant, though usually a competent businessman, does not have overwhelming economic power. Neither does he have the support of competent engineers and laboratories, so his demands on a technological level, including quality of product, are only rudimentary. This technological ignorance characterizes the entire distribution chain and is at its worst in the case of the ultimate consumer, whose ignorance is complete.

In consequence, the profit picture for spare parts business is rather rosy. The ultimate consumer, because he has no real choice, pays the repair bills. From these payments there is ample money to provide a profit to all links in the spare parts distribution chain, including the manufacturer.

The evil hidden in all this is that the vendor relies on spare parts business to give him his total profit, both for sale of spares and for sale to OEM companies. He continues to sell to OEM companies mainly because such sales make it easier for him to sell the spares. The distribution chain logically concludes that the vendor who got his product by the OEM engineers is more likely to have a sound design than the vendor who did not. (This logic is not complete either, since in subsequent production, the lots that are not up to OEM standards are likely to be shipped out as spares.)

What is presented here is a spectacle of the ultimate users living behind some protective dikes of quality control when the vendors have a vested interest in leaky dikes. What OEM companies save in driving down the profit of vendors is paid for, over and over again, in the repair bills of the ultimate consumer. The system is a disgrace to the economy, and we ought to get rid of it.

OEM people have plenty to answer for, partly for driving the prices down to a point that they know is a poor return for the vendors, but mainly for clinging to a concept of optimizing the manufacturers' costs instead of the users' costs. (I will shortly deal with this problem.) I believe it is time for our OEM people to take the full responsibility for what happens to long life apparatus over the entire life span, and not abdicate this to the spare parts merchants and repair shops.

OPTIMIZING THE USERS' COSTS

It would be a giant step forward if our manufacturers adopted the policy "We will optimize the users' costs." Today OEM manufacturers optimize their own costs. So do companies in the wholesale distribution chain. So do companies who retail the products. So do the repair shops. These suboptimizations do not optimize the users' costs. Sometimes, as in the case of spare parts, they are squarely antagonistic to the users' costs.

The starting point in adopting such a policy is to understand what are the users' costs. It is simply astonishing that our manufacturers know so little about the users' economics. As a corollary, the opportunity for original, creative work, and for identifying new market opportunities is simply breathtaking. To those who are looking for virgin territory in which to discover hidden gold, this is about the most exciting possibility for a high return on the costs of prospecting.

Recently a friend of mine had such a satisfying experience. He is quality manager of a company making power-driven tools used in the construction and lumber industries. On one line of these products, he had successfully completed a program to improve the reliability of the tools. He then proposed that the company raise its prices, but the marketing manager was unwilling to go along on the grounds that standard tools must sell at competitive rather than premium prices. On appeal, the president backed up the marketing manager.

However, the quality manager did secure approval for a field study to discover the value of the improved reliability to users of the tools. A study team visited a number of users. Some of them were of no help. They had inadequate records, or no records. However, some users had excellent records through which their costs could be quantified.

It was found that the value of the improved reliability was very real in the form of less repair time and less spare parts. However, even more important was the reduction in down time, that is, when a tool failed, not only did the user take a loss due to the idle tool and the idle operator; there was a much bigger loss due to idle time of heavy equipment waiting on the work performed by these tools.

Armed with this data, my friend was able to justify a price increase to the president, the marketing manager, the sales force, and the customers. The company gained $500,000 in annual income and lost no customers in the process.

In this example, what stands out is the fact that the users' costs of down time were decisive, yet the conventional quality cost studies of the manufacturer would fail to disclose this, and thereby would fail to disclose the market opportunity present. Only a study of the users' economics can disclose such opportunities.

A generalization of this principle leads us directly into what has been labeled as life cycle costing, which does look at the users' costs. The concept is one of looking at the total costs of securing service from long-life hardware. In many instances these costs, over the useful life span, are several times the original purchase price, which is plenty to think about.

We might note that users are pushing to force the manufacturers to consider these users' costs. In the printing industry, it is common for paper mills to compensate users for down time of presses in the event of paper breaks. The same practice is emerging in the case of synthetic yarn breaks in the textile industry. The airlines buy engines under a contract that guarantees the cost of maintenance; the excess is charged to the manufacturer. We can expect a continuing expansion of this trend, and we should welcome it. Such provisions make the user's costs a direct factor in the manufacturers' thinking, which is as it should be.

These user's cost considerations are not limited to long-lived apparatus; they apply to consumables as well.

A manufacturer of abrasive cloth was losing share of market and couldn't understand why. His laboratory tests showed good compliance with specification. When he checked with key customers, he found that they exhibited little interest in the specification. What concerned them was something called "cost per hundred pieces polished," and his cloth had the highest costs, as seen by the user.

There is also some initiative by manufacturers. There is a trend in the manufacture of heavy equipment to quantify availability as one of the design parameters. Where this is based on the user's economics, it is a most constructive step forward.

The trend of some manufacturers and some merchant companies to establish their own service shops is a step in the direction of optimizing the user's costs. The resulting service contracts and feedback give companies a superior knowledge of the user's needs and lead to redesigns, both in contract and in hardware, which will optimize the user's costs.

EFFECT OF QUALITY ON INCOME

Quality affects the economics of the manufacturing company in two basic ways:

- The effect on costs, that is, scrap rework, returns, inspection, test
- The effect on income, that is, prices, share of market, success in bidding

Notice that the word "quality" is used here in two different meanings. The "quality" that affects costs is conformance to specification. The "quality" that affects income is fitness for use.

By now most companies have learned how to measure and analyze their quality costs—the costs of planning quality, of inspection and test, of control and prevention, of internal and external failures. Analysis of these costs can point to opportunities not disclosed in the conventional accounting reports, and many companies have developed great skills in using these analyses.

In contrast, we are still amateurs on the problem of how to measure the effect of quality on income, and how to identify opportunities to improve income thereby. It is well to look at this topic in some detail, since the effect of quality on income is normally much greater than the effect of quality on costs.

Our quality as seen by the user (fitness for use) may be superior, competitive, or adequate, and our source of income is different in each case.

When our fitness for use is *superior*, we derive our income through a combination of:

- High share of market (if we price competitively)
- Premium prices (if we market selectively)
- Greater ease in bidding and in negotiating contract terms

When our fitness for use is *competitive*, our income is decided not by the minor quality differences. (By definition, the user is unaware of, or uninterested in such differences.) In such cases, prices must also be competitive, and our income depends on share of market which is decided by our marketing skills: attractive packaging, imaginative promotion, personable selling, and seemingly a dash of dancing girls and din. We make ample use of the concept that "If the steaks are alike, sell the sizzle."

When our fitness for use is only adequate, our prices are commonly low, and we rely on these low prices to give us a high share of market.

The role of quality (fitness for use) in securing income becomes evident. At the outset we face a basic policy decision—should we structure our business on a base of quality superiority, competitiveness, or adequacy. It is a most important policy question, and too few companies have faced it squarely. It is time to bring this question of policy out in the open.

I don't mean we should look at these three options and sagely opt for superiority, because anything else sounds like a disgrace. That just sweeps it all under the rug. What we need to do is to examine the situation as seen by the user—his costs, his problems, his convenience. Only when we have done the job of studying the facts as seen by the user can we discover the opportunities and act on them.

There is also plenty of room for creativity through invention of new tools for study. For example, we gain some customers (and lose others) because of our quality. We can identify who are these customers and what they buy. We can quantify this to determine the effect on our income and profit. For the 1970s we should dig deeply into this problem of the effect of quality on income.

Important as is the problem of quality costs, it is dwarfed by the problem of income due to quality. We have been studying the smaller problem first; now it is time to put first things first.

PERFECTIONISM

There are two sides to the coin of fitness for use:

1. We should put forth whatever effort is required to meet the needs of fitness for use.

2. We should avoid any effort that does not contribute to fitness for use. What I mean by "perfectionism" is this fruitless effort.

All this seems very obvious, but there are in fact some powerful forces in the economy that are ever pushing us toward perfectionism. Let me identify the most influential of these:

1. Top management and marketing managers who want something "superior" when this superiority does not contribute to fitness for use and hence will increase costs without increasing income

2. Government regulators and industrial quality managers who are obsessed with conformance to specification in the face of clear evidence that the product is fit for use

3. Theoreticians in all camps who equate tighter specifications with greater fitness for use

4. The enthusiasts and fanatics of the motivational programs who urge that nothing short of perfection will do

5. The reformers and legislators who publicize evidence of failure to conform to specification as proof of unfitness for use

Collectively, this is a big wind, and it has been blowing down anyone who has the temerity to stand up to it. But it is high time to stand up because we are confusing perfection with fitness for use. So far as the user is concerned, the one is not noticeably better than the other. However, the costs of perfection are enormously greater.

The man who stands up to the big wind soon finds himself accused of being indifferent to public safety and health. Motor vehicle safety is a good case in point. We have by now added over $100 of new costs per car for safety devices, perhaps closer to $200. All this will have only a minor effect on the motor vehicle accident rate simply because the vehicle had already been developed to where it was a minor contributor to these accidents. The same billions of dollars if spent on the major causes: alcohol, speeding, irresponsible youngsters, and so on, would have gotten us somewhere.

There is nothing theoretical about this. Look at the strange "job action" incident that took place during the recent protest of the Long Island Parkway police. They were unhappy over their contract package, and they showed their displeasure by enforcing the law. During those two weeks, traffic accidents on that parkway dropped to under one-quarter of the usual level, all without any change in the vehicle.

A severe complicating factor has been the rise of the new world of space systems and ultra-complex defense systems. For these systems we need a quality and reliability well beyond that needed in the civilian sector. But we are utter fools if we try to apply to the civilian sector the degree of reliability required by these systems, since the stakes and the economics are totally different. In the one case, national safety and prestige are at stake. In the other case, it is a matter of making the best use of available assets, so that what should be decisive is not perfection but optimum economics.

The advocates of perfectionism all have some characteristics in common. For the most part:

- They are sincere believers that greater precision, and so on, is "better."

- They are oriented to specifications, not fitness for use.

- They have no responsibility for the costs involved.

The main weapon for dealing with these people is the evidence of fitness for use. Curiously, even the so-called practical people do not utilize adequately the evidence available. We have legions of instances in which products have for years proved their fitness through actual usage. This actual usage constitutes an immense laboratory in which a fantastic number of tests has been conducted, under an equally fantastic assortment of environmental conditions.

In dealing with perfectionism, the road to sanity is marked "fitness for use." During the 1970s, we will have plenty of occasion to travel this road.

MOTIVATION

I hope that in the 1970s we will make an orderly reexamination of the entire question of motivation for quality.

During the 1960s, we have endured quite a bit of nonsense under the guise of motivation for quality. The defense and space industries undertook programs that were largely based on the premise that industry's quality troubles could be solved if the people at the bottom would get interested in their jobs, make fewer blunders, find the causes of errors, and so on. These programs were launched with much fanfare and exhibitionism. Pledge cards were signed "voluntarily," and there emerged periodic communiqués about how well the programs were going. To the uninitiated it seemed that miracles were being achieved, and (illustrated by moving pictures in color) all concerned had become deliriously happy.

The advocates of these programs had unwittingly (or wittingly) struck an axiomatic belief of many managers—the belief that because the people at the bottom have the ability to sabotage quality in spite of management's well-laid plans, they also have the ability to create good quality in spite of poor management planning. The former premise is correct; the latter is not.

It is time to face squarely some stubborn facts:

1. Most quality failures are management-controllable, not operator-controllable.

2. Most operator-controllable failures are the result not of willful errors but of other causes: inadvertence, conflicting standards, lack of skill, and so on, for which motivation is of little avail.

3. The concept of craftsmanship has little application in repetitive, boresome jobs. If this concept is to be reawakened in modern industry, we will have to restructure the jobs, or change radically our concepts of employee participation.

I would hope that in the 1970s we take a new look at motivation for quality. My belief is that the need for motivation for quality is greatest at the top. I don't mean that our managers like poor quality. I mean that despite their sincere efforts and eloquent pleas, they have not dug into the problem enough to discover what they themselves need to contribute. I will discuss this somewhat under the heading of Top Management Leadership.

In the case of worker motivation, I have recently analyzed that question and must refer you to the published paper.[1]

Suffice it to say that we have overemphasized the talk and propaganda, and have underemphasized the study and analysis. There is a big opportunity to discover, through analysis, the knack that distinguishes good from bad performances. There is another big opportunity to go further in fool proofing the operations. It is time to change our emphasis.

TRAINING

Our training in quality control is badly distributed. We have numerous specialists who are well trained in the skills and tools needed for achieving and controlling quality and reliability. However, we have great difficulty in making these skills and tools effective, because our line people are not sufficiently trained in the quality function to make adequate use of these well-trained quality specialists.

We might contrast this pattern of training with that used by the Japanese. They have gone for a massive training program in which managers, supervisors, and specialists at all levels and in all functions learn to be at home in the quality function. As a consequence, these line people carry out, as part of their daily work, numerous activities that we must assign to quality specialists. Thereby they avoid many of the problems of coordination, selling, and so on, that arise from having two men in the picture when one will do. As I have noted elsewhere, this training achievement has also made it possible for the Japanese to enlist the time and energy of nonsupervisors through the device known as the QC Circle.[2]

I have serious doubt that our present approach of teaming up highly trained quality specialists with poorly trained or untrained line people will keep us competitive in the race for world-quality leadership. Right now the Japanese are winning that race. The new need is to bring line managers, supervisors, and specialists into a do-it-yourself situation with respect to the quality function. This involves a battery of training programs:

- Top management to be trained in setting quality policies and goals, in broad quality planning, in design of organization for quality, in the effect of quality on cost and income, in motivation for quality, in executive reports on quality

- Middle managers and supervisors to be trained in process planning and regulation, in analysis of sporadic troubles, in quality improvement, and in data feedback and analysis

- Researchers, developers, and designers to be trained in reliability quantification and analysis, in design of experiments and in other tools associated with launching new designs

- Manufacturing planners to be trained in matters of process capability, instrumentation, process control systems, and so on

- Purchasing agents to be trained in vendor surveillance, vendor rating, joint planning

- Service people to be trained in data systems, field performance analysis, reporting systems

- Accountants to be trained in quality costs and quality reports

(I have omitted use of the QC Circle concept because as yet I am not convinced that this can be adapted into Western culture.)

ORGANIZATION

The patterns of organization for quality differ remarkably around the earth, and it is useful to examine these patterns. I will restrict this examination to the four main patterns that collectively preside over the bulk of the world's efforts to achieve fitness for use.

1. *The United States.* During the 20th century we have revolutionized organization for quality in our large and middle-sized companies by creating centralized QC departments that are manned by trained specialists. However, our line supervisors, in manufacture, in

design, in marketing, and so on, lack such training. As a consequence, we have much difficulty in coordinating the work of these trained specialists with the work of line supervisors to whom we look to execute the planning done by staff specialists.

2. *The Western Europeans.* They, too, have revolutionized their large companies, though not as drastically as have the Americans. They have not made as sharp a separation between planning and execution so that even their large companies have fewer staff specialists than their American counterparts, and their line supervisors thereby retain greater planning responsibilities. Their middle-sized and smaller companies cannot be said to have revolutionized their organizations for quality—they retain much of the concept of the master as supervisor and the craftsman as workman.

   Moreover, the Western Europeans have not concentrated their industry into a relatively few huge companies to the extent that the Americans have. Because of this concentration, American industry is conducted mainly in large, widely owned, professionally managed companies, whereas West European industry is conducted mainly in smaller, owner managed companies. These owner-managed companies have been slower to develop the concept of professional management. They rely instead on their experience and dedication.

3. *The Eastern Europeans.* The "socialist" countries exhibit a basic organization form that differs remarkably from that of any of the capitalistic groups. Following their political revolutions, the East European countries organized their means of production and distribution into government-owned monopolies. Super-imposed on these are central planning and control agencies with wide powers for planning the direction of the economy and for reviewing the work of the monopolies. This planning and review applies to quality as well as to other aspects of their national life.

   In my observation, this organizational form imposes some distinct handicaps on the ability of their industries to achieve fitness for use, in several ways:

   - Central planning tends to insulate companies from the needs of the marketplace. The preoccupation is with specifications and standards rather than with fitness for use.

- Absence of competition multiplies the difficulty of solving specific quality problems.

- Continuing shortages of goods breed their own quality deterioration. It is significant that in those fields where this organization form seems to be bypassed, their quality performance seems to be at its best (competitive exports, defense, and space)

4. *Japan.* Their revolution has been the quality miracle of the century, and we would do well to understand it. The decisive element in their revolution has been their training programs, which have extended to their line people in all functions and at all levels. Through this training, their line managers and supervisors understand how to achieve fitness for use. In consequence, the Japanese have not developed quality specialists and central quality control departments to anything like the degree done in the United States. They do have specialists, but their use is mainly in consulting and auditing.

Looking ahead to the 1970s, I feel that the Japanese organization form has considerable promise of taking them to world leadership in quality. The American attempt to coordinate staff quality specialists with line managers carries a built-in difficulty because of the great difference in training. Aside from this, it is time to reexamine the entire question of retaining our wide separation of planning from execution. This had its origin in the Taylor movement, late in the 19th century, and was justified on the ground that the line supervisor and the workman lacked the education needed to do good planning. That premise was valid in the 1890s but is highly questionable today. Yet we have retained the organizational form anyhow.

I would like to see us embark on a movement to turn more of the planning work back to the line managers and supervisors. Before we can do this, we must do the training job discussed elsewhere in this article.

In spite of the present organization form, Americans should give a good account of themselves in world competition for quality. Western Europeans are handicapped because they have been slower in developing the concept of professional management. Eastern Europeans are handicapped even more (and perhaps fatally) because of their cumbersome, centralized economic setup. The real competitor for world quality leadership is Japan, and I doubt that our present organization form can stand up to their competition.

GOVERNMENT REGULATION
OF QUALITY

Governments have concerned themselves with quality from time immemorial. Until recently, this concern centered around several needs:

1. To protect the safety and health of the citizenry. At first this was control after the fact—punishment of those responsible for the failure of a bridge or for deaths from adulterated food. In due course this extended to control before the fact—licensing of physicians and engineers, approval of ships for seaworthiness, and so on.

2. To protect the purse of the government. Commonly the government controlled the major facilities for production and distribution. The supervision of these facilities required that quality and other specifications be established and met.

3. To protect the foreign trade of the community. This took the form of quality controls on the export of goods, but often the controls extended to process specification and regulation.

4. To protect the purse of the citizenry. This commonly received short shrift. Most purchased goods consisted of natural or semiprocessed materials, widely used and well understood. There were few mysterious qualities known only to the manufacturer; and authorities took the sensible view that the purchaser should be able to protect himself against fraud.

We have recently witnessed a considerable expansion of government intervention on matters of public safety and health. Some of this has been in traditional industries, for example, drugs, and some has been in industries which heretofore have been self-regulating, for example, motor vehicles. In addition, we are seeing all the signs of an attempt to impose government regulation on the grounds of a need to protect the purse of the citizenry. We can be sure that this drive will continue into the 1970s

To date, I have grave doubt that all this agitation will have much effect on the public's health, safety, or assets. In some future paper, I will examine these things in more detail. What should concern us now is the problem of industry's response to this urge to expand government regulation of quality.

In my observation, an individual company cannot by itself head off such regulation. It can, however, contribute leadership to an industry approach. In turn, this industry approach must go down all the main roads:

1. *Examine the facts and the climate of opinion.* Get the facts on those matters that give the public a cause for complaint: safety, health, deceit, incompetence, and so on. Examine the prevailing beliefs and accusations that beset the industry. From these analyses, which should be insured for objectivity, discover whether there is a real need to impose regulation on the industry. If there is no such need, publicize the results, especially the factual base. If, however, there is a need for regulation, then

2. *Draft a plan for self-regulation.* Get it adopted by the industry and have a go at self-regulation by the industry. Publicize this as well. If, in spite of this, it becomes clear that there is risk of government regulation, then

3. *Take the initiative in drafting the legislation.* The matter of who takes the initiative is very important, since it puts on the other fellow the burden of proving the draft is wrong.

To date, neither our companies nor our industry associations have been very effective in dealing with these matters. Some of their responses have been downright inept: denouncing government regulations on ideological grounds, defenses without facts, personal attacks on the reformers, and so on. It has been a sorry spectacle, and I hope we have seen the last of it. The need is for leadership in the companies to achieve an initiative in the industry.

Let there be no delusions that achieving unity in the industry is simple. On the contrary, one of the heavy prices we pay for benefits of competition is the difficulty of getting these same competitors to agree on a common program and, especially, to carry out the agreements. Maybe it just can't be done. If not, we are going to see a lot more government regulation of quality in the 1970s.

PRODUCT LIABILITY

The explosive growth in use of manufactured products has sharply increased the number of injuries users have suffered from these products. These injuries come from a variety of causes: defective design, manufacture, or installation; misuse; ignorance; and still others.

As the number (not the rate) of injuries has risen, legal defenses of the manufacturers have eroded away. The injured party no longer needs to prove he had a contract relationship with the manufacturer. Neither does he need to prove that the manufacturer was negligent. The manufacturers' disclaimers are ruled out as contrary to public policy. The result is essentially one of liability without negligence, and a theory that the injuries should be paid for by whomever has the most assets, that is, the manufacturer.

All this is being whipped up into a thriving business—there is money in it. There have been some extraordinarily large verdicts from juries. These are well publicized by the lawyers who are in this business in an organized way. This publicity, aided by the publicity of product recalls, is building claims consciousness into sizable proportions.

The defense to all this is not merely insurance, since rates have a way of penalizing the worst record. The basic defense is in deeds which will reduce incidence of injuries and of unjustified claims. All hands in the company can contribute to these defenses:

- *Top management* can promulgate a policy on product safety and product recalls. It can structure an organized approach through product safety committees and formal programs; demand dating of the product and good traceability; set up an audit of the entire program; and support industry programs that go beyond the capacity of the unaided company.

- *Design* can adopt product safety as a design parameter. It can require a fail-safe philosophy of design, organize formal design reviews, follow the established codes and secure listings from established laboratories, publish ratings, and arm itself with the modern tools of design technique.

- *Manufacture* can establish a sound quality control program to include systems and procedures for foolproofing matters of product safety. It can train supervisors and operators in use of the product as part of the motivation plan, open the suggestion plans to ideas on product safety and set up the documentation needed to provide tractability and historical evidence.

- *Sales* can train its field force in the contract provisions. It can supply safety information to distributors and dealers, set up exhibits on safety procedures, conduct tests after installation and train uses in safety, publish the list of do's and don'ts that contribute to safety, and maintain a climate of customer relations that minimizes animosity and claims.

- *Advertising* can set up to secure technological and legal review of its copy. It can propagandize product safety through education and warnings.

- *Sales service* can observe use of the product, discover hazards inherent in this use, and feed the information back to all concerned, including the warning and training of users.

- *Accident investigation* should be done promptly and by qualified experts, with early notification to the insurance company. There should be a team review of claims and provision for retaining the failed hardware as evidence. There should be defense of borderline claims to deter unjustified claims.

- *Contracts* should be drawn to avoid unrealistic commitments and "save harmless" provisions. Judicious disclaimers should be included, again to discourage unjustified claims.

VENDOR ON THE TEAM

In a recent paper[3] I examined the new problem of vendor relations in some detail. I will, therefore, merely note the main points of that review.

The big change in the 20th century has been that a vast array of sub-contracting of engineered products has been superimposed on top of the standard materials that formerly dominated vendor-vendee relations. These engineered products call for a revolution in vendor relations, and the slogan in that revolution is "interdependence." The pattern of vendor relations for these new products requires that there be joint planning on several fronts: product design, process development, quality planning, instrumentation, documentation, and others.

The effect of all this is that for these new products, the vendor must be treated like an in-house department in many respects: technological assistance, exchange visits, exchange of data, and so on. At the same time, care must be taken not to encumber vendors of standard, noncritical materials with the more elaborate planning and documentation required by 20th century hardware.

NEW PRODUCT DEVELOPMENT

During the 1970s we should see a continuation of four movements that have already gained momentum:

1. *Early warning devices.* For our 20th century products, the greatest single source of field failures is weaknesses in the inherent design. Since product development and design precedes

usage by several years, managers have long been aware of the desirability of early warning devices that will discover design weaknesses before we go into manufacture, marketing, and use. With the swifter pace of obsolescence and with an accelerating birth rate of new, complex. products, what was once desirable has become essential.

It was this combination of circumstances that gave rise to the reliability engineer. As he gained acceptance, he brought to new product development an unprecedented completeness and formality of analysis. The price paid for this analysis plus its supporting services has been high, and there has undoubtedly been much waste. Yet we have paid the price, and we believe that without it, our exotic hardware would hardly have reached the levels of reliability achieved.

Our civilian industries have been reluctant to go into these elaborate, costly analysis and documentation programs. They certainly want reliable products. and they want early warnings of the design failures. However, the price paid for the defense and space reliability programs is positively frightening to a commercial manufacturer.

The answer, it seems to me, is seen in the list of early warning signals available to any manufacturer:

- During preproduction

  - Design review

  - Prototype testing

  - Environmental testing

  - Overstressing

- During pilot lot production

  - In-house use testing (kitchen, road)

  - Consumer use panels

  - Customers as test laboratories

  - Limited marketing area

- During full scale production

  - Prompt feedback

I believe the day is gone when we can leave these early warnings to be developed by informal discussion, by hunch, by experience. We now need a structured countdown.

2. *Quantification of design parameters.* As a corollary to the concept of fitness for use, our long-lived hardware must now provide essentially continuous service, with prompt restoration of service in the event of failure. The signs are abundant that we are not satisfied to define this fitness for use in terms such as "essentially continuous" or "prompt restoration." What is coming up fast is the quantification of these needs as design parameters. In other words, users are demanding that these products provide a measured continuity of service (availability). To back up these demands, they are quantifying the requirements for mean time between failure, for time to restore service, for cost of maintenance, and so on.

   This is a big change for the designers. To quantify these things will require new data banks, new forms of feedback to designers, new training for designers and still other changes.

3. *Breaking the designer's monopoly.* In all companies, we give to one and only one department a monopoly on publishing the specification. In many of these same companies, this monopoly on publication has come to be regarded as a monopoly on deciding the contents of the specification as well, for example, tolerances, configurations, and so on. The first monopoly is sound; the second is a mistake.

   Decision-making on designs should be based on inputs from all who have a contribution to make. The designer is normally the best informed on matters of structural integrity. However, there are others in the company who are better informed on manufacturing economics, instrumentation, field usage environments, and so on. In those companies where the designer has a monopoly on decision-making, the risk is that his design has not considered all these inputs adequately. Then, having prepared this design, he resists changing it for cultural reasons—he defends "his" design against attack.

   I believe the answer is to formalize the community character at the design inputs. We can retain for the designer or project manager the coordination of all these inputs.

Certainly we must give the designer the benefit of the doubt and the last word on matters of structural integrity. However, the era of the designer's monopoly is over.

4. *Systems design.* Finally, our designs must look not merely to our "products" but to the entire system of providing service to the user. This concept is best exemplified by some imaginative breakthroughs of the past, for example, centrally generated gas and electricity instead of wood fires and oil lamps, self-lubricating bearings, ready-mixed concrete; soluble coffee. In these instances, much or all of the work formerly done by numerous ultimate users has been transferred upstream in the distribution system, mainly to the manufacturers, with gains in cost, quality, convenience, everything.

TOP MANAGEMENT LEADERSHIP

The leadership of our quality function seldom comes from our top managements. More often it comes from our quality control specialists, from inspired middle managers, from determined customers, or from no one. In contrast are other functions, notably finance and marketing, where top management leadership is the rule. What makes the difference?

In part, the difference is historical. Only recently has the quality function risen to top management importance. Hence, the tradition of top management leadership is too new to make this leadership widespread in the quality function. However, in part the difference lies in the maturity of the tools and skills through which top management can make its leadership effective. We would all make a big contribution to our companies if, during the 1970s, we were to make effective the concept of the annual quality program—the equivalent, in the quality function, of the budget of the financial function.

The financial budget sounds like a page full of accounting figures. It certainly ends up that way, but it starts out as a list of deeds we intend to accomplish next year. Each line department is asked to set out its list of intended deeds, within a framework of overall results to be achieved by the company. A staff coordinator called the budget officer summarizes all this for review by higher and higher levels, including top management. The great diversity of deeds requires that they be expressed in the common language of money. The final budget is, therefore, the agreed-on list of deeds "dollarized," or expressed in money.

The quality function lends itself to precisely such an approach, and it is high time that the quality program became a regular use tool of our companies.

The preparation of the quality program should start with a meeting of the minds on quality policies. What markets do we intend to serve? Within these markets, how does quality affect income? What standards do we need to establish—quality leadership, competitiveness, or adequacy? What internal standards will we set for conduct of the quality function? How will we divide up the work of achieving fitness for use among the various company departments, among the various levels of supervision, between line and staff, between supervisors and nonsupervisors, between the company and its vendors, and so on?

Such an agreement on policies greatly simplifies the next step in the quality program, which is the setting of broad goals or objectives. These objectives should cover the essential aspects of user satisfaction: downtime, repairs, returns, complaints. In addition, the objectives should cover other parameters that are familiar to all of us: critical characteristics of the product, costs of inspection and test, internal losses due to defects, costs of planning, of prevention, and so on.

It is important to separate our objectives for improvement or breakthrough from the objectives for control. This means two separate programs, but that is what we should do, since the approach to breakthrough differs so remarkably from the approach to control.

These quantified objectives become the basis of detailed planning, with each department setting out the deeds it must perform as its contribution to the overall quality goals; the manpower, facilities, and so on, it will need to perform these deeds, the associated organization, timetable; and so on.

We already have a working model of the use of a quality program in the President's Audit used by the Japanese. As described by Prof. S. Mizuno[4] at the 1968 conference of the European Organization for Quality Control, this parallels closely the general approach to financial budgeting in U.S. companies. Under this approach, there is an annual (or semiannual) review of quality performance in all departments. Based on this review, programs are proposed for the year ahead. These programs are summarized and reviewed at higher and higher levels, culminating in a review by the president. At this top review meeting, approval is given for the quality program to be undertaken in the following year.

In this Japanese approach, leadership is in the hands of the line managers (as it is in our financial budgeting), with the quality control people serving in an advisory capacity (as do our financial budget officers). Our approach to quality programming would involve more leadership from our quality control specialists, since our line managers are as yet not so well trained in these matters as are their Japanese counterparts. But the concept of the program is as valid in the quality function as it is in finance, and quality managers would do well to study the financial budgetary process and adapt its proven merits to the preparation of such quality programs.

Once the concept of the quality program has been grasped, the way is open for retaining continuing top management participation through executive reports on quality. This parallels the achievement of continuing top management participation in the finance or marketing functions through standardized periodic reporting of sales, profits, assets, and so on.

To date, the design of the executive report on quality has not reached the standardization achieved in the balance sheet or profit-and-loss statement. However, the usual ingredients of these executive reports on quality are well enough known. They consist of converting myriads of small quality facts, none of which merits top management participation, into a few big facts, each worthy of top management participation.

Typically, the system of quality reports summarizes how the company is doing on:

- Customer relations, for example, complaints, returns, service calls, loss of customers, new business

- Direct measures on the product, for example, specific qualities, rating of conformance, reliability, quality versus competitors

- Quality costs, for example, failure costs, inspection, test

- Results of surveys, audits

- Status of solution of major quality problems

SOME OPPORTUNITIES

Inevitably, a broad array of challenges presents a corresponding array of opportunities for creativity and leadership. It would be appropriate to close this article by listing some of the interesting roles waiting for an actor or an entire cast of characters.

1. We need badly a form of objective appraisal of each industry to discover those quality weaknesses to which it has become shock-proof or calloused. Lacking such appraisals, the industries are sitting ducks for a traumatic shock. The shock may come from alert competition outside the industry, with a serious effect on share of market. Alternatively, the shock may come from some skilled

publicist who succeeds in saddling the industry with new
regulations and constraints.

These are times when skilled publicists are on the warpath—
there is fame and fortune in it. Nor is it all bad. Where the publicist
discovers a basic weakness that the industry has overlooked or
ignored, he is performing a useful public service. However, more
usually they seize on scattered instances of inadvertence and
misconduct to build a plausible case, relying on a bumbling
industry defense to clinch it. In sympathizing with such industries,
we cannot help wondering what they were doing all those years
and with all their resources.

The professional society has a potential role to play here and, in
my opinion, a duty to play it. I do not share the view of those
professional society leaders who want to keep the society out of
"controversial" matters. Such abdication leaves a vacuum to be
filled by the amateurs, who will then write the rules for the
professionals.

2. We need to develop strong, numerous linkages with the
   consuming public. It is simply astonishing that in quality
   matters vitally affecting the consuming public, those who are
   professionals in achieving fitness find themselves as spectators
   on the sidelines rather than as participants in the arena.

   It is time for our industry and technical committees to take a
   look, to identify the live consumer quality problems, to alert
   all concerned to the dangers and opportunities present, and to
   offer some objective proposals.

3. We need a better dialogue with top management. It has long
   been evident to me that top management regards quality as a
   business problem, whereas the "professionals" have regarded
   it as a technological problem.[5] A wide gulf separates these two
   viewpoints, and it will take a long time to build a connecting
   bridge.

   Of course, each company presents the local professionals
   with an opportunity for a dialogue. However, many reflexes
   and restraints complicate this relationship. A dispassionate
   dialogue should be free from these local restraints.

   Here again, there is opportunity for committees of the
   professional societies to strike out boldly. They can set up a form
   of dialogue with top managers. They can use this dialogue to
   break into the self-sealing thought system of the professionals

(as well as that of the top managers). They can disseminate the findings to all concerned so as to broaden the base of action.

4. We need to conduct a major invasion of the service industries. The revolution in quality control methodology has to date been extensive in our manufacturing industries but sparse in our service industries. These service industries (banking, insurance, hospitals, schools, maintenance shops, transportation, and so on) offer an exciting prospect for specialists looking for the frontier. Whether as salaried insiders or as outside consultants,[6] these specialists have the opportunity to become the quality leaders for their respective industries by designing the pioneering installations, writing the leading papers, writing the manuals and handbooks, and conducting the training courses. It is a most rewarding life for the person who prefers the professional career to the hierarchical career.

5. We need a good deal of research to acquire, analyze, and publish useful data of several varieties:

   • What are prevailing industry costs for various categories of quality control effort and waste, for example, inspection, test, scrap, rework, field returns, guarantee charges?

   • What are the prevailing failure rates for components, subsystems, and so on? A number of local data banks have been started, all with limitations that restrict their use as a universal bank. We must break through this somehow. The example of the Swedish concept (that all data on the performance of electronic components are public property) should be studied carefully.

   • What is the experience with vendor performance? To date, I have not been convinced that our vendor surveys are useful predictors of future vendor performance. What we need is the quality equivalent to the financial credit rating, for which we do have a national data bank in the form of the Dun & Bradstreet service.

   • What is the precision of processes? It should be feasible to prepare manuals of process capability along with the relative cost of precision for various competing processes. These manuals would be quite helpful in product design, manufacturing planning, control planning, and other ways.

The foregoing list is only a sample. At no time in my 45 years of association with the quality function have I seen so many opportunities for creativity and leadership. Some of these opportunities can be seized and realized by individuals, but more usually they require a team effort under some professional sponsorship.

ASQC is admirably structured to provide sponsorship for those who are willing to go after these opportunities. However, to date ASQC has been mainly preoccupied with internal matters. A quick tally of the membership on various Society committees, councils, boards, and so on, shows that of 630 names,

- 555, or 88 percent serve on bodies devoted mainly to internal matters

- 75, or 12 percent serve on bodies devoted mainly to external matters

For a body of specialists to be accepted as professional requires that they meet their obligations to society at large with respect to that specialty. None of us wants to become a professional through self-appointment. The deep-down satisfaction comes when others regard us as having earned the status of professional through our deeds on behalf of society. While I welcome the ASQC efforts to date, I believe we need quite an enlargement of these efforts before our professionalism can become a reality.

ENDNOTES

1. Juran, J. M. 1968. Operator errors—time for a new look. *Quality Progress* (February) 1(2): 9–11.
2. Juran, J. M. 1967. The QC Circle phenomenon. *Industrial Quality Control* (January) 23(7): 329–36.
3. Juran, J. M. 1968. Vendor relations—an overview. *Quality Progress* (July) 1(7): 10–16.
4. Mizuno, S. 1968. Quality systems analysis. 12th EOQC Conference, Madrid, September 17th–19th.
5. Juran, J. M. 1964. The two worlds of quality control. *Industrial Quality Control* (November) 24(5): 238–44.
6. Juran, J. M. 1966. So your want to be a quality control consultant. *Industrial Quality Control* (December) 23(6): 265–70.

11

Management Interface

THE TAYLOR SYSTEM
AND QUALITY CONTROL

Early in the 20th century, an American engineer, Frederick W. Taylor, proposed a revolutionary approach to management, based on his experience as a manager and as a consultant. Taylor's proposals may be summarized as follows: the methods for doing work should be based on scientific study, not on the empirical judgment of foremen or workmen; the standards of what constitutes a day's work should likewise be based on scientific study; selection and training of workmen should also be based on scientific study; piecework payment should be employed to motivate the selected and trained workmen to use the engineered methods and to meet the standards of a day's work.

To make these proposals effective, Taylor separated work planning from execution. Next, he created industrial engineers and other specialists to prepare work methods and standards of a day's work. He then limited the foremen and workmen to "control," that is, to execute the plans and meet the standards. The system "worked"—it achieved spectacular improvements in productivity. Under Taylor's competent advocacy, the system was widely adopted by American industry, took firm root, and remains as the principal base on which our managerial structures have been erected. Now, more than half a century later, we are able to identify with clarity the then-existing premises behind the Taylor system: the foremen and workmen of

Editor's Note: The paper appearing here in Chapter 11 was published as one of a series of papers under a column entitled, "Management Interface," in *Quality Progress*, May through December, 1973.[1]

that day lacked the technological literacy needed to plan work methods, to establish standards of a day's work, and so on. The standard of living was so low that piecework incentives could provide a powerful stimulus to employees to meet standards. The economic power of the employers was sufficient to prevail over employee resistance to such a system of management. These premises were quite valid in Taylor's day, but they have since become increasingly obsolete. Today's foremen and workmen are well educated, including education in technology. Rising standards of living have sharply diminished the influence of piecework as an incentive to productivity. The rise of labor unions has required that many decisions affecting productivity be based on collective bargaining rather than on unilateral planning.

Despite this obsolescence of Taylor's premises, we retain the Taylor system, with all the detriments inherent in use of a system that is based on obsolete premises. The most obvious and serious of these detriments is the underemployment of the intelligence and creative capacity of millions of human beings.

All of the foregoing has profoundly influenced our management of the quality function. The Taylor system provided a strong impulse to the movement to separate inspection from production, that is, to use full-time inspectors for product inspection and process control rather than to rely on the workmen. The proliferation of Taylor's piecework systems was a strong influence on the decisions to create independent inspection departments to take over the command of inspectors (who had previously been under the command of production foremen). The evolution of quality specialists (quality control engineers, reliability engineers) was again an extension of the concept of separation of planning from execution.

At the time these and other steps were taken, there was a logic to support them. Now we suddenly find the system to be suspect. It is under attack from within as evidenced by a growing resistance of employees, especially young employees, to spend years of their lives doing work that poses little challenge, that makes little use of their education or their creativity. The system is also under attack from the outside, as we discover that there are entire industries in that we are outperformed by countries that operate under different systems.

It seems clear that we need a counterrevolution, and I believe that this has already begun. Because of the massive forces involved, today's quality managers and specialists will very likely spend a lifetime dealing with this counterrevolution as it affects the quality function.

In the remainder of this article, I will identify some of the major steps being taken to dismantle the outdated aspects of the Taylor system. In future issues, I will discuss these steps individually and in some detail.

1. We are returning some of the work of job planning to the operators, inspectors and still other nonsupervisors at the bottom of the company hierarchy. This is a direct reversal of the Taylor concept.

2. We are continuing to abolish Taylor's piecework incentive. Piecework was indeed effective in those days of low standards of living. Since then, our growing affluence has demonstrated that piecework does not remain viable once human physiological needs have been met. However, while we have largely abandoned use of piecework, we have yet to agree on a universal form of industrial motivation applicable to an affluent society. We are clear on what we want to abandon but not on what we want to adopt.

3. We are engaged in some useful experimentation on new forms of participation and motivation, not merely for meeting standards but for quality improvement as well.

4. We are in the early stages of returning product inspection to the production force. This is not to be confused with a transfer of the inspection department to production. In the latter transfer, the same people continue to do the same work they have been doing, but under a different chain of command. What is happening is rather an abolition of full-time inspectors, with the work of inspection being taken up by production operators.

5. We are beginning to look to the assignments of our quality staff specialists so that they will turn to unsolved problems while delegating solved problems to the line organizations.

6. We are looking for new ways of organizing the broad quality function to be responsive to modern needs, while at the same time getting rid of outworn and outdated organization machinery.

In discussing these steps, it is well to refer periodically to the nature of the Taylor system and to the premises on which it was based. To a degree far greater than is generally realized, our managerial approach is rooted in the Taylor system. The fact that we must now dismantle the system will be no discredit to Taylor. He was an uncommonly incisive thinker, a forceful doer and a persuasive advocate. His advocacy of a technocratic industrial society was in any case doomed in a political democracy, but for the most part, his system was a logical response to the forces prevailing in his time. Our present dilemma is mainly the result of Taylor's followers (ourselves) having retained the system despite the obsolescence of its premises. I doubt that so objective a man as Taylor would have retained the system as long as have his followers.

ENDNOTE

1. The reader may want to review all of these papers from the column "Management Interface." in ASQC's *Quality Progress,* 1973. The series of papers were: (1) The Taylor system and quality control, *Quality Progress* (May) 6(5):42; (2) The redelegation of quality planning, *Quality Progress* (June) 6(6):33; (3) Inspection returns to its origins, *Quality Progress* (July) 6(7):34, 48; (4) The motivation to meet quality standards, *Quality Progress* (August) 6(8):41, 49; (5) The motivation to improve quality, *Quality Progress* (September) 6(9):33; (6) The future of the inspection department, *Quality Progress* (October) 6(10):26, 40; (7) The quality staff specialist: an emerging role, *Quality Progress* (November) 6(11):36, 40; and (8) The emerging quality control department, *Quality Progress* (December) 6(12):31–32.

12

The Non-Pareto Principle—Mea Culpa

T he "Pareto Principle" has by this time become deeply rooted in our industrial literature. It is a shorthand name for the phenomenon in any population that contributes to a common effect, a relative few of the contributors account for the bulk of the effect.

Years ago I gave the name "Pareto" to this principle of the "vital few and trivial many." On subsequent challenge, I was forced to confess that I had mistakenly applied the wrong name to the principle.[1] This confession changed nothing—the name *Pareto Principle* has continued in force, and seems destined to become a permanent label for the phenomenon.

The matter has not stopped with my own error. On various occasions, contemporary authors, when referring to the Pareto Principle, have fabricated some embellishments and otherwise attributed to Vilfredo Pareto additional things that he did not do. My motive in offering the present paper is in part to minimize this tendency to embroider the work of a distinguished Italian economist. In addition, I have for some time felt an urge to narrate just how it came about that some early experiences in seemingly unrelated fields (quality control, cryptanalysis, industrial engineering, government administration, management research) nevertheless converged to misname the Pareto Principle.

It began in the mid-1920s when as a young engineer, I observed (as had many others before me) that quality defects are unequal in frequency, that is, when a long list of defects was arranged in the order of frequency, a relative few of the defects accounted for the bulk of the defectiveness. As I moved

---

Editor's Note: The paper appearing here in Chapter 12 was published in 1975 in *Quality Progress* (May) 8(5):8–9.

into quality management posts in the late 1920s and the 1930s, I observed (as had many others before me) that a similar phenomenon existed with respect to employee absenteeism, causes of accidents, and so on.

During the late 1930s, I moved out of the field of quality control to become the corporate industrial engineer for Western Electric Company. In this capacity, one of my responsibilities was to visit other companies to exchange experiences in industrial engineering practices. One of the most exhilarating of these visits was to General Motors Corporation's head-quarters. There I found an uncommonly competent team of managers facing up to the then-new problems of collective bargaining. As an incidental tool, they had put together an assortment of data processing machinery to enable them to compute the cost of any new labor union proposal. This they did by programming the machines and then running the (punched) employee record cards through the program. It was an ingenious concept, and their system was quite advanced for those days. However, the electro-magnetic machinery then in use took hours and even days to process those hundreds of thousands of cards, so that the managers often found them-selves waiting for the machines to grind out the results.

It is a part of our chronicle that these General Motors managers were a keen, inquisitive lot, and were ever on the alert for anything new. Thus, when it happened on one occasion that the card readers were producing gibberish, the managers not only found the cause to be a miswired plug board, they also realized that they had stumbled onto a means for creating messages in cipher. As a form of comic relief from the grueling hours to which they were often subjected, they used some of the waiting time to dig further into this enciphering system. The more they got into it, the more convinced they became that they had evolved a cipher system that could not be broken.

During the relaxation of a luncheon, they told me of this unbreakable cipher system, and I laughed at them. As it happened, I was no slouch in such matters, since my work in the Signal Corps Reserve was precisely on this subject. Naturally, one thing led to another, and before the day was done, I had rashly accepted their tender of an enciphered message to break. Break it I did, although it took until three o'clock in the morning. (Thereafter my sleep was short but blissful.)

They were stunned by the news that the unbreakable had been broken, and for the rest of the visit the agreeable aura of a miracle man followed me about. As a byproduct, some hitherto secret doors were opened up to me. It was one of these doors which led me, for the first time, to the work of Vilfredo Pareto. The man who opened that door was Merle Hale, who presided over the executive salary program of General Motors.

Hale showed me research he had conducted by comparing the executive salary pattern prevailing in General Motors with one of the mathematical models that Pareto had once constructed. The fit was surprisingly close. I registered the incident in my memory, along with the fact that Pareto had made extensive studies of the unequal distribution of wealth, and had in addition formulated mathematical models to quantify this maldistribution.

In December 1941, the month in which the United States entered World War II, I took a "temporary" assignment as a federal government administrator. The original six weeks stretched into four years and as a byproduct gave me an insight into the problems of managing the federal government. Of course, the principle of the vital few and trivial many had wide application. At the end of the war (1945), I embarked on a career dedicated to the field of management: research, writing, teaching, consulting, and so on. By the late 1940s, as a result of my courses at New York University and my seminars at American Management Association, I had recognized the principle of the "vital few and trivial many" as a true "universal," applicable not only in numerous managerial functions but in the physical and biological worlds generally. Other investigators may well have been aware of this universal principle, but to my knowledge no one had ever before reduced it to writing.

It was during the late 1940s, when I was preparing the manuscript for *Quality Control Handbook*, First Edition, that I was faced squarely with the need for giving a short name to the universal. In the resulting write-up[2] under the heading "Maldistribution of Quality Losses," I listed numerous instances of such maldistribution as a basis for generalization. I also noted that Pareto had found wealth to be maldistributed. In addition, I showed examples of the now familiar cumulative curves, one for maldistribution of wealth and the other for maldistribution of quality losses. The caption under these curves reads "Pareto's principle of unequal distribution applied to distribution of wealth and to distribution of quality losses." Although the accompanying text makes clear that Pareto's contributions specialized in the study of wealth, the caption implies that he had generalized the principle of unequal distribution into a universal. This implication is erroneous. The Pareto Principle as a universal was not original with Pareto.

Where then did the universal originate? To my knowledge, the first exposition was by myself. Had I been structured along different lines, assuredly I would have called it the Juran principle. However, I was not structured that way. Yet I did need a shorthand designation, and I had no qualms about Pareto's name. Hence the Pareto Principle.

The matter might well have rested there had there been a less-than-enthusiastic response to the universal. Instead, the new universal became the subject of wide use and reference. I contributed to this dissemination by coining and popularizing the term "vital few and trivial many" in the widely read "universals" paper,[3] and in the moving picture film I prepared for American Management Association on the "breakthrough" process. The resulting wide usage also brought me some challenges (from Dorian Shainin and others) as to the attribution to Pareto. These challenges forced me to do what I should have done in the first place—to inform myself on just what was it that Pareto had done. It was this examination that made clear to me what I had seen only dimly—that Pareto's work had been in the economic sphere and that his models were not intended to be applied to other fields. To make matters worse, the cumulative curves used in *Quality Control Handbook*, First Edition, should have been properly identified with Lorenz.[4]

To summarize, and to set the record straight:

1. Numerous men, over the centuries, have observed the existence of the phenomenon of vital few and trivial many as it applied to their local sphere of activity.

2. Pareto observed this phenomenon as applied to distribution of wealth, and advanced the theory of a logarithmic law of income distribution to fit the phenomenon.

3. Lorenz developed a form of cumulative curve to depict the distribution of wealth graphically.

4. Juran was (seemingly) the first to identify the phenomenon of the vital few and trivial many as a "universal," applicable to many fields.

5. Juran applied the name "The Pareto Principle" to this universal. He also coined the phrase "vital few and trivial many" and applied the Lorenz curves to depict this Universal in graphic form.[5]

ENDNOTES

1. Juran, J. M., Pareto. Lorenz, Cournot Bernoulli, Juran, and others. 1950. *Industrial Quality Control* (October) 17(4):25.

2. Juran, J. M., ed. 1951. *Quality control handbook*, 1st ed. New York: McGraw-Hill: 37–41.

3. The first published use of this term was likely in my paper: Juran, J. M. 1954. Universals in management planning and controlling. *The Management Review* (November).

4. Lorenz, M. O. Methods of measuring the concentration of wealth. *American Statistical Association Publication* 9 (1904–1905): 200–19.

5. See also, Juran, J. M., ed. 1974. *Quality control handbook*, 3rd ed. New York: McGraw-Hill: 2-16 to 2-19.

13

That Uninterested Top Management

Too often, quality specialists and upper management have different ideas about the word "quality."

A major concern of any specialized department is the extent to which upper management has an interest in the specialty. The extent of this upper management interest affects everything that the specialist holds dear: his access to information, his ability to secure action on his proposals, his status and emoluments, and even the continued life of his specialty. With such vital matters at stake, it is not surprising that one of the questions most frequently raised by quality managers and quality specialists in my courses and seminars is: "How can I get my top management interested in quality?"

By this time, I have discussed "quality" with a good many top managers around the world. *Without exception,* they all want satisfied customers, a good quality reputation, minimal factory waste, and all the other recognized fruits of good quality. Moreover, they do not need to be convinced that these are good goals.

I have also discussed, with a good many quality managers and specialists the specific problems they face in their own companies in securing upper managers' interest in "quality." All too often, it emerges that what the specialists have in mind by the word "quality" is quite different from what upper management has in mind. These instances have been so numerous that it is helpful to look at some of the more usual cases encountered.

Editor's Note: The paper appearing here in Chapter 13 was published in 1977 in *Quality Progress* (December) 10(12): 18–19.

Case 1. This involves long-standing debates over command of specific departments. For example, in one company, the inspection department was responsible to the head of production. The quality manager's role was mainly of a staff nature. He felt that the inspection department should be placed under his command to make the inspectors more "independent." I played the role of devil's advocate and asked whether the lack of inspection independence had resulted in unfit product going to the field. He was of the opinion that the outgoing product was, in fact, fit for use. However, he believed that the extent of nonconformance to specification was being affected by the lack of organizational independence of the inspectors. I agreed with him, but I also felt that so long as the product was fit for use, there was little likelihood that top management would force an organizational change on an unwilling production manager. If anything, they would regard such a proposal as an avoidable form of internal abrasion. I also thought that the quality manager could, through audit, do something about improving inspection performance. It then became evident (to me) that his main interest was one of empire building.

Case 2. Here the problem is that the quality manager makes proposals for adopting techniques on which he is sold, but for which he has not presented persuasive evidence that company performance will be improved thereby. A typical example was that of a quality manager who proposed to introduce a comprehensive, formalized, quality control program into the company involving more formal quality planning at work stations and inspection stations, a more complete feedback of quality data to all concerned, design review and reliability quantification for new products, quality cost reporting on a broad scale, and so on. He had gotten a weak reception from the line managers but was thoroughly sold on his own proposals. His top managers had then told him, in effect, to secure the support of the line managers first. Again I played the role of critic, and asked him to explain to me just what would be the tangible effects of his proposals. Which present losses could we avoid? What new sales could we create? He was unable to be specific enough to convince me that the present system (or lack of system) had enough deficiencies to warrant taking a major step into the unknown. I later confirmed that his top managers had much the same judgment.

Case 3. This concerns proposals for refining further the status of solved problems despite the fact that some major unsolved problems are going on and on. For example, in one company I found the corporate quality manager to be openly critical of the quality consciousness of the upper managers because of their seeming lack of response to various proposals for refining controls. However, in due course, I had a visit with the chief executive officer and discussed with him my estimate of the losses due to internal scrap and rework, and my associated estimate of the potential improvement. The chief executive was shocked by the amounts involved—such a picture had never before been brought to him. He promptly convened his vice presidents to discuss the implications and to formulate a plan of action.

What runs through these and many other kinds of cases is a difference in basic outlook between the upper managers and many quality managers. The upper managers regard themselves as businesspeople. Their concepts of "quality" derive from the way in which quality has an impact on the business scoreboard—on volume of sales, share of market, costs, return on investment, employee relations, customer relations, and so on. It is the performance on such parameters that measures the effectiveness of an enterprise, and thereby of the upper managers of that enterprise.

Publication of business results permits direct comparisons to be made among competing companies. These comparisons impose their imperatives on the respective managers and, to an important degree, determine their conduct as to the various functions in the company, including the quality function. What the upper managers demand of all functions is:

- A predictable assurance that current goals will be met. This is "control" and provides freedom from crises and other unpleasant surprises.

- A continuing series of improvements or "breakthroughs" that will keep the company competitive in the years ahead.

The upper managers are generally aware that both control and breakthrough are activities vital to the health of the company (current and future health, respectively). However, these two vital activities do not have equal status in the eyes of upper management. Breakthrough is the favorite—it is associated with creativity and progress. In contrast, control, while accepted as necessary, can readily decline to the status of a necessary evil—a parasitic tax. All too often, this view then colors the upper manager's view of those engaged as controllers. Of course, the upper managers should not look at control in this way, but many of them do, and thereby they become part of the problem.

In my experience, it is futile to defend control departments before such upper managers. They have long ago made up their minds that the control departments "do not contribute anything," taking for granted (or forgetting) the contribution the control departments made by aiding these same upper managers to meet their current goals. What is really decisive is that these managers have concluded that control is a low-caste activity, in contrast to the high-caste activity of breakthrough. In such cases the lesson for the control managers, including the quality control manager, is clear: see to it that you engage in both breakthrough and control, and orient these activities to the business objectives of the company.

In my observation, the quality manager who engages in both breakthrough and control, with a clear emphasis on business objectives, has little problem with lack of interest on the part of his upper management. The fact that the quality manager has engaged in successful breakthroughs qualifies him to step across the border and to qualify his overall activity as high-caste. In the process, his credit is enlarged in several directions:

- His proposals for further breakthrough projects move up on the priority list.

- He receives the benefit of the doubt on proposals that are not fully documented.

- His proposals on refining controls may be accepted on faith derived from his record on breakthroughs.

14

Japanese and Western Quality—A Contrast

Using the color television set as an example, the author provides some in-depth comparisons. The purpose of this paper is to:

1. Compare the quality of Japanese and Western product.

2. Identify and evaluate the differences.

3. Discover the reasons behind the differences.

4. Judge the trends of the past and the implications for the future.

Because Japan and the West compete in a great many product lines, I have chosen the color television set as a case example for comparison. It is a good case. The color television set is a complex and demanding piece of apparatus embodying some of the most advanced technology known. Its price makes it one of the most expensive products bought by consumers. It is produced and sold in such large numbers that it constitutes an important industry—a significant element in the economy of many nations.

Obviously, any case example has some degree of uniqueness due to its special technology. However, as we shall see, the reasons for the quality differences between Japanese color television sets and those of the West include many which are common to a wide list of industries. This conclusion (of the existence of wide commonality among multiple industries) is one I have drawn from close observation of international quality control practice during the last several decades. This same conclusion is in general

---

Editor's Note: The paper appearing here in Chapter 14 was first presented in 1978 as *Japanese and Western Quality* in the Proceedings of International Conference on Quality Control, October 17-20, Tokyo, Japan.

agreement with those drawn by other widely-traveled practitioners such as Dr. Kaoru Ishikawa.

COLOR TELEVISION SET QUALITY

Commercial television and the color television set had their origin in the West. At the outset, the problems were those of finding technological principles that could transmit and receive pictures by wire or wireless methods. Then came the solution of problems of manufacture and marketing in ways which could bring the benefits of television within the reach of the bulk of the population. A major initial quality weakness of the industry was the high failure rate of the electron tubes used in the color television set. The invention of the transistor and its descendants then made possible a remarkable reduction in this failure rate. While these solid-state devices were invented in the West, it was the Japanese, aided by government subsidy, who brought out the first all-solid-state color television sets (1968). U.S. adoption of solid state was slower, mainly for manufacturers' economic reasons.[1] As these fundamental technological problems were solved, it became feasible for many manufacturers to make color television sets, so conventional national and international competition set in.

The quality of a color television set is generally judged with respect to three interrelated product features:

1. Picture quality, or "function," which is judged by the extent to which the image on the screen correctly reproduces the original scene in its proportions, color, and so on.

2. "Product appeal" which is judged by styling, finish, convenience of operation, ease of transport and placement, smoothness of control mechanisms, and so on.

3. Reliability, which is synonymous with freedom from failures in service.

Obviously, all manufacturers (both in Japan and in the West) would prefer to make products that are excellent with respect to all of these features. This is no simple undertaking, since making, marketing, and servicing color television sets involves a delicate balance among many conflicting variables in technology, economics, and so on. As a consequence, there are compromises or "tradeoffs."

Broadly speaking, Western manufacturers have in the past emphasized what is obvious to consumers—picture quality and product appeal. Through frequent model change, they brought out various useful innovations, that is, remote controls, random access, automatic tuning, smaller bulk, and so on, along with a degree of just gadgetry. Through this emphasis, the Western manufacturers attained and for years retained marketplace leadership in picture quality and product appeal. They were able to exhibit these features to consumers through direct comparison of competing models, side by side, in the showrooms. The consumers could sense these differences. The effect on share of market was significant if the innovations were significant.

In the early years of Japanese color television, consumers were also strongly influenced by function and product appeal. However, in recent years consumer emphasis has been on reliability and function. (Evidently operating hours in Japan are significantly longer in the West.) In response to this emphasis, Japanese manufacturers attained a clear leadership in reliability—a leadership which they hold to this day. More recently, the Japanese have, in addition, narrowed or closed the gap in picture quality and product appeal.

(One widely experienced U.S. director feels that the real Japanese emphasis has been on "value," that is, high reliability at low cost. "While one of their objectives was high reliability which they have achieved, reliability at low cost was and continues to be the principle objective.")

The present situation with respect to picture quality and product appeal is essentially one of distinctions without much difference. At least the difference no longer seems to be so significant a factor in share of market as once was the case. In contrast, the difference in reliability is striking. During the middle 1970s, the Western color television sets were failing in service at a rate of about five times that prevailing in Japanese sets.[2] Obviously, the consumers were not aware of this difference. However, the merchants, leasing companies, and large buyers (such as hotel chains) became keenly aware of such a difference. As the influence of important clients began to have its effect on share of market; the Western manufacturers reacted and have been working ever since to narrow the gap. I have been shown data which make clear that Western companies have, in fact, been improving their reliability. However, the Japanese, meanwhile, have also been improving. It is not easy to quantify the present status with precision. My best estimate is that the present Western products have from two to four times the failure rates of the Japanese sets.

All of these shifts in emphasis have been having an effect on share of market. In the early years in the United States, quality did have significance but was a secondary factor in share of market when compared with the price of the set and the margins available to the dealers. As price competitions have minimized these margins, quality has emerged as the dominant factor for deciding which of two equally priced sets is bought.

What is central to this paper is that, in the case of the color television set, quality is now a major element in share of market. What has already become evident in the case of color television sets may be incubating with respect to other major products, for example, automobiles.[3]

In the remainder of this paper, I will examine the various forces which have brought about the present state of affairs in color television sets. While some of these forces are unique to color television set manufacture, most of them are applicable to all industries.

THE BROAD, NATIONAL APPROACHES TO QUALITY

Japan and the countries of the West exhibit a good deal of commonality in their approach to product quality. This commonality is traceable to their use of a capitalistic form of economy along with competition in the market place. There are also important differences which are traceable to differences in history and culture.[4] To oversimplify, the moods since the end of World War II have been:

- Japan: a mood of dissatisfaction with quality and a program of revolution

- The West: a mood of satisfaction with quality and a program of evolution

Each of these moods is quite logical in relation to the background histories of the respective countries.

The Industrial Revolution had its origin in Europe about two centuries ago. The Europeans thereby became the early leaders in industrial development and in product quality. During the decades which followed, European preeminence in quality became widely accepted. Today's European directors are quite aware that, meanwhile, other countries have become competitive in quality. This awareness is causing some discomfort and alarm, but it has not yet reached a level that could stimulate a revolution in the approach to product quality. (A revolution is a risky adventure since its outcome is not fully predictable.)

Industrial development in the United States followed later—at the beginning of World War I the United States was still mainly a developing country. Thereafter, it developed at a very rapid rate, attaining a degree of competitiveness in quality as well as world leadership in productivity. (It actually became a "superpower"—industrially, economically, and militarily.) Due to intense emphasis on productivity, attainment of quality did involve a revolution of sorts—the creation of large quality control departments with broad responsibilities for quality, and staffed with numerous quality specialists. As with the Europeans, the U.S. directors are aware of growing competition in quality. (I have seen information evidencing this awareness on the part of the top managements of every one of the three major automobile manufacturers in the United States.) However, as in Europe, the U.S. directors have not concluded that a revolution is necessary. Most of them believe that their problems in selling their products are mainly those of price competition.

Japanese industrial development started still later—their emergence from feudalism is only about a century old. By the end of World War II, Japan was still a developing country. It had a low standard of living when compared to the West, and Japanese product quality had the worst reputation of all.

Following World War II, the Japanese industrialists were drawn into posts of national leadership. They wanted to develop their country industrially but found that their product quality was a major obstacle. No one wanted to buy such low quality goods. For a country so lacking in raw materials, this inability to sell finished goods for export was also an inability to earn foreign exchange, and hence an inability to buy the materials needed to create an upward spiral in industrial development. A revolution in quality became essential, and the Japanese industrialists became the leaders of the revolution. The methods used to create that revolution have been well documented,[5] so I will not go into the details here. However, several aspects of quality policy are pertinent to my subject, and as to these I will now elaborate.

POLICY ON REMOVING QUALITY TROUBLES BEFORE "GOING TO MARKET"

In all countries, the launching of a new product model is done in accordance with a master schedule. This schedule allocates time for all the major activities needed to put the product on the market: market research, product development, manufacture, marketing, and so on. As work progresses, the imperatives of the schedule grow progressively more severe. Failure to adhere to schedule is progressively more costly as more and more investment is committed. Even worse, there is a risk of having no product to ship to merchants who have meanwhile been phased out of the old models by the same schedule.

A major obstacle to meeting the schedule is solution of the quality problems. For long-life products such as color television sets, it is typical to find that the field failures have their origin as follows:[6]

- In development and design 20–40 percent

- In quality of components 40–65 percent

- In quality of workmanship 15–20 percent

For each of these sources of failures, there are solutions, and it is most desirable to find and apply these solutions before going to market. This is a process known as "debugging" or "scrub-down" of the new model. Such scrub-down takes investment as well as a good deal of time on the part of the managers, engineers, and workforce.

The evidence is overwhelming that in the case of the color television set, the Japanese do a more complete scrub-down than do their competitors in the West. This difference is mainly due to upper management policy. Meanwhile, let me note that there are differences in basic financial policy. Manufacturers in the West tend to make major capital investments only on assurance of relatively prompt "payout"—several years at most. Japanese manufacturers tend to accept much longer payouts and, thereby, greater risks. However, the Japanese are encouraged in this by favorable government tax policies. The U.S. government has over the years vacillated considerably in this respect. The present administration has exhibited little awareness of the importance of stimulating industrial investment.

The collective consequence of these policies is that the Japanese models are well debugged, and the Japanese know this at the time of going to market. In the West, the scrub-down is less complete, and the manufacturers are usually aware that the quality problems have not been fully solved. However, the decision is nearly always to go to market anyway because of the pressures of the schedule. The decision to go to market contemplates two compensating actions:

1. Good field service will be provided to compensate for the field failures.

2. A follow-through will be made to complete the scrub-down after the model has gone to market.

In practice, neither of these hopes is fully realized. The field service is never as good as intended[7] In addition, the follow-through is seldom made since the engineers and others involved have meanwhile been assigned to the next new models which have new schedules to be met.

I might add my own speculation that a further reason for the more thorough Japanese scrub-down is the extent to which their quality revolution has had its influence on their domestic market. This market seems to have developed an intolerance toward poor quality that goes beyond anything I have observed in the West.[8] A comparable phenomenon is the high standard demanded in some European countries with respect to quality of meal service. In such countries, a high status is conferred on superior restaurants and chefs, with corresponding impacts on share of market.

THE COLOR TELEVISION SET
MARKETING STRUCTURE

For users to have the benefits of color television reception requires, among other things:

1. A manufacturer to design and build the set

2. A merchant to sell it

3. A repair service shop to restore service in case of failure

In the West, it is usual for these three major functions are usually carried out by three independent organizations. Manufacture is done by a few large companies. Marketing is done mainly by numerous independent distributors and retailers. Repair service is done mainly by numerous independent repair shops.

In Japan, as in the West, manufacture is also done by a few large companies. However, marketing in Japan is done mainly by captive markets owned (or essentially controlled) by these same manufacturers. (They also have some "open" markets.) In addition, repair service is done mainly by service shop networks which are likewise owned by the large manufacturers.

These differences in marketing structure have a profound influence on manufacturers' quality policies:

1. *Emphasis on picture quality and product appeal versus reliability.* Under the system of independent merchant companies that prevails in the West, it is common for the merchant to sell models made by many manufacturers. (In one large merchant shop I counted 70 models made by eight different manufacturers.) In such a shop, the consumer sees competing models side by side and tends to be heavily influenced by what he can sense then and

there, that is, picture quality and product appeal. In the case of captive markets, there would be fewer comparisons and more reliance on the reputation of the manufacturer.

2. *Payment for service calls.* In the West, it is a perennial complaint of merchants, service shops, and users that they bear a substantial part of the cost of in-warranty service.[9] (Out-of-warranty costs are, of course, borne by the user.)[10] Under the usual Japanese arrangement, all in-warranty costs are borne by the single company, which carries out the multiple roles of manufacturer, merchant, and service shop. One U.S. merchant company has suggested that manufacturers in the United States have little incentive to improve reliability since much of the resulting savings in service costs would benefit the merchant, service shop, and user rather than the manufacturer. Support of this theory is seen in the experience of service companies such as the Bell Telephone System. They do not sell their equipment—they sell only the service. In consequence, they tend to design their apparatus on a life-cycle-cost basis. If need be, they incur higher original costs provided they can thereby avoid the still-higher costs of service calls.

3 *Feedback of field service data.* In the West, it is difficult to secure good field failure data due to the independent nature of the service shops. Under the Japanese system of captive service chains, this problem is simplified, as are the problems of collecting failed components and analyzing causes.

It is seen that the concept of independent merchants may be beneficial in stimulating greater competition in picture quality and product appeal. However, the concept of integrated companies is clearly beneficial for stimulating higher reliability.

QUALITY PLANNING

Both in Japan and the West, there is a clear awareness of the need for quality planning. By "quality planning" I mean the preparatory steps required to identify the quality characteristics needed by the users and to assure that the activities of design, manufacture, and so on, will, in fact, provide for attainment of those qualities. These preparatory steps are well known and consist of market research, design review, model construction and test, environmental and life testing, trial lot production and test, and so on. [11]

All of these steps are well known and carried out by virtually all manufacturers. However, there are important differences in the emphasis given to various quality characteristics, as we have seen. In addition, the intensity of the planning varies considerably, which, in turn, results in variations in the extent of assurance provided. I will discuss these differences in intensity under the next few headings.

PRODUCT DESIGN

Any new product model is a breeding ground for new quality troubles. The product design is a major contributor to these troubles. All companies devote much effort to minimizing the extent to which design weaknesses end up as manufacturing difficulties and/or field failures. This preventive effort takes numerous forms but is concentrated in the following:

1. *Training of designers.*[12] It is commonplace to require designers to be formally trained in the technological disciplines needed by the industry. In the case of the color television set, these technological disciplines include electronics, metallurgy, solid-state physics, and so on. To my knowledge, there is no significant difference in the training levels of Japanese and Western designers with respect to these disciplines.

   A second aspect of training of designers is "practical experience." One major area for such experience is in the production shop, to give the designer an awareness of some of the realities faced by the production personnel; this gives him a better understanding of how to design for "producibility." A second major area for designer experience acquisition is in field service work. Through such experience the designer learns much about the conditions of use, the problems of diagnosing field failures, the difficulties of making repairs, and so on. As a result, he understands better how to design for reliability and maintainability.

   With respect to such "training by practical experience," there are wide differences between Japan and the West. It is common, though not invariable, for Japanese companies to require that designers acquire such shop and field experience before being assigned to key responsibilities in product design. In the West, the requirement for such experience is unusual.

   A third area of designer training is in the quality control disciplines—variation, sampling, reliability analysis, design of experiment, analysis of variance, Weibull analysis, and so on. In Japan, it is the rule that designers must receive such training. In one published account, the training courses for those in charge of design and research add up to 144 hours in length.[13] In the West, such training programs are available but are rarely mandated. Some companies provide a climate that is favorable for designers to take such courses, but progress has been slow. In fact, many designers whose skills lie in the scientific and engineering disciplines remain scornful of the statistical discipline.

2. *Design for reliability.* As noted previously, Japanese practice is oriented to a strict scrub-down of field failure problems. An example in the color television set is the tradeoff between reliability and other parameters. A wide angle (110 degrees) picture tube results in a less bulky piece of furniture but generates more heat during operation. In like manner, a thick-necked (36mm) picture tube gives better resolution at the edges but requires more power during operation. Generally, Western manufacturers chose the smaller bulk sets and superior resolution, but their sets ran hotter and so were more susceptible to failure.

   A second form of tradeoff concerns the "factor of safety" applied to component design. Lower factors of safety or smaller sizes of components mean lower costs of components, but also higher operating temperatures and hence higher failure rates. In general, Japanese designers do not push their components as far as their Western counterparts. One evidence of this practice is the extent of heat dissipation. Data quoted to me by one manufacturer showed Japanese sets generally run well under 100 watts, while U.S. sets run in the range of 120–140 watts, with some as high as 165 watts.[14]

   A further aspect of design for reliability is the willingness to invest in improvement projects, even small improvements. Japanese QC literature teems with case histories of numerous small projects (and some not so small) tackled by QC circles and other groups.[15] In the West, such projects are not undertaken due to low return on the investment (when done by engineers and managers).

3. *Qualification testing.* All companies provide for laboratory tests of components to assure that the designs are adequate before permitting the designers to specify them for use in the color television set. These qualification tests are multienvironmental in nature. Many include over stressing as well to assure adequate factors of safety.

The comparative severity and extent of this testing is difficult to assess. What has impressed me is that several Japanese companies (and one Western company), all assert that most Western sets are unable to meet certain Japanese tests, for example, thermal stress and humidity. However, there are also assertions in the other direction, such as flame retardancy.

4. *Trial lots.* In all companies there are provisions to build trial lots (also known as pilot lots, preproduction lots, and so on.) These trial lots serve as early warnings by identifying weaknesses in the model which may result in high production costs, high field failures, and so on.

Some companies use two subspecies of pilot lots:

1. An "engineering" trial lot run on a special assembly line (not a regular factory line) by experienced production employees who are supported by engineering personnel. Such special assembly lines are specially equipped to permit experimentation and analysis for improvement.

2. A "production" trial lot, run on the regular production line under regular conditions. This serves as a measure of attainment of goals before turning the responsibility over to the production department.

Here again, it is difficult to make a useful judgment as to the differences in practice. What does stand out is the intensity of analysis of failures down to the precise failure mode, followed by remedial action. There is, in my mind, little doubt that the Japanese engage in relentless pursuit of such analysis and remedy.

VENDOR RELATIONS

Color television set quality depends heavily on component quality. All manufacturers know this, and all go to great lengths to structure their s in ways that will assure the adequacy of component quality. The methods used for attaining this assurance have been widely published, but there remain important differences in emphasis between Japan and the West.

The most fundamental of these differences is in the policy followed as to the basic relationship between vendor and buyer. This relationship can range over a wide spectrum. At one extreme is the adversary concept, that is, mutual doubt if not mistrust; reliance on contract provisions, documents, and penalties; and other elements of an arm's-length relationship. At the other extreme is the teamwork concept: mutual trust and confidence, cooperation, joint commitment to the consumer, and so on. This policy on basic relationship is of the utmost importance. It is decisive on such questions as extent of joint planning, mutual visits, technical assistance, exchange of data, and so on.

The large Japanese manufacturers are heavily committed to the teamwork concept. So, to a considerable degree, are the Europeans. In the United States, the manufacturers are emerging from an era in which the adversary concept was the rule. The directions for the future all seem to point to a policy of treating the vendor as a member of the team. In my judgement, the adversary policy is no longer a viable basis for vendor relations on products such as the color television set.

Beyond this basic policy question, there remain numerous important elements of practice and technique.

1. *Design qualification.* Before component designs are "listed" they are commonly required to undergo environmental tests and life tests. These tests are similar in concept to those discussed above under "qualification testing." (Such testing is done whether the designs originate with the buyer or the vendor.) The resulting design qualification is quite separate from the problems of vendor or process qualification.

2. *Vendor selection.* To a considerable extent, color television set manufacturers "buy" components from sister divisions in the same company. However, the residue that must be bought in the competitive marketplace is also considerable, and many independent component makers compete with each other for the available business. To reduce these many to a manageable few, the color television set manufacturers make use of a vendor selection process and apply criteria in accordance with their policies and objectives. Wide use is made of questionnaires and preliminary screening to eliminate would-be suppliers who are clearly deficient on grounds of finance, facilities, and so on. Following this screening, it is common to conduct "surveys," that is, visits to vendors to determine in greater detail whether the vendors meet the buyer's criteria for quality, delivery schedule, price, and so on.

3. *Criteria for predicting quality performance.* All surveys involve a look at production and laboratory facilities to judge their adequacy for production and test. Beyond these and other

technological essentials, there is a divergence. In the United States, great emphasis is placed on organization form, written procedures, manuals, audits, documentary proof, and so on. In contrast, the Japanese emphasis is on the following:

a. *Process "validation."* Quantifying process capabilities so that it is known in advance whether the vendor's processes can hold the tolerance.

b. *Process controls.* The plans of control which will be used to keep the processes doing good work.

c *Management policies.* The vendor's willingness to operate in a teamwork atmosphere requiring mutual confidence, exchange visits, technical assistance, improvement programs, and so on.

d. *Training in quality control.* The extent to which the vendor's managers, supervisors, and the workforce have been trained in quality control methodology. (Deficiencies are remedied by conducting training courses for the vendor's people in all levels.)

e. *Quality of prior deliveries for similar products.*

These differences in emphasis are, or course, traceable back to the basic policy on vendor relations, that is, adversary versus teamwork.[16]

4. *Joint quality planning.* The ingredients of joint planning are universal, but again there are important differences in emphasis. Generally there is little difference in practice with respect to such matters as measurement correlation, lot traceability, or exchange of test data. The differences are mainly in the following:

a. *Use of AQLs.* In the United States, the contracts embody agreed levels of acceptable quality level (AQL). These AQLs, once agreed on, serve to unify the parties on the sampling to be used, as well as providing a basis for adjudicating of disputes; for example, if the AQLs are exceeded, the buyer has a clear basis for a claim. Under this approach, many U.S. manufacturers tend also to view the AQLs as tolerable limits. This view is reinforced by some of the efforts that have been made to standardize AQLs in the industry.

The Japanese approach is quite different. They take the view that the AQLs tend to reduce the incentive for quality improvement. Hence, while for contract purposes they may quantify

AQLs, their real purpose is to find the best vendor, not merely one whose AQL is competitive.

The reasoning behind the Japanese view is evident from two major imperatives of color television set reliability. In the first place, component failures have been the major cause of color television set field failures and of in-house "fall off" rates. Secondly, the number of components in the color television set runs over 1000. Such numbers can convert component defect rates of the order of 0.1 percent into set failure rates of the order of 100 percent. This multiplying effect has been a factor in the Japanese use of parts per million (ppm) as a unit of measure for component quality.[17]

Clearly for defect rates in the range of ppm, the AQL concept is useless. In the design qualification stage, resort must be had to overstressing, environmental testing, and so on, to bring the component weaknesses out into the open. In addition, there must be a strict discipline of discovering the precise failure modes so that remedial action can be taken. Subsequently, during production, defects at the ppm level can be dealt with only on an automated sorting basis.

b. *Inspection data feedback to vendors.* In the United States, wide use is made of computerized data systems to provide manufacturers with summaries of vendor performance. These data are then used for tracking corrective action as well as for stimulating vendor improvement. In addition, there is some use of vendor rating systems for judging the comparative quality performance of vendors. The resulting ratings are usually made known to vendors and become the basis of awards for superior performance as well as penalties for inferior performance. Vendors are expected to share in the initiative to make the quality improvements needed to improve their ratings.[18]

c. *Product performance feedback.* The Japanese emphasis is on failure analysis, during assembly and in the field. These analyses go down to the precise failure mode. The resulting findings, along with samples of failed components, are presented to the vendor as part of the program of technical assistance. There is little doubt that the Japanese have secured much improvement in quality of components through their close working with vendors in failure analysis.

MANUFACTURE

There are hard data available to suggest that as to internal failures (discovered in the factory), the Japanese have an overwhelming superiority over the West. Prior to coming under Japanese management, the Motorola factory ran at a "fall-off" rate of 150 to 180 per 100 sets packed. This means that 150 to 180 defects were found for every 100 sets packed, or 1.5 to 1.8 per set. Three years later, the fall-off rate at Quasar (the new name of the factory) had gone down to a level of about 3 or 4 per 100 sets, or only about one-fortieth of the previous level. In Japan, the fall-off rates are about 0.5 per 100 sets, which is more than two orders of magnitude lower than the Motorola performance.[19]

There are other, unpublished data that tend to support the above example as being typical rather than extreme.

There are also hard data to suggest that Japanese productivity in color television set manufacture likewise exceeds that of the West, although by margins much less spectacular.[20]

On closer examination, these two performances are seen to be complementary. They are traceable to these practices:

1. *The prior design for producibility.* The benefit conferred by such design is obvious.

2. *Component quality.* This quality is derived not merely from the program of vendor relations; there is an extensive added program of sorting purchased components to keep the defectives out of the assembly lines and out of the marketplace. I observed such a program at Quasar. It involves a considerable investment in automated testing machinery and occupies the time of numerous people to set up and tend the machines. Similar practices have been observed in other plants by visiting journalists.

   While it takes substantial investment and personnel to sort the components, the benefits are spectacular. The Motorola assembly lines required about 15 employees per assembly line to perform line inspection and repair work. At the reduced fall-off rates, this number is in the range of one or two. This reduction, when applied to about eight assembly lines, is far greater than the number of people associated with component sorting.[21]

3. *Process design.* The processes used for color television set manufacture are quite similar from one company to another. There are differences in emphasis, however, and it is clear that the

Japanese's primary emphasis is on quality. Examples of this emphasis include:

   a. More extensive use of the "sequence" process for automatic insertion of discrete electronic components into printed circuit boards.

   b. Design of assembly conveyors to permit each assembler to disengage the set from the conveyor. This tends to avoid the quality problems created when the worker is unable to keep up with the conveyor.

   c. Design to automate and to minimize human handling. This design is evident throughout, even to the packing of the final product.

4. *Process control.* Here again there are many commonalities among all manufacturers. There is a worldwide trend toward returning process inspection to the workforce. There is some, but not conclusive, evidence that Japanese study and control of critical process variables, for example the solder bath, may be more complete than in the West. In the case of feedback to the workforce, the evidence is stronger. Of course, this aspect of manufacture is strongly influenced by the general state of employee relations.

5. *Final test.* All color television sets go through a final adjustment operation where each demonstrates its ability to perform its basic function. These final adjustments are typically made after operating temperatures have been stabilized. In addition, there are programs of audit on a sampling basis, consisting of extensive testing. It is usual to keep the entire day's product on hold to await the results of this audit. More comparative data would be required on final test practices to be able to make a useful judgment on contrasts.

ORGANIZATION

Japan and the United States are strikingly different in their organization for quality. In Japan, the revolution in quality was based primarily on a massive training program that started with the upper management—directors and managers. Through this training, these upper managers have acquired the capability and the tradition of directing the product quality affairs of the company as a part of their regular duties. Hence, they have little need for large central quality control departments and numerous quality specialists.

A further feature of the Japanese approach is the concept of group agreement before undertaking new projects or programs. This tends to slow down the decision-making process but assures unity of action once agreements have been reached.

In the United States, the organizational forms are radically different. The trend has been toward formally planned systems that define departmental responsibilities as well as setting up the procedures, methods, data networks, and so on, to carry out the plans. Wide use is made of central quality control departments staffed with quality specialists. Some specialists draft the plans and secure line department approval. Other specialists then audit performance against plan. Still others conduct analytical studies, report results, provide coordination, and so on.

The European organization forms are not so easy to classify. Their very large companies have tended to go to formalized systems, though with less elaborate quality control departments. Those who are suppliers to NATO or to large U.S. companies have, of course, had such systems imposed on them by their clients. Smaller European companies tend to operate with minimal formalized systems, including systems for quality.[22]

EMPLOYEE RELATIONS

One of the most striking effects of Japanese takeover of Western factories has been a simultaneous improvement in quality and in productivity. Such is the record in Europe (Great Britain and Germany) as well as in the United States. Still more striking is the fact that three different Japanese manufacturers have been involved. The results achieved by these recent takeovers have stirred new interest in the Japanese "style of management." It had been supposed that the Japanese revolution in quality was something that could thrive only in Japan—that it could not be exported. Now there is a gathering awareness that some of the benefits of the Japanese style of management may be exportable. Otherwise, how was it possible for those factories in the West, operated by the same Western personnel as before, to make such improvements under Japanese management?

It is obviously desirable for the West to understand, with some precision, the reasons behind those improvements. As we have seen, some of them involve broad policies as to marketing structure, launching of new products, product design, vendor relations, and so on. Beyond these broad policies, and their effect on technology, are other policies of a human relations nature, and these should also be understood by the West. In Japan, these human relations policies have somehow made possible the growth of QC Circles.[23] These QC Circles and their accomplishments, in morale as well as in quality, have aroused the admiration of all industrially developed and developing countries. Yet to date, the QC Circle concept has made negligible headway in the West

To understand the nature of these human relations policies, the Westerners must first look at the nature or the Japanese pattern of culture. Observed phenomena, such as the QC Circles, are logical only when examined in the light of that culture. The main elements of the Japanese industrial culture as it affects quality are well known and include:

- A tradition of lifelong employment with freedom from fear or layoffs; use of seniority as a major influence in salary increases and in promotions; strong mutual loyalties between company and employees with associated mutual responsibilities during the life of the employee.

- A successful revolution in quality, led by top management, based mainly on extensive educational programs and with resulting immense benefits to every Japanese; a consequent dedication to quality at all levels.

- A tradition of union organization paralleling company organization patterns rather than industrywide patterns; a conciliatory relationship between the company and the union, rather than an adversarial relationship; extensive participation by the union and the employee body in decision-making; a high level of industrial democracy.

Study of these elements of the Japanese culture should aid in identifying those concepts that can readily be adapted to other cultures and those that will present grave difficulties. To illustrate, "extensive educational programs" are entirely compatible with industrial policies in the West, whereas union organization along company lines would run into prohibitive obstacles.

Additionally, there is need to look closely at the cultural pattern in the West as it affects employee relations and product quality. In the United States, there remains a considerable residue of the Taylor system of shop management, based on a concept of separating planning from execution. Planning was delegated to engineers, leaving to the shop supervisors and workers only the job of executing the plans. The rationale behind this concept was that the supervisors and workers of that day (early in our century) lacked the education needed to establish work methods, conduct training, set standards of a day's work, and so on. The Taylor system, spectacularly successful in increasing shop productivity, was widely adopted in the United States, and was without doubt a major contributor to making the United States the world leader in productivity. However, the effect on product quality was adverse and led to the creation of independent inspection departments in an effort to restore the balance.

Meanwhile, the education levels of shop supervisors and workers have risen remarkably. As a consequence, these employees now have education, experience, and creativity that could be utilized on the job. However, under the division of work inherent in the Taylor system, they are severely limited in using these assets. In my judgment, the collective worker education experience and creativity is the major underemployed asset in the economy of the United States.[24] Attempts to make use of this underemployed asset are running into a good deal of cultural resistance. Some of this comes from the workers and unions. However, most of the resistance comes from the managers and staff specialists, including quality control specialists, who have acquired vested interests in the status quo. Nevertheless, the climate for experimenting with new ways is now more favorable than at any other time.

The Europeans also adopted a degree of separation of planning from execution, but on a scale far below that of the United States. As a result, they have less to undo. In addition, they are relatively more active in experimenting with new ways than their counterparts in the United States.

Cultural differences have been elaborated on to make clear that use of employee education, experience, and creativity is a matter far more profound than the specific mechanism adopted. As a mechanism, the QC Circles are merely the visible evidence of invisible prerequisites—mutual respect, industrial democracy, spirit of participation, and so on. These prerequisites are the real essentials and commonalities; the specific mechanisms adopted will vary widely with the culture.

IMPLICATIONS FOR THE FUTURE

The color television set provides a good insight into the relative progress of Japanese and Western quality. The television industry was created in the West; it was the West that contributed the technological and managerial know-how needed to bring the industry to a viable state. The Japanese, despite their late entry, brought to the industry all the fervor of their postwar revolution in quality. That revolution was led by the top industrialists and had its origin in the need to make Japanese products salable in the world market. As the revolution progressed, it became evident that it contained the seeds for world quality leadership.[25] The Japanese have recognized this potentiality and have continued to support their revolution. As a result, they have already attained quality leadership in some product lines (of which the color television set is one). The prospect is for this leadership to invade more and more product lines in the decades to come.

Until now, the West has made no vigorous general response to this Japanese revolution. There have been "Quality Year" programs in some countries and these have received a degree of support from top industrialists. However, the programs have been mainly in the nature of providing a favorable climate for action at the company level. Whether the companies took action depended entirely on the extent to which their management felt an acute need to act, that is, to take advantage of an opportunity or meet a threat.

Will the West take forceful action to respond to the Japanese revolution? In my judgment, they will, but only after things have gotten noticeably worse. Once there is clear evidence that significant sales are being lost due to quality competition, the upper management will move in. Similarly, once there is clear evidence of jobs being lost ("exported") due to quality competition, the governments and unions will move in. Lacking such clear evidence, evolution will continue to prevail.

Extensive sales and jobs have already been lost for quality reasons. However, the West has long believed these losses to be due to price competition. Originally, this belief was entirely valid. Lately, the quality competition has been growing while price competition has been declining. This trend has yet to be understood by the majority of the economic analysts in the West and especially by the press.

Where will this clear evidence materialize? It already has materialized in the case of the color television set. In the automobile industry, the evidence is already sufficient to be of widespread concern to upper managers in several Western countries.[26] Reading the trends leaves no hesitancy in predicting that, by the end of the 1980s, Japanese quality leadership will be the subject of far more discussion and action than has been the case to date. This discussion will not be limited to those industrial companies that will be on the defensive. The discussion will extend to the legislative bodies, the labor unions, the press, and still other organs of society.

The hope is that the companies in the West do not wait for things to become noticeably worse. Time is already here when these companies should take some of the steps needed to accelerate their progress. These steps involve such matters as:

- *Market research* to understand the importance of various qualities as seen by the user and also the competitive status of the company with respect to the key qualities.

- *Visits abroad* to learn how quality is attained in other cultures. Of these visits, none is now more important than visits to Japan. If I were head of a company in the West, I would not only visit

Japan—I would invite the head of the union to go along with me to see at first hand the nature of the competition faced by the company and its employees.

- *Training.* The central ingredient of the Japanese revolution has been a massive training program. This training started at the top and progressed downward through all levels in the hierarchy as well as sideways through all functions. Since it took nearly a decade for this training program to work its way through the levels of the hierarchy, it follows that planning for training should receive one of the highest priorities in any program.

We are all aware of the potential benefits of competition in the marketplace. With the greatly increased role of quality in human affairs ("life behind the dikes of quality control"), competition in quality must be regarded as conferring benefits of uncommon importance. It is also true that competition in the marketplace can create short-term disruptions due to declines in sales, loss of jobs, and so on. The prospect is for these disruptions to grow as product quality becomes a larger and larger factor in share of market. Those who would avoid such disruptions would be well advised to prepare now for the increased competition which lies ahead.

ACKNOWLEDGEMENTS

Numerous individuals have helped in the preparation of this paper through contribution of data, critiques, ideas, and other forms of assistance. In most cases, it has not been possible to attribute specific assistance due to the classified nature of the data or comments. In still other cases, the contributors declined to be identified at all, so that their assistance is known only to me. I do have the privilege of publicly thanking the following:

Hitachi: Keizo Nukada

Japanese Union of Scientists and Engineers: Junji Noguchi

Matsushita Electric Industries: Takao Funahashi

Sony Corporation: Nobuto Yamada

Tokyo-Shibaura Electric: Sadashige Morikawa and Masaya Murakami

N.V. Philips' Gloeilampen Fabrieken, B.L. Kaper: H. van der Weiden

Philips Electronics: D.W. Ritchie

GTE Sylvania: John J. Gonet

Quasar Electronics: A.J. Hitzelberger, Gary Griffin, and James J. O'Hara

Sears and Roebuck, M.C. Hill, Jr. and R.W. Peach

Abraham & Straus: George Ouellette

Hitchcock Publishing: Loren M.Walsh

Dr. Frank M. Gryna, Jr.

Dr. Lennart Sandholm

AEG-Telefunken Ing.: E. Schlotel

ITT Europe, Dipl Ing.: Lotar Kozina

ENDNOTES

1. The Center for Policy Alternatives. 1974. "The Productivity of Servicing Consumer Durable Products." Massachusetts Institute of Technology with the Charles Stark Draper Laboratory: 51. (Available from RANN Document Center, National Science Foundation, Washington, D.C. 22230.)

2. The ratio of five to one is quoted from unpublished information provided to me by European and American managers. Mainly, I acquired these inputs at the 18 (or so) courses in "Management of Quality Control" which I conduct annually in about eight countries and that are attended annually by about 1000 managers and specialists from all industries. Some information is also available from the trend-in-failure rate reduction when Western television-making companies came under Japanese management. In the Quasar factory (formerly Motorola), the cost of service calls dropped from $22 million in 1974 to less than $4 million in 1976. (Private communication to J. M. Juran.) In Whirlpool Corporation's Warwick factory (now a Sanyo facility), the retail failure rate of close to 10 percent was brought to below 2 percent. *Business Week* (December 12, 1977): 160.

3. In the case or plain paper copiers, a Japanese machine (Ricoh) is asserted to have a mean time between failures (MTBF) of about 17,000 copies compared to the leading Western copier (Xerox) with a MTBF of 6,000–10,000 copies. In combination with a shorter repair time, the resulting number of machines serviced by a serviceman is 100 versus 50. *Fortune* (March 13, 1978):86.

4. Juran, J. M. 1974. *Quality control handbook*, 3rd ed. New York: McGraw-Hill: 48-1 to 48-14.

5. Ibid. 48-6 to 48-11.

6. Private communications to J. M. Juran.

7. In the United States, service on color television sets is surrounded with numerous difficulties arising from inadequate organization, skills and ethics; see The Center for Policy Alternatives. 1974. "The Productivity of Servicing Consumer Durable Products," Massachusetts Institute of Technology with the Charles Stark Draper Laboratory: 109.

8. During October 1974, I had occasion to moderate a three day conference in Tokyo, at which 15 Japanese service companies presented papers on the subject of quality control in the service industries. My summary for dissemination in the West included the following: "The quality-cost relationship became pertinent during discussions of the economics of attaining perfection, whether in pollution, product quality, or clerical errors. There was an awareness that perfection is, in theory, an uneconomic standard. Yet surprisingly, the audience of industrial managers did not readily accept a standard short of perfection." Juran, J. M. 1975. Quality control of service—The 1974 Japanese symposium. *Quality Progress* (April): 10–13.

9. The Center for Policy Alternatives. 1974. "The Productivity of Servicing Consumer Durable Products," Massachusetts Institute of Technology with the Charles Stark Draper Laboratory: 87–94.

10. In the United States, the service costs for 1972 color television sets were estimated to equal 66 percent of the purchase price and 33 percent of the life cycle costs. The Center for Policy Alternatives. 1974. "The Productivity of Servicing Consumer Durable Products," Massachusetts Institute of Technology with the Charles Stark Draper Laboratory: 78; see also pages 87–94 for a discussion of the warranty system.

11. For a good description, see Gonet, John J. 1973. A total quality system for consumer electronics products. *ASQC 1973 Technical Conference Transactions:* 381–392.

12. One Japanese company pointed out to me that the Japanese economy does not include large military or space industries. As a result, the engineers who would otherwise be drawn off by such industries become available for the civilian sector of the economy.

13. Ishikawa, K. Education for Quality Control in Japanese Industry. Japanese Union of Scientists and Engineers, *Reports of Statistical Application Research* 16(3): 21–40.

14. Private communication to J. M. Juran.

15. The best of these case histories are published in the monthly FQC (in Japanese) with a circulation of about 70,000 copies per month. The Japanese Union of Scientists and Engineers also publishes some prize papers in English.

16. For an example of the Japanese emphasis, see Murakami, M., T. Kishii, and E. Inamura. 1977. PPM control for electronic parts. Japanese Union of Scientists and Engineers. *7th Symposium on Reliability and Maintainability.*

17. Ibid.

18. See Gonet, John J. 1973. A total quality system. *ASQC 1973 Technical Conference Transactions:* 381–392. See also Breibach, Paul J. 1978. Vendor quality assurance and reliability. *ASQC 1978 Technical Conference Transactions:* 11–20.

19. Hitzelberger, A. J. 1975. "Quality Control-Japanese Style." Talk before the Chicago Section, ASQC. November 12; see also, No Miracle. *Quality* (February 1978): 22–24; also, discussion between A. J. Hitzelberger and J. M. Juran, October 3, 1977.

20. *Fortune* (January 30, 1978): 56–62.; *Business Week* (December 12, 1977): 156–160; No Miracle-Just Good Management. *Quality* (February 1978): 22–24.

21. Hitzelberger, A. J. 1975. "Quality Control-Japanese Style." Talk before the Chicago Section, ASQC. November 12; No Miracle. *Quality* (February 1978): 22–24.

22. Juran, J. M. 1974. *Quality control handbook*, 3rd ed. New York: McGraw-Hill: 48-2 to 48-14.

23. Ibid. 18-34 to 18-37; also 18-51 and 18-52, plus references cited.

24. Juran, J. M. 1973. The Taylor system and quality control. A series of eight articles appearing in *Quality Progress* (May through December).

25. As a Westerner who was privileged to be an early observer of (and modes contribution to) the Japanese quality revolution, I had little hesitancy in making the following prediction in 1966:

> *This prediction is based on seeing, at first hand, the trend of events in Japan and in a good many other countries over the last two decades. During those decades the Japanese, through a revolution in quality control practices, have already attained a world competitive position, although starting with the worst quality reputation among the industrial nations. Now there is evidence that the energy that created this revolution, far from being spent, is still in full vigor.*
>
> *In my observation, no other nation is so completely unified on the importance of good quality achievement, so eager to discover and adopt the best practices being followed in other countries, so avid in training all company levels and functions in modern methods of controlling quality, so vigilant in regulating the quality of exported goods. To be sure, there is progress along these fronts in all countries, but nowhere else is there the broad-based sense of devotion and, especially, the sense of urgency that is so evident among the Japanese. Witnessing their accelerated pace, and comparing this with the pedestrian progress of other countries, the conclusion is inescapable: The Japanese are headed for world quality leadership and will attain it in the next two decades because no one else is moving there at the same pace.*

Quoted from Juran, J. M. 1967. The QC Circle phenomenon. *Industrial Quality Control* (January): 336.

26. Private communication to J. M. Juran.

15

Quality Control in Service Industries

INTRODUCTION

All institutions, whether for manufacture, service, or other purposes, face problems of attaining quality. In the case of the manufacturing industries, extensive work has been done in the last three decades to identify the quality problems that are common to all manufacture, and to discover common solutions to these problems. This search for commonality has led to identification and successful application of various universals of quality control. Some of these universals (for example, process capability, the Pareto Principle, quality cost analysis, statistical methodology) have been of great aid to practitioners.

The present article examines the problems of commonality as it applies to quality control in service industries.

WHAT IS SERVICE?

Service, as used here, is work performed for someone else. The recipient of the service (often called the client) may be:

- An individual user, for example, the housewife (often called a consumer)

Editor's Note: The paper appearing here in Chapter 15 was published in 1979 as Standards for quality control in service industries. *Quality Progress* (January) 12(1): 32–34.

- An institution, for example, a company occupying office space under a lease

- Both, for example, users of electrical energy from a central source.

Service work exists for a variety of reasons, principally to:

1. Enable the client to meet needs which he would otherwise be unable to meet, for example, distant voice communication.

2. Offer the client alternatives that are superior in cost, time, convenience, and so on, for example, public transportation.

3. Meet a wide variety of human psychological and physiological needs, for example, amusement, freedom from disagreeable tasks, opportunity for learning and creativity.

Service work may include sale of a product, for example, food in restaurants, spare parts used during automobile repair. However, such sale of a product is normally incidental to the work performed for the client.

Definitions of "service industries" usually exclude manufacture, agriculture, mining and construction. The definitions usually include:

- Public transportation

- Public utilities (telephone communication, energy services, sanitation services)

- Restaurants, hotels and motels

- Marketing (retail food, apparel, automotive, wholesale trade, department stores)

- Finance (commercial banks, insurance, sales finance, investment)

- News media

- Personal services (amusements, laundry and cleaning, barber and beauty shops)

- Professional services (physicians, lawyers)

- Government (defense, health, education, welfare, municipal services)

CHARACTERISTICS OF A SERVICE COMPANY

A service company is a system of special facilities and skills, organized to provide services to clients.[1] It sells the benefits of this system to its clients in a variety of ways, for example:

- Lease of facilities, for example, apartments, office space

- Use of facilities, for example, bus rides, telephone calls

- Professional advice, for example, medical, legal

- Health maintenance, for example, hospital service

- Product maintenance, for example, automobile repairs

- Relief from self-service, for example, restaurant service

In carrying out its mission, the service company usually sells directly to the user. This is true not only for large industrial users but also for numerous small users as well. In this latter respect, the service company differs sharply from the manufacturing company.

These direct sales bring the service company into multiple contact with large numbers of consumers, giving rise to huge numbers of individual transactions. All of these transactions have their impact on human beings, many of whom are articulate.

A favorable aspect of these direct contacts with the consumer is the opportunity for good feedback as to fitness for use. In this respect, the service company has an easier job than the manufacturing company, which is comparatively insulated from the consumer, and must resort to special studies to secure adequate feedback.

The extensive personal contact also sets up some relationships that are inherently uncomfortable for the consumer. To secure some services he surrenders his property into the custody of the service company, for example, baggage for transport. The service company holds this property in captivity, and a failure or a delay in returning it can greatly inconvenience the consumer. In other cases, it is the consumer himself who feels he is held captive. The most usual form of this is waiting in line in a queue, or waiting for service when there are no effective alternatives.

For some service failures, the consumer can make a direct complaint and claim. He may be compensated for loss of property, but he is seldom compensated for loss of time or for his annoyance. What he can do is to turn to competing services, if they exist. He can also do damage to the company by publicizing the trouble he has had. If the service is a monopoly, he can join other disgruntled consumers in collective efforts to force improvements through publicity or political action.

DESIGN OF SERVICE QUALITY

In establishing their quality of design, the service industries are bound by the same broad considerations as are the manufacturing companies: identification of what constitutes fitness for use, choice of a design concept that is responsive to the identified needs of the user, and translation of this concept into specifications. Beyond these basic needs, the service industries must give special emphasis to several added aspects of quality of design that are inherent in dealing with a clientele of many consumers.

Made-to-Order Designs

Human beings exhibit a wide spectrum of needs and likes, all stemming from differences in status, personal taste, and so on. The service industries respond to this spectrum by such methods as:

1. Creating a range of choice for the client, for example, the restaurant menu.

2. Providing a modular system design that permits the user to direct the system in accordance with his special needs. The classic example is the automated telephone system, which permits the consumer to reach millions of destinations, unaided by human intervention.

3. Providing assistance to meet that residue of "to order" needs that the engineered system cannot provide directly to the consumer, for example, tailoring clothes to measure.

While these made-to-order designs are an essential aspect of service quality design, they are also a breeding ground for errors, that is, in interpreting the special needs and in conforming to them. In addition, the special designs may require special pricing, again multiplying the chances of error.

Technical Assistance

The consumer has extensive need for such assistance. In some cases, his technological ignorance requires that qualified specialists be available to diagnose his needs, for example, human illness or a television set that is out of service. In other cases, the need is mainly for explanation, for example, complex contract provisions; train time tables.

Simplicity

In offering a design of service to thousands or millions of clients, the need for simplicity is absolute. Some consumers are unable to understand printed instructions. Many more consumers are unwilling to take the time to learn, and their unwillingness creates trouble for them and the company as well.

Auxiliary Services

In some countries, the service industries teem with "free" services which are provided to clients as part of the quality of design. For example, an automobile service station will clean the client's windshield and check the status of oil, batteries, and tires while the pump is filling the fuel tank. It also provides washroom facilities for the travelers. Such auxiliary services are designed partly to meet competition and partly to meet a special need of consumers for "well-being."

TIME AS A PARAMETER OF SERVICE QUALITY

A striking feature of the service industries is that the time required to provide service is regarded as an element of "quality." In manufacturing companies, delivery time is certainly regarded as a vital parameter of overall customer relations. However, delivery time is not regarded as a part of "quality"; it is a wholly separate parameter. The organization setup reflects this. A separate department (production control, materials management, and so on) is designated to establish standards (schedules), measure delivery performance, and report on adherence to schedule.

Some service industries distinguish sharply between different subdivisions of time.

Access Time

This is the length of time that elapses from the client's first effort to gain the service company's attention until he has that attention. The standard for this "accessibility" is expressed, for example, in the form: 80 percent of the incoming phone calls should be answered within 15 seconds after the first ring.

Measurement of some types of access time can be done by automated recorders. More usually, special observers must conduct sampling studies.

Queuing Time

Some services involve a queuing of clients due to variable loads or to considerations of economy. In such cases the consumer is concerned with:

- The length of the queue and therefore the waiting time. The service company is in a position to plan this based on past history and probability considerations (queuing theory).

- The integrity of the queue, that is, adherence to the principle of first-come, first-served. Some companies organize this by use of assigned serial numbers. This also permits the clients to sit while they wait, and to occupy themselves with reading material provided for the purpose. This may be embellished by play facilities for children.

Action Time

This is commonly defined as the interval between taking the customer's order and providing him with the service requested.

In designing the time aspect of service, it is important to stress the customer's viewpoint of elapsed time. To a railroad or an airline, the emphasis on travel time may be from terminal to terminal, and this is clearly important. To the shipper or passenger, the emphasis is from dock to dock or from point of origin to point of final destination. The customer will make his decisions on this point-to-point basis, no matter what the carrier thinks.

A second major reason for the critical importance of service time is the cumulative effect of delays. A byproduct of organizing human affairs around complex systems is that when those systems fail, a great deal of human activity is disrupted. For example, a vital machine tool is delayed eight days during railroad shipment. Because the machine is critical to a factory production line, the entire factory is delayed for eight days. Some or all of this delay may extend to the factory's customers, and to their customers, and so on.

As a corollary of the critical nature of service time, the service industries should:

1. Establish standards for the various components of service time, and set up controls to enforce these standards.

2. Improve present service time by studying enough cases of service to find out just where the time is being consumed.

3. Make service time a major parameter in design of future systems. For example, an entire new industry of "fast food" has arisen in the United States to meet the needs of many clients who choose not to devote time either to food preparation or to waiting in restaurants.

DESIGN FOR CONSUMER "WELL-BEING"

A further parameter of service quality is consumer "well-being." This parameter is difficult to define, but easy to exemplify. For instance, a serviceman repairs a household appliance. He does so promptly and with competence. His charges are fair. What the housewife remembers is that he tracked mud into her kitchen and was rude.

The service industries recognize that there are positive and negative aspects that affect consumer well-being. On the positive side are such matters as:

Atmosphere

Some service industries take active steps to create an "atmosphere" that will meet the tastes of their clientele. Obvious examples are seen in the industries devoted to travel, leisure, and entertainment. The clients are a mixed lot: commercial travelers; older, retired citizens; young unmarried people; couples with young children, and so on. These categories differ in their tastes to such an extent that the service industries design differences in decorations, furnishings, refreshments, provisions for leisure time, and so on.

Feeling of Importance

Because service is work done for someone else, many consumers view the relationship between client and service company as one akin to master and servant. This viewpoint is flattering to the ego of the consumer and leads him to expect attention, courtesy, respect, and still other elements common to a master-servant relationship. Service companies are well aware of this viewpoint, and some design into their plan of customer relations some elements that enforce the consumer's feeling of importance: formal "welcome" symbols, various forms of continuing attention, free souvenirs, "thank you" letters, and so on.

Information

Still another element of well-being is to know what to expect. For example, when a train is late, the passengers waiting in the station to board that train want to be informed as to the expected departure time. This "need to know" is not for the purpose of enabling the traveler to change plans depending on the length of delay. (Unless the delay is overwhelming, virtually all the passengers will wait it out anyway). Instead, the need to know is based on an instinctive human desire for mastery over the environment. The consumer who knows what to expect derives a feeling of well-being from this knowledge, since he has the information needed for predictability and, at this option, for choice of alternatives. Lacking knowledge of what to expect, he is at the mercy of rumors and surprises, with the result that his anxiety rises.

Safety

Because the user entrusts his person, property, and well-being to the custody of the service industries, "service safety" becomes as vital as product safety. The hotel, the restaurant, the carrier, and so on., all have responsibilities for this safety. These responsibilities were on the statute books for centuries before the current wave of activity in product liability

Continuity of Service

Many designs include provisions for maintaining continuity of service despite failures. Telephone companies and airlines make use of alternative routings in the event of unavailability of standard routings. Professional service groups (doctors, lawyers) organize their work in a way that permits continuity in the absence of any member.

CONFORMANCE TO DESIGN

In the service industries, it is necessary to distinguish clearly between two very different kinds of conformance, "internal" and "external."

Internal Conformance

Internal conformance relates to those aspects of the service company's operations that cannot be sensed by the clientele. For example, the electric power company establishes standards for quality of fuel bought and for energy yield per ton of fuel.

Generally the service industries' approach to internal conformance is similar to that used in the manufacturing industries for process control, cost control, and so on.

External Conformance

Other aspects of service company operation can be sensed by the consumer. These aspects are by no means limited to the obvious, *sine qua non* elements of the design, for example, wholesome restaurant food, clean hotel beds, correct telephone connections. They include also the features that contribute to timeliness and well-being.

In many cases, what appears to be "internal," that is, the system, processes and equipment, can have severe impacts on the consumer. For example, the control of hospital medication errors is, on the face of it, squarely up to the personnel, notably the nurses. On closer examination, the "system" is seen to be a major contributor to these errors. Similarly, because many service companies serve large numbers of small clients, the adequacy and maintenance of the data processing system is an important factor in the accuracy and timeliness of invoices, credit for payments, and so on.

This interrelation between internal and external conformance requires that the review of internal conformance not be limited to that carried out by the departmental supervision. Many service companies recognize this need, and set up independent audits that are all-pervasive.

Standards of Conformance

Adherence to service specifications poses the universal problem of finding the optimum level of conformance. One approach is to use a "market" standard based on analysis of performance attained by multiple members of the same large service organization. This approach is widely used in the Bell System, which operates hundreds of telephone exchanges, by the U.S. Postal Service, by the Howard Johnson chain of hundreds of restaurants, and by numerous other multi-unit service companies. A second approach is to study the performance of competitors. It is common practice for managers of service companies to make use of competitors' services with an incidental purpose of appraising quality. In addition, there are periodic special studies which follow generally the principles of market research.

The conventional array of ratios used in managerial and financial control carry hidden risks to service quality. For example, when the manufacturing industries undertook to automate, their traditional ratios of support personnel to production personnel became meaningless. Similarly, when a service company automates, efforts to hold a constant ratio between maintenance and production forces can result in deterioration of service. Similarly, improvements in other aspects of operating performance can affect quality of service as seen by the consumer. For example, in the hospital, the bed patient has traditionally called for service by pressing a call button to which a nurse responded in person. The trend has been to centralize the response to these patient calls by directing them to a switchboard operator. The operator answers this call via a loudspeaker located behind the patient's bed. In turn, the patient makes his wants known to the operator via a microphone located "somewhere" near his bed. The new system achieves some needed improvement in hospital manpower productivity, and may well reduce the "access time" for the patient. However, some patients feel that the anonymous voice response represents a severe drop in well-being when compared with a response through the personal appearance of a nurse.

MEASURES OF SERVICE QUALITY

For internal conformance, the measures of quality have much in common with the well-known measures widely used in control of manufacturing processes. Measure of external conformance is more complex due to the abstract nature of some of the qualities and the subjective reactions of consumers.

An obvious source of data on external conformance is the crosssection of consumer complaints and claims, although many annoyed consumers will not take the trouble to complain. However, the complaints received do represent a sample of the types of annoyance to which all consumers are subject.

A second method of measure of external performance is through solicitation of consumer comments. A typical form of this is the appraisal card made available to consumers in hotel rooms and restaurants. Some companies use the summaries of these cards as the basis for a regular management report.

Additionally, some companies design special surveys of customer reaction, through letter questionnaires, telephone contacts and personal interview. The techniques used follow conventional market research practice.

Measures of service quality have to date been on an industry-by-industry basis, and this will continue for the foreseeable future.

Some service companies supplement their regular measures of quality by use of periodic audits. These audits are all-pervasive, covering both internal and external aspects of quality. As is common in formal audit plans, the service industry audit covers many incidents, observations, documents, and so on. To reduce these findings to a simple score suitable for management reports (or for motivation plans) requires systems of summary, weighting, demerit values, ratings, and so on.

Audit or review of the work of professional categories of personnel (for example, researchers, physicians) runs into a special obstacle. These professional categories tend to feel that the review must be by a "peer group," for example, only physicians should review the work of physicians. When audit of such professional work is done by administrative personnel, the findings are not accepted wholeheartedly.

ORGANIZATION FOR QUALITY

Service industry organization for quality differs considerably from that used by manufacturing industries. There are also extensive differences among the service industries themselves. However, in general, the service industry organization exhibits the following features:

1. The day-to-day regulation and decision-making on conformance to standards are largely in the hands of the line departments, without the presence of independent inspection and test personnel who have powers to hold up the delivery of nonconforming "product."

2. The concept of a separate staff of specialists in quality control has only a minority acceptance.

3. The concept of a high-level manager devoting full time to the quality function likewise has only minority acceptance. Where this organization form is used, the title of this manager is usually something other than Quality Manager.

4. Organized coordination of the quality function seldom exists in continuing form. For specific projects or crises, coordination may be set up through temporary committees of departmental heads.

The service industries' approach to organization for quality is adequate for establishing specifications and standards, for planning of day-to-day controls, and for executing those controls. In addition, their approach to coordination appears to be adequate for dealing with crises and with specific, agreed-on projects. However, their organization forms do not appear to be well suited for programs of quality improvement, since:

- The concept of an organized approach to quality improvement has not been fully grasped

- Their basic training in the nature of the quality function has been limited

- There is a lack of trained specialists to carry out the details of diagnosis for quality improvement.

QUALITY IMPROVEMENT

The service industries abound in chronic quality problems, and thereby in opportunities for quality improvement. The general approach to such improvement, as used in some manufacturing companies, could also be used by most service industries. However, as noted above, the service industries are not well organized for quality improvement.

These weaknesses in organization form do not preclude quality improvements if top management provides the leadership. For example, the Howard Johnson restaurant chain has engaged in massive programs for improving quality through:

- Transferring most of the food processing to centralized factories

- Shifting from franchised restaurants to owned restaurants

Additional improvement projects are the result of vendor initiative. Equipment manufacturers and materials suppliers are active in studying the problems of the service industries as a source of ideas for new equipment and materials that will improve productivity, quality, and so on. Purchase of such new equipment usually involves substantial investments for the service company, and thereby requires the approval of top management.

Large service companies maintain a staff of full-time technologists, particularly with respect to facilities and equipment. These technologists are active in studying ways to make improvements in productivity, quality, and so on, through changes in facilities and equipment.

Where top management does not provide the leadership for quality improvement, the initiative, if any, must come from the middle management. However, in the absence of a manager devoted full time to the quality function, it is difficult and unusual for the line managers to evolve programs for quality improvement.

Study of Quality Costs

In manufacturing companies, study of quality costs is a fruitful technique for identifying promising projects and for proving their promise to upper management. This technique is applicable to the service industries, including the standardized quality cost categories.

While the quality cost concept is clearly applicable to the service industries, the published cases of application have been too few to permit sound conclusions as to whether the potential benefits to the service industries would match those experienced by manufacturing industries.

Effect of Quality on Income

This is a most promising field of study. The most dramatic examples have involved improvement in competitive position through shortening the time required to render service. In some cases, existing companies have made use of operations research techniques for planning delivery operations amid a complex interrelationship of vehicles, drivers, customer needs, product types, alternative routes, delivery frequencies, and so on. Aside from the effect on customer relations, these deliveries are a major factor in cost of service, for example, in some industries, delivery costs run to about 20 percent of sales.

One way of translating service quality improvements into income is through making the sales contract contingent on prompt delivery. Such contract provisions, for example, penalty clauses, give a competitive advantage to the service company which has the firmest grip on its delivery interval.

MOTIVATION FOR QUALITY

To a considerable degree, the approaches to motivation used by manufacturing companies are applicable to the service industries. There is the same need for observing the principles and implications of self-control, controllability, subspecies of operator error, and so on. However, the problems of quality motivation for non-supervisory employees exhibit some features that differ from those found in manufacturing industries:

- Service employees have extensive direct contact with consumers, and can thereby directly affect the company's customer relations.

- This same direct contact gives many service employees prompt, useful feedback of the effect of their actions on fitness for use. This direct feedback is in sharp contrast to the "meaningless" features of many factory jobs.

- The fact that service employees do have extensive contacts with customers requires that the company develop the means of appraising the quality of this contact through sampling observation, customer feedback, and so on.

Despite the manpower problems inherent in a labor-intensive and (often) low-wage industry, service companies have evolved ways of establishing successful motivational programs. Some of these are highly formalized, being based on a comprehensive system of data feedback. At the other extreme are the rather informal systems of employee rating, employee of the month award, and so on.

COMMONALITY IN SERVICE INDUSTRIES

To discuss this commonality, it is useful first to look sideways at the parallel problem of commonality in manufacturing industries. These industries differ remarkably in products, processes, materials and underlying technology. Despite such diversity, the manufacturing industries have evolved an extensive commonality in their approach to the quality function. (A major reason for this evolution of commonality has been the traditional gregariousness of manufacturing managers, plus their willingness to participate in expositions, conferences, seminars, and so on, and to contribute papers, discussions and exchanges of experience and ideas)

This evolution of commonality has been of great assistance to all manufacturing industries. As the universals have become identified, and as the case histories of application have been published, it has become possible to:

1. Understand the nature of the quality function as something universal and distinct from the specialized technology of each industry.

2. Structure seminars and training programs related to these universals.

3. Develop quality specialists and quality managers who can make themselves effective in any manufacturing situation.

Individual service industries also hold expositions, conferences, and so on, in which their executives and specialists participate. However, these are insular in nature, being oriented to the problems of that industry and not to the universal problems of the quality function. Conferences to deal with quality problems that are common to all service industries are a rarity. As a result, while all service industries are keenly aware of the need for quality, and have evolved programs specially suited to their respective needs, these programs are likewise insular, that is, every industry on its own. There has to date been no significant movement to identify what are the common problems of service industry quality, and what are the common solutions.

SUMMARY ON COMMONALITY

The manufacturing industries have based their commonality on:

1. Universal elements of the managerial process, that is, policies, objectives, plans, organization, manning, motivation, and so on. These universals apply fully to the service industries.

2. Universal parameters of quality (fitness for use). These have extensive application to service industries as well. However, the service industries make use of additional, important parameters, and these need to be studied in depth to evolve the universals which underlie them.

3. Universal functional activities through which fitness for use is achieved: product development, manufacturing planning, vendor relations, process control, test, sale, use, field maintenance, feedback, and so on. These activities are common to service industries as well, but with important differences in emphasis.

4. Universal skills, tools and techniques. These have extensive application to the service industries, but it is likely that there will need to be some new inventions to meet the special problems of the service industries.

The service industries would be well advised to take steps to evolve the universals and commonalities that underlie quality of service. These steps would parallel those taken in the manufacturing industries:

- Conferences, seminars and training courses on service quality, with attendance by managers and specialists from a variety of service industries. (When attendance is restricted to one industry, there arise inhibitions, since competitors are asked to learn from each other. When attendance is from a variety of industries, these inhibitions are minimal).

- A professional society that structures its activities around service industry quality.

- Journals, books and other publications to exchange experiences and expound principles.

- In all likelihood, all of these activities can be set up under the programs of existing institutions, without the need for creating new ones.

ENDNOTE

1. *Company* is used here in a generic sense. It may include government departments and still other institutions created for service

This article is derived from the more exhaustive analysis "Quality Control in Service Industries" (by J. M. Juran and R. S. Bingham Jr.) that constitutes Section 47 of the forthcoming Third Edition of *Quality Control Handbook.* J. M. Juran, ed. 1974. New York: McGraw-Hill.

16

Product Quality—A Prescription for the West

The West is in serious trouble with respect to product quality. A major reason is the immediate threat posed by the Japanese revolution in quality.

THE NEW COMPETITION IN QUALITY

A simple diagram (see Figure 16.1) shows what has happened.

During the early 1950s, Western product quality was regarded as the best. The label "Made in USA" (or Germany, Switzerland and so on) was a distinct asset to product salability. In the subsequent decades, Western quality has continued to get better as it had been doing for centuries. (Those who contend that Western quality has deteriorated are usually generalizing from isolated cases.)

Prior to World War II, Japanese product quality was poor—it was widely regarded as among the worst. Such products could be sold but only at ridiculously low prices, even then it was difficult to secure repeat sales.

Soon after World War II, Japanese quality began to improve, and the pace of improvement has been remarkable. My estimate is that by the mid-1970s this pace had brought the Japanese to a state of equality with the West. Within this broad state of equality, the West retained quality leadership in some product lines. In other product lines, the Japanese had attained quality superiority. A well publicized example is the color television set. In

---

Editor's Note: The paper appearing here in Chapter 16 was presented in 1981 at the closing session of the 25th conference of the European Organization for Quality Control, Paris, June.

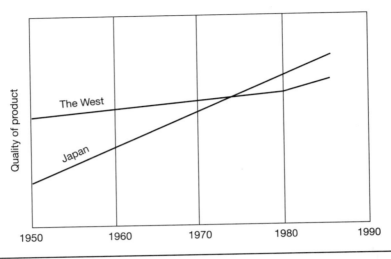

Figure 16.1 World competition in quality.

that case, Japanese quality superiority was a major reason for a dramatic shift in share of market from the West to Japan.

Figure 16.1 also shows that ever since the mid-1970s the two lines have been diverging. The prospect is that during the 1980s the situation will get worse much worse. The scenario of the color television set is being rerun in many product lines, including such essentials as automobiles and large-scale integrated circuits. The magnitude of this threat has yet to be grasped by the West.

WHAT HAS MADE JAPANESE QUALITY SO GOOD?

In any competition, an important element of grand strategy is to understand the strengths of the competitor. The more that Western companies under-stand what are the ingredients of the Japanese revolution in quality, the more effective will be the Western response.

The Japanese could have chosen an evolutionary approach—gradually learn by experience how to compete with the West. Instead, the Japanese industrialists chose to create a revolution in quality. To this end, they made three radical departures from prior practice:

1. A massive, quality-related training program

2. Annual programs of quality improvement

3. Upper management leadership of the quality function

The Japanese massive training program. Massive is the word for describing a program of training hundreds of thousands of managers and supervisors at all organization levels and in all company departments plus millions of non-supervisors. That massive training program has made Japanese managers, specialists, and workers the best-trained forces on earth so far as quality is concerned. With respect to such training, it is not possible for the West to overtake the Japanese before the end of this decade. The reason is that it took the Japanese an entire decade to train all those levels of managers and supervisors. Not until the early 1960s (1962) did they begin to train non-supervisors.

Japanese annual programs of quality improvement. Armed with their new know-how and prodded by grim necessity, the Japanese proceeded to make many improvements in product quality—millions of them. (Again, massive.) Because the training programs had included all departments, improvements came from all functions—product design, purchase of components, manufacture inspection, and test field service. In addition, because the training was carried on at all levels, it became possible to utilize the experience and creativity of the entire company hierarchies, including much of the workforce.

One thing leads to another. The application of new know-how creates an added source of know-how—the experience that comes from applying concepts and tools in the environment of reality. Over the years, the accumulated experience has developed its own imperatives—the precious *habit of improvement.* All organizations evolve the habit of "control"—of meeting the day-to-day schedules and putting out the fires. If they do a good job of control, they will meet this year's budgets and targets. They will also *fall a year behind* any competitors who have acquired the habit of improvement.

It is this habit of annual quality improvement that has put the Japanese on that steep upward climb. Each year they have gained on the West because their pace of improvement has exceeded that of the West. The Japanese will continue to make these gains year after year until the West can develop a pace of annual quality improvement that matches that of the Japanese.

Japanese upper management leadership of the quality function. In Japan, it is quite usual for the upper managers—the presidents and the general managers—to provide leadership to the quality function. The Japanese upper managers first assumed this leadership during the quality emergency of the late 1940s and early 1950s. It was these upper managers who launched those massive training programs and those programs of annual quality improvement. Having created a successful revolution, the presidents have shown no disposition to give up their leadership role—they have become lifelong revolutionaries. In addition, they are entirely comfortable in this leadership role. They have the needed training, and they are quite familiar with the underlying concepts and methods. In these matters of quality, they have the support of the best-trained forces on earth. And they have an understandable pride in their national attainment as to quality.

FUNDAMENTAL CHANGES
FOR THE WEST

Those diverging lines tell us that the West keeps getting better but that the pace is not fast enough—the Japanese pace is faster. Clearly the West must accelerate its pace and should start this promptly. For the West to catch up with the Japanese (and hopefully to overtake them) requires some very fundamental changes in approach. The really fundamental changes to be considered by the West have a marked resemblance to those already undergone by the Japanese:

- Structured annual improvements in quality

- A massive, quality-oriented training program

- Upper management leadership of the company's approach to product quality

ANNUAL QUALITY IMPROVEMENT
FOR THE WEST

Of all the fundamental changes needed, the structured annual improvement program has the shortest lead time. It can be made effective this year or any year. It provides tangible results in a matter of months.

The broad objective for these improvement programs should be to develop among all managers specialists and (ultimately) workers:

- A sense of *responsibility* for active participation in making improvements

- The *skills* needed to make improvements

- The *habit* of annual improvements so that each year the company's quality is significantly better than it was a year ago

Large scale integrated circuits: a case example. To illustrate the limitations of responsibility and skills, consider the case of the silicon chips that carry the large-scale integrated circuits (LSI) used in computers. I have acquired some solid but limited data that suggest that Japanese yields in manufacture of LSI chips are higher than those of the West by a factor of two or three. If these limited data are representative of the entire industry, it would be very serious indeed.

I have also examined the practices of some Western companies relative to improving these yields. I always ask the upper managers: "Who is responsible for improving the yields?" The usual answer is: "The process engineers. " Then when I talk to the process engineers, their reaction is: (1) they have never been given any such clear responsibility; and (2) in any case, they would have no time to carry out such a responsibility, since they are under intense pressure to plan the manufacture of a never ending procession of new designs of these LSI chips.

Beyond the reaction of these upper managers and process engineers, I have an added reaction. The process engineers would be unlikely to improve the yields even if they had the time. The limitation is not in the technology—they are well trained in the pertinent technology. The limitation is mainly in the problems of data collection and analysis. The LSI manufacturing process involves numerous steps, each exhibiting numerous variables. The crux of the solution is to discover which are the key variables and how they affect product quality. It is a complex exercise in design of experiments and analysis of variance, and the process engineers lack the training needed to carry out this exercise.

The universal sequence for making quality improvements. There is a universal sequence of events for making quality improvements. This sequence is built around the project concept. A project is a problem scheduled for solution. All improvement (breakthrough) is made project by project and in no other way.

In practice, the company sets up a committee of managers to guide the annual improvement program. The committee solicits nominations for projects, screens them, and chooses the projects to be tackled in the year ahead.

For each project, a team or task force is appointed. This team then mobilizes the necessary company resources to:

- Study the symptoms of the defects and failures.

- Theorize as to the causes of these symptoms.

- Test the theories until the cause(s) is known.

- Stimulate remedial action by the appropriate line department.

This universal sequence is now well known and is widely used. The Japanese make extraordinary application of this sequence annually. In the West, the application varies widely from company to company. Some Western companies have well-structured annual quality improvement programs. Most do not. In companies that lack such structured programs, any improvements must come from the initiatives of specific middle managers. It takes a good deal of determination by such middle managers to secure results, since they lack the legitimacy and support that comes from an official, structured program.

Why has the West lagged? We may well ask: Why hasn't the West gone ahead on that well traveled universal sequence to secure all those benefits? The matter has not really been researched in depth, but some of the major reasons are evident to experienced observers.

In the early 1950s the Japanese faced a grim reality. No alarm signal is as insistent to industrial managers as inability to sell the product. Since their major limitation was quality, not price, they directed their revolution at quality. They learned how to improve quality, became proficient at it, and have acquired the habit. Their managers are equally at home in meeting current goals and in making improvements for the future.

During most of those same years, the grim reality facing the West has been price competition, not quality competition. The improvement programs of the West reflected this reality. (For example much labor-intensive manufacture was subcontracted to countries in Asia.) Meanwhile, there have been sharp rises in Japanese pay scales so that price competition has been declining while quality competition has been rising. However, the alarm signals of the West have been slow to detect these trends. Lacking loud, insistent alarm signals, the Western companies continued until very recently to respond to alarms that had become increasingly out of date. In the case of the color television set, we may be sure that the surviving Western companies have mounted some heroic efforts to close the quality gap between their products and those of the Japanese.

A MASSIVE TRAINING PROGRAM
FOR THE WEST

At the very outset, we must make clear what subject matter we are talking about, that is, training in what? We are *not* talking about training in technology. Western designers, process engineers, production supervisors, workers, and so on, are quite as well trained as any one else in science, technology, machines tools, methods, and so on. What we are talking about is training in the "quality sciences" or "quality disciplines —a body of quality-oriented concepts, methods, tools, techniques, and skills through which we manage the quality function. We can best understand the nature of the quality sciences by looking sideways at the finance function.

The financial analogy. All companies, no matter what their product, exhibit wide commonalities with respect to finance. They receive income from multiple sources and they spend money for multiple purposes. They face severe consequences if they fail to keep income and outgo in proper balance, both short run and long run. The companies can help to avoid these consequences by making use of the *tools of financial management*. These tools have been evolved over the centuries and consist of such things as budgets, return on investment evaluation, profit statements, balance sheets, sales analysis, expense and cost reports, and financial audits. Through such tools trained managers can plan the financial direction of the company review actual performance and make decisions accordingly. (Behind these financial tools is an infrastructure of accounting concepts, methods, techniques, and skills: double entry bookkeeping, charts of accounts, journals, ledgers, time records, materials requisitions, accruals, and depreciations. The accountants and financial specialists have the expertise to prepare budgets, reports, and so on, from the infrastructure.)

Within the quality function, there is a corresponding array of tools for managers, and a corresponding infrastructure, as well as an associated body of specialists. The striking difference between the worlds of finance and quality is in the extent to which the managers are trained in use of the respective available tools.

To date, selective training. In the West training in the quality sciences has been largely confined to members of the specialized quality departments: quality managers, quality engineers, reliability engineers, inspection supervisors, and quality auditors. Such categories constitute only about 5 percent of the managerial and specialist forces in the companies. In contrast, the Japanese have trained close to 100 percent of their managers and specialists in the quality sciences. With such an imbalance in training, there is no possibility for the West to overtake the Japanese.

Once again, the financial analogy is in point. Consider two companies, A and B. In Company A, the line managers and specialists have undergone training to enable them to participate actively in setting budgets, understand and use expense and cost controls, evaluate return on investment, and so on.

In Company B, only the finance department has such training. Which company will have the best financial performance'?

Variation in training needs. Some training needs are common to many categories of managers and specialists. The major commonalities include:

- The universal sequence of events for improving quality and reducing quality-related costs (creation of beneficial change)

- The universal feedback loop for control (prevention of adverse change)

- Fundamentals of data collection and analysis

Other training needs vary widely. Here are some examples relative to specific functional departments:

- *Product design.* Design review; reliability analysis; maintainability analysis; safety analysis; failure mode and effect analysis; fault tree analysis; design of experiments and analysis of variance; and life-cycle costing.

- *Purchasing.* Vendor survey; vendor qualification; audit of decisions; and vendor rating.

- *Process engineering.* Process capability analysis; quality cost analysis; process control; concepts of operator self-control and self-inspection; measurement error; design of experiments and analysis of variance, production, quality cost analysis; process capability analysis; concepts of operator self-control and self-inspection; process control; equipment maintenance; audit of decisions; and troubleshooting.

Massive training requires thorough planning. The need for such planning becomes evident when we realize that:

- The massive training program will take years, even a decade, to work its way through the hierarchy.

- The special needs of each functional department and job category should be identified and provided for.

- The costs are substantial.

My recommendation to companies had been: Establish a special task force to do the planning on a companywide basis. The task force should consist of selected line managers plus a training manager and a quality manager. The mission of the task force is to:

- Identify the subject matter of the training needed by each job category.

- Identify possible sources for training materials and for leaders to do the training.

- Estimate the investment required in money, facilities, and personnel.

- Recommend a program including training media, locations, leaders, and a time schedule.

A major limitation in setting up these training programs is a shortage of adequate training materials. We need badly an extensive array of training materials that cover management of quality for all functions and at all levels. Moreover, these materials should be designed to facilitate in-house training, or at least, training by local leaders. Otherwise, companies will face the heavy burdens of sending managers to distant cities, at high cost and with associated interruptions in work schedules.

To illustrate, when I prepared the Fourth Edition (1981) of the notes for my course on Management of Quality, I designed them specifically to facilitate their use as in-house training materials. In like manner, I am currently in the process of recording some of these materials on color video cassettes, again to facilitate in-house training (see Table 16.1).

(There is no such problem with "statistical quality control." Written texts are available in abundance, and video cassettes are emerging in increasing numbers.)

Table 16.1 Recordings of training materials.

Topic	Hours
Role of top management in implementing QC	1.5
QC in new product development	2.0
Statistical methods	3.5
Management of QC	3.5
QC in manufacture	3.5
QC in purchasing and sales	3.5
Quality assurance	3.5
QC in Japan and in the world	3.5
Group discussions on promoting QC in the companies	3.0
Reports of group discussions	3.0
Total	30.5

Upper managers should by all means become trainees in the program. Their training will be partly by the book and partly by the extent to which they participate in leadership of the quality function.

It is useful in this connection to look at the training program that the Japanese Union of Scientists and Engineers was offering in 1980 to Japanese top managers:

UPPER MANAGEMENT LEADERSHIP

To understand what is meant by such leadership, we can again look sideways at the finance function. In the West, it is quite common for upper managers to be trained in how to make use of budgets, balance sheets, profit statements, and financial controls of all sorts. Most upper managers actively use these devices. They participate actively in formulating the financial goals, in reviewing results against goals, and in taking action based on these reviews. Through these means the upper managers maintain effective leadership of their company's financial performance.

In Japan, the upper managers maintain effective leadership not only of the company's financial performance but of the quality performance as well. In the West, this has been rare. However, it has not been rare in the case of those Western companies that have clearly lost share of market for quality reasons. (Again, the color television set is a case in point.) The bigger the crisis, the more has been the upper managers' involvement. During the 1980s, the imperatives of those diverging lines suggest that we will see more and more Western upper managers moving in to participate in leadership of the quality function.

Leadership to do what? The need for upper management leadership stems from the need to create major changes. We have already discussed two of the needed major changes:

- A structured program of annual quality improvement and cost reduction

- A massive training program in the quality sciences

Beyond these needed changes, we do not really know the extent to which Western upper managers should take leadership of the quality function. We do know the need varies widely from company to company, since the impact of Japanese competition and other forces varies widely from company to company. We also know that most Western upper managers are handicapped in charting an optimal course. They lack knowledge in depth as to what is going on in the quality function. What I have been recommending to these upper managers is to undertake a comprehensive review—an audit—of what is going on in the company with respect to quality. Then, based on the inputs secured from this audit, make the needed revisions in quality policies, organization, human relations, and so on, including a decision on the extent to which upper management should take leadership of the quality function.

The comprehensive audit. The West has little experience with upper management audits of the quality function, so some awkwardness is inevitable. The areas to be audited should certainly include such major functional activities as product development; purchasing and materials management; manufacture; inspection and test; marketing; and field service. One scenario for such audits is to schedule them about two months apart. For each area, and prior to the audit, a designated task force puts together some pertinent information including open questions of an upper management nature: policy formation, organization, coordination, and so on.

There is little need for upper management audits to get into matters such as conformance to government regulations, product standards, or established procedures. Such matters are generally already being covered by conventional company audits. What is missing is a review of broad matters to provide answers to questions such as:

- What should be the quality mission of the company?

- What are the key qualities as seen by the clients?

- As to the key qualities, what is our state of competitiveness?

- What opportunities do we have for quality improvement and reduction of quality-related costs?

- What can we do to make better use of the human resources in the company?

- What threats are coming over the horizon?

The quality mission of the company is a good case in point. There is a school of thought that contends that the company's mission is one of conformance to specifications, standards, and so on. This contention is mostly valid when applied to the *mission of individuals and departments* in the company. However, it is mostly a serious misconception as to the mission of the company. The quality *mission of the company* is fitness for use. (We may be sure that the makers of the drug Thalidomide met all specifications and standards.)

Beyond the basic quality mission, there are other policy questions that turn up in the audits. In many Western countries, matters of high policy are, in fact, being decided in the functional departments solely because these matters have never come to the attention of upper management:

- Should products be designed based on intended use or based on actual use (and misuse)?

- Should we treat vendors as adversaries or as team members?

Another broad category of questions turned up in the audits relates to organization and coordination. There are many ways in which actions taken by one department can create severe problems elsewhere in the company. For example:

- Some new product designs are made and tested successfully in the model shop but turn out to be costly to make in the production shop, fail excessively under the realities of field usage, or are shockingly difficult to service.

- Some components purchased solely on the basis of price turn out to be the most expensive due to the quality problems they create during further processing.

The coordination needed to optimize company performance requires interdepartmental machinery of all sorts: early warning systems, communication. committees, and so on. Upper management is well poised to create this machinery. However, it must first learn what are the needs and what are the obstacles behind the needs.

A further and major element of upper management review will be that of the basic company organizational structure for quality. In the United States, this organizational structure features a large central quality department with numerous functions of quality planning, coordination, and auditing. In many of the U.S. companies, this same department also has direct command of the inspection and test personnel. All of this contrasts sharply with the organizational forms prevailing in Japan. There most of these quality-oriented functions are carried out by line personnel (who have the necessary training to carry out such functions). The Japanese do have quality departments, but they are small in terms of personnel, and they perform a limited array of functions: broad planning, audit, and consulting services.

As the West expands its training of line personnel, it is inevitable that the organizational structures will change. There will be a gradual shift away from the forms so prevalent in the United States and toward those used by the Japanese.

EMPLOYEE RELATIONS, QC CIRCLES

By now, the West has learned that employee relations in Japan differ markedly from those in the West. One aspect of that relationship has belatedly excited the companies of the West—the phenomenon of QC Circles (QCC). The West is in the process of conducting an extensive test of this concept, and some sort of uncontrolled "movement is in the making. Hence, while employee relations is a broad subject indeed, I will restrict this discussion to the implications of the QCC concept as it applies to the West.

In Japan a QC Circle is a group of about 10 employees within a single company department. They have undergone training in problem solving and they spend part of their time (about an hour each week) studying and solving job-related problems. Between the origin of the concept (1962) and now (1981), about 10 million Japanese employees have undergone this training. During that same interval, they have completed over 15 million projects. Some of these projects (about a third) are quality-oriented. The rest are oriented to productivity, cost reduction, safety, and so on.

Western companies that are trying out the QCC concept are usually hoping to improve their effectiveness in one or more of the following areas: quality, productivity, and human relations. We will examine each of these briefly.

Improvement in quality. There is no possibility for the workforce to make a major contribution to solving the company's quality problems. It has not happened in Japan, and it will not happen in the West. The reason is that the "vital few" field failures and factory defects have their origin in matters that are inherently beyond the capacity of the workforce to diagnose and remedy: management policies, interdepartmental coordination, product designs, process designs, vendor relations practice, and so on. What the workforce can tackle is the "trivial many" intradepartmental problems. However, these give rise to only a small fraction of the overall quality troubles. In my discussions with the Japanese, their general feeling has been that the QC Circles have at best accounted for no more than about 10 percent of the overall Japanese revolution in quality.

Accordingly, a company that tries to solve its quality problems through the QCC concept is not putting first things first. It may well make progress—on the trivial many, the minor part of the total. In doing, so it will delay action on the vital few, where action is the most urgent. Meanwhile, those two diverging lines on the chart continue to diverge.

Improvement in productivity. Many, perhaps most, of the projects of QC Circles in Japan are now oriented to productivity and cost. From the employee viewpoint, such studies help to improve the company's health. In turn, the healthier the company, the more secure the employee, since most Japanese join a company for life and most are free from fear of layoff. From the company's viewpoint, the time spent by employees on such projects is cost effective, although the matter has not been easy to research.

In the West, the early experiences with QC Circles also suggest that projects oriented to productivity are cost effective in the aggregate. However, the pattern of motivation is different due to cultural differences. In the West, most employees do not join a company for life nor are they free from fear of layoff. It remains to be seen what will be the effect of these fears, since in the West improvements in productivity can jeopardize the jobs of employees.

Improvement in human relations. Here we come to what may emerge as the most exciting potential of the QC Circle. All of those projects involve a continuing procession of mutual dialogues between the workforce and the managers. These dialogues constitute a form of communication on common problems. The resulting threshing out of differences brings out into the open the thought processes of all concerned. It is difficult to envision a better way for each to discover why the others behave the way they do. The efforts to carry out projects yield a byproduct in the form of constructive teamwork between workers and managers. Some managers feel that this byproduct is more important than the subject matter of the projects.

PSEUDOSOLUTIONS AND NONSOLUTIONS

We have said that the West is in serious trouble with respect to product quality. The underlying causes have been building slowly. The growth has hardly been noticeable from one year to the next. Such slow growth provides no obvious alarm signals—it escapes notice until the crisis point is reached. At that point, the effects become painfully evident and the demand is for "action now." The stage is then set for application of remedies before the disease has been diagnosed. War is declared before the enemy has been identified.

Certainly the West should scrupulously avoid going down various attractive byways which lead only to pseudosolutions and nonsolutions:

- Attempts to defeat competition not in the marketplace but in the courts, the legislatures, the press.

- Acceptance of the status quo as a fate rather than treating it as a problem.

- Exhortations that urge everyone to "improve" but that make no provision for identifying projects, assigning clear responsibility, providing support, and so on.

- Campaigns to motivate the workforce to solve the company's quality problems by doing perfect work These campaigns have marched under various banners, for example, "Zero Detects." Generally, such campaigns fail to secure useful results because they are based on two fatally defective premises: (1) that the company's quality problems have their origin in worker-controllable errors, and (2) that workers know how to do perfect work but lack adequate motivation (or awareness, involvement, and so on). In addition, these campaigns have generally failed to supply specific answers to the worker's proper question: "What should I do different than I am doing now?" Of all the pseudosolutions, *this one has done the most damage to the West,* since it has done the most to divert attention from the main road.

- "Bring in the miracle men." A segment of the Western press has come up with the conclusion that the Japanese miracle was not Japanese at all. Instead, it was due to two Americans, Deming and Juran, who lectured to the Japanese soon after World War II Deming will have to speak for himself. As for Juran, I am agreeably flattered, but I regard the conclusion as ludicrous. I did indeed lecture in Japan as reported, and I did bring something new to them—a structured approach to managing for quality. I also did the same thing for a great many other countries, yet none of these attained the results achieved by the Japanese. So who performed the miracle? For that matter, let it be recalled that the Japanese had built a huge arsenal of sophisticated weaponry and used it with devastating effect during World War II—all before they had ever heard of Deming or Juran. If that were not enough, let it be recalled that their navy sank the Czar's navy at Tsushima Strait in 1950—a time when neither Deming nor Juran amounted to very much.

PROGNOSIS

In venturing a prognosis, let me first recall an earlier conference of the European Organization for Quality Control; the place was Stockholm and the time was June 1966.

On that occasion, I was still in a state of enthusiasm from having revisited Japan two months before. I concluded my address as follows:

> *In my observation, no other nation is so completely unified on the importance of good quality achievement, so eager to discover and adopt the best practices being followed in other countries, so avid in training all company levels and functions in modern methods of controlling quality, so vigilant in regulating the quality of exported goods. To be sure, there is progress along these fronts in all countries, but nowhere else is there the broad-based sense of devotion and especially, the sense of urgency that is so evident among the Japanese. Witnessing their accelerated pace, and comparing this with the pedestrian progress of other countries, the conclusion is inescapable: The Japanese are headed for world quality leadership, and will attain it in the next two decades, because no one else is moving there at the same pace.*

In offering my present prescription for the West, I am under no delusions. The West comprises an exceedingly diverse mixture of industries and companies. For some, the threats of foreign quality competition are severe and immediate; for others the threats are not immediate. In addition, the West comprises a diverse mixture of national and local cultures, each with built-in stabilizers that resist radical change. Given so many permutations of need for change and resistance to change, we can safely predict a diverse response to a prescription so seemingly radical. Managers are quite willing to listen to radical proposals, but they tend to be convinced only after seeing successful results achieved by the venturesome few.

In this case, I wish it were otherwise. In my judgment, most Western managers have not fully grasped the seriousness and the immediacy of the threats. In addition, I believe that most Western managers are seriously underestimating the time required for a successful response to meet these threats.

My gloomy prediction is that during the 1980s we will witness a dismaying number of casualties of the kind that took place among Western manufacturers of color television sets. I see no way to avert such casualties in view of the imperatives of those diverging lines and in view of the built-in cultural resistance of the forces that control the companies of the West. Things will get worse before they get better.

Beyond the 1980s, my prediction is much more optimistic. The West is now clearly on the defensive, but its competitive position in matters of quality is not at all as severe that faced by Japan in the early 1950s. Moreover, the West has enormous natural resources as well as the managerial and technological skills required to harness those resources to the needs of industrialized societies. Historically the industrial West has demonstrated that once it sets clear priorities and goals, it can accomplish astounding results. In my opinion, during the 1980s, the West will clarify its priorities and goals with respect to product quality. By the late 1980s and during the 1990s, those astounding results should be forthcoming.

These two decades—the 1980s and 1990s—should provide all of us with exciting opportunities for rewarding results. I do not know where your European Organization for Quality Control will hold its annual conference during the year 2001. However, if I am still ambulatory at that time, I will be glad to accept your invitation to review what went on during the 20th century and to provide an updated prognosis for the 21st century.

17

The Quality Trilogy—
A Universal Approach to
Managing for Quality

S everal premises have led me to conclude that our companies need to chart a new direction in managing for quality. These premises are as follows:

1. There is a crisis in quality. The most obvious outward evidence is the loss of sales to foreign competition in quality and the huge costs of poor quality.

2. The crisis will not go away in the foreseeable future. Competition in quality will go on and on. So will the impact of poor quality on society. In the industrialized countries, society lives behind protective "quality dikes."

3. Our traditional ways are not adequate to deal with the quality crisis. In a sense, our adherence to those traditional ways has helped to create the crisis.

4. To deal with the crisis requires some major breaks with tradition. A new course must be charted.

5. Charting a new course requires that we create a universal way of thinking about quality—a way applicable to all functions and to all levels in the hierarchy, from the chief executive officer to the worker in the office or the factory.

Editor's Note: The paper appearing here in Chapter 17 was published in 1986 in *Quality Progress* (August) 19(8): 19–24.

6. Charting a new course also requires extensive personal leadership and participation by upper managers.

7. An obstacle to participation by upper managers is their limited experience and training in managing for quality. They have extensive experience in the management of business and finance but not in managing for quality.

8. An essential element in meeting the quality crisis is to arm upper managers with experience and training in how to manage for quality, and to do so on a time scale compatible with the prevailing sense of urgency.

9. Charting a new course also requires that we design a basis for management of quality that can readily be implanted into the company's strategic business planning, and that has minimal risk of rejection by the company's immune system.

A company that wants to chart a new course in managing for quality obviously should create an all-pervasive unity so that everyone will know which is the new direction, and will be stimulated to go there. Creating such unity requires dealing with some powerful forces that resist a unified approach. These forces are for the most part due to certain nonuniformities inherent in any company. These nonuniformities include:

- Multiple functions in the company: product development, manufacture, office operations, and so on. Each regards its function as something unique and special.

- Multiple levels in the company hierarchy, from the chief executive officer to the nonsupervisory worker. These levels differ with respect to responsibility, prerequisite experience, and training, and so on.

- Multiple product lines: large and complex systems, mass production, regulated products, and so on. These product lines differ in their markets, technology, constraints, and so on.

Such inherent nonuniformities and the associated beliefs in uniqueness are a reality in any company, and they constitute a serious obstacle to unity of direction. Such an obstacle can be overcome if we are able to find a universal thought process—a universal way of thinking about quality—that fits all functions, all levels, all product lines. That brings me to the concept of the "quality trilogy."

(Let me add parenthetically that my colleagues in Juran Institute have urged me to let them call it the "Juran Trilogy." Their reasons are purely mercenary. I have yielded to their wishes. In Juran Institute we also need unity.)

The underlying concept of the quality trilogy is that managing for quality consists of three basic, quality-oriented processes:

- Quality planning
- Quality control
- Quality improvement

Each of these processes is universal; it is carried out by an unvarying sequence of activities. (A brief description of each of these sequences appears in Table 17.1.) Furthermore, these universal processes are interrelated in ways we can depict on a simple diagram. (See Figure 17.1.)

Table 17.1 Basic quality processes.

Quality Planning

- Identify the customers, both external and internal.
- Determine customer needs.
- Develop product features that respond to customer needs. (Products include both goods and services.)
- Establish quality goals that meet the needs of customers and suppliers alike, and do so at a minimum combined cost.
- Develop a process that can produce the needed product features.
- Prove process capability—prove that the process can meet the quality goals under operating conditions.

Control

- Choose control subjects—what to control.
- Choose units of measurement.
- Establish measurement.
- Establish standards of performance.
- Interpret the difference (actual versus standard).
- Take action on the difference.

Improvement

- Prove the need for improvement.
- Identify specific projects for improvement.
- Organize to guide the projects.
- Organize for diagnosis—for discovery of causes.
- Diagnose to find the causes.
- Provide remedies.
- Prove that the remedies are effective under operating conditions.
- Provide for control to hold the gains.

The starting point is quality planning—creating a process that will be able to meet established goals and do so under operating conditions. The subject matter of the planning can be anything: an office process for producing documents; an engineering process for designing products; a factory process for producing goods; a service process for responding to customers' requests.

Following the planning, the process is turned over to the operating forces. Their responsibility is to run the process at optimal effectiveness. Due to deficiencies in the original planning, the process runs at a high level of chronic waste. That waste has been planned into the process, in the sense that the planning process failed to plan it out. Because the chronic waste is inherent in the process, the operating forces are unable to get rid of it. What they do instead is to carry out "quality control"—keep the waste from getting worse. If it does get worse (sporadic spike), a fire-fighting team is brought in to determine the cause or causes of this abnormal variation. Once the cause(s) has been determined, and corrective action is taken, the process again falls into the zone defined by the "quality control" limits.

Figure 17.1 also shows that in due course the chronic waste falls to a much lower level. Such a reduction does not happen of its own accord. It results from purposeful action taken by upper management to introduce a new managerial process into the system of managers' responsibilities—the quality improvement process. This quality improvement process is superimposed on the quality control process—a process implemented in addition to quality control, not instead of it.

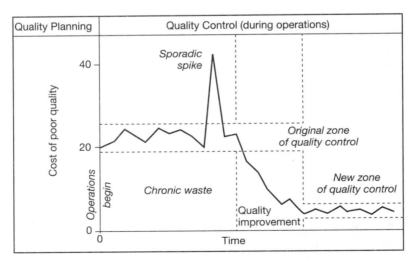

Figure 17.1 The quality trilogy.

We can now elaborate the trilogy descriptions somewhat as follows:

1. *Process*:   Quality planning—the process for preparing to meet quality goals
   End result: A process capable of meeting quality goals under operating conditions

2. *Process*:   Quality control—the process for meeting quality goals during operations
   End result: Conduct of operations in accordance with the quality plan

3. *Process*:   Quality improvement—the process for breaking through to unprecedented levels of performance
   End result: Conduct of operations at levels of quality distinctly superior to planned performance

The trilogy is not entirely "new." If we look sideways at how we manage finance, we notice some interesting parallels, as shown in Table 17.2. (I have often used the financial parallels to help explain the trilogy to upper managers. It does help.)

In recent seminars, I have been collecting upper managers' conclusions on their companies' performance relative to the basic processes of the trilogy. The results are quite similar from one seminar to another, and they can be summarized as shown in Table 17.3.

Table 17.2   Quality and finance parallels.

Trilogy processes	Financial processes
Quality planning	Budgeting
Quality control	Cost control/expense control
Quality improvement	Cost reduction/profit improvement

Table 17.3   Quality process performance (Upper managers' ratings of their companies' performance).

Trilogy processes	Good	Passing	Not passing
Quality planning	13%	40%	47%
Quality control	44%	36%	20%
Quality improvement	6%	39%	55%

These summarized data point to several conclusions:

1. The managers are not happy with their performance relative to quality planning.

2. The managers rate their companies well with respect to quality control, that is, meeting the established goals. Note that since these goals have traditionally been based mainly on past performance, the effect is mainly to perpetuate past performance—the very performance that is at the root of the quality crisis.

3. The managers are decidedly unhappy with their performance relative to quality improvement.

My own observations of company performance (during consultations) strongly confirm the above self-assessment by company managers. During my visits to companies, I have found a recurring pattern of priorities and assets devoted to the processes within the trilogy. This pattern is shown in Table 17.4.

As Table 17.4 shows, the prevailing priorities are not consistent with the managers' self-assessment of their own effectiveness. That assessment would suggest that they should put the control process on hold while increasing the emphasis on quality planning and especially on quality improvement.

To elaborate on the need for raising the priority on quality improvement, let me present several baffling case examples.

1. Several years ago the executive vice president of a large multinational rubber company made a round-the-world-trip with his chairman. They made the trip in order to visit their major subsidiaries with a view to securing inputs for strategic business planning. They found much similarity with respect to productivity, quality, and so on, except for Japan. The Japanese company was outperforming all others, and by a wide margin. Yet the Americans were completely mystified as to why. The Americans had toured the Japanese plant, and to the Americans' eyes, the Japanese were using the same materials, equipment, processes, and so on, as everyone else. After much discussion the reason emerged: The Japanese had been carrying out many, many quality improvement projects year after year. Through the resulting improvements, they made more and better products from the same facilities. The key point relative to "ignorance" is that the Americans did not know what to look for.

2. A foundry that made aluminum castings had an identical experience. The foundry was losing share of market to a Japanese competitor, mainly for quality reasons. Arrangements were made for a delegation of Americans to visit the Japanese factory. The delegation came away completely mystified. The Japanese were using the same types of equipment and processes as were used by the Americans. Yet the Japanese results in quality and productivity were clearly superior. To this day, the Americans don't know why.

3. A few years ago, I conducted research into the yields of the processes that make large-scale integrated circuits. To assure comparability, I concentrated on a single product type—the 16K random access memory (16K RAM). I found that Japanese yields were two to three times the Western yields despite similarity in the basic processes. It came as no surprise to me that the Japanese have since become dominant in the market for 64K RAMs and up.

4. My final example relates to the steel industry. The managers of American steel companies report that their cost of poor quality (just for factory processes) runs at about 10–15 percent of sales. Some of these steel companies have business connections with Japanese steel companies, and the respective managers exchange visits. During these visits the Americans learn that in Japanese steel mills, which use comparable equipment and processes, the cost of poor quality runs at about 1–2 percent of sales. Again, the American managers don't know why. Some of them don't even believe the Japanese figures.

My own explanation is that the Japanese, since the early 1950s, have undertaken to improve quality at a pace far greater than that of the West. The slopes of those two lines are an index of the rate of improvement (see Figure 17.2). That rate is in turn dependent on the number of quality

Table 17.4 Priorities for quality processes.

Trilogy processes	Self-assessment by upper managers	Prevailing priorities
Quality planning	Weak	Limited priority
Quality control	Very strong	Top priority, by a wide margin
Quality improvement	Very weak	Very low priority

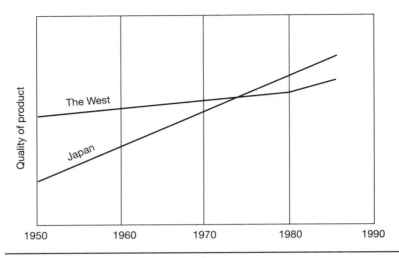

Figure 17.2 World competition in quality.

improvement projects completed. (A project is a problem scheduled for solution.) My estimate is that in terms of numbers of improvement projects completed, the Japanese pace has been exceeding that of the West by an order of magnitude, year after year.

It seems clear that we must change our priorities with regard to the three quality processes. This change in priorities represents a new course. Underlying this new course is the quality trilogy. As a universal way of thinking about quality, the trilogy offers a unified approach for multiple purposes. Let us look at two of these purposes: training in managing for quality and strategic quality planning.

With respect to training, many of our companies have decided to break with tradition. In the past, their training in managing for quality has been limited to managers and engineers in the quality department. The break with tradition is to extend such training to all functions. Since this is a size-able undertaking, the companies have set up corporate task forces to plan the approach.

These task forces have run into serious obstacles due to those same systems of variables mentioned earlier. It is hopeless to establish numerous training courses in managing for quality, each specifically designed to fit specific functions, specific levels in the hierarchy, specific product lines, and so on. Instead, the need is for a universal training course that will apply to all audiences, but with provision for plugging in special case examples as warranted. The trilogy concept meets that need.

The training courses then consist of fleshing out the three sequences of steps described in Table 17.1. Those sequences have been field tested and proven to be applicable to all functions, levels, and product lines.

We have already seen that the trilogy parallels our approach to strategic business planning. Our companies are experienced in business planning; they are familiar and comfortable with the concepts of financial budgets, cost control, and cost reduction. We can take advantage of all that experience by grafting the quality trilogy onto the existing business planning structure. Such a graft reduces the risk that the implant will be rejected by the company's immune system.

The usual starting point is to set up a quality planning council to formulate and coordinate the activity companywide. The council membership consists of high-ranking managers—corporate officers. The chairman is usually the chief executive officer or an executive vice president. The functions of this council parallel closely the functions of the company's finance committee, but apply to quality instead of finance.

The council prepares a written list of its responsibilities. These typically involve the following:

- Establish corporate quality policies.

- Establish corporate quality goals; review quality goals of divisions and major functions.

- Establish corporate quality plans; review divisional and functional plans.

- Provide the infrastructure and resources needed to carry out the plans.

- Review quality performance against plans and goals.

- Revise the managerial merit rating system to reflect performance against quality goals.

It is all quite logical, and some companies are already securing gratifying benefits from going into strategic quality planning. However, other companies are failing to get results, and the main reasons for these failures are becoming evident. They relate to some areas that I will now discuss: goal setting; providing the infrastructure; providing resources; and upper management leadership.

Setting goals. Goal setting has traditionally been heavily based on past performance. This practice has tended to perpetuate the sins of the past. Failure-prone designs were carried over into new models. Wasteful processes were not challenged if managers had met the budgets—budgets that had in turn assumed that the wastes were a fate to be endured.

All this must change. Goals for parameters that affect external customers must be based on meeting competition in the marketplace. Goals for parameters that affect internal customers must be based on getting rid of the traditional wastes.

Infrastructure. Strategic quality planning requires an infrastructure to be set up. The nature of this is evident when we look sideways at the infrastructure needed for strategic business planning: a budgetary process; an accounting system to evaluate performance; associated procedures, audits, and so on.

Much of this structure has long been in place to serve various local needs: divisions, functions, factories, and so on. This structure must now be supplemented to enable it to meet strategic quality needs as well. This is especially the case in large corporations that traditionally have delegated matters of quality to the autonomous divisions. The quality crisis has caused some large corporations to revise this delegation. They now require corporate review of divisional quality goals, plans, and reports of performance. The new approach has required revision of the infrastructure.

Resources. It takes resources to carry out plans and meet goals. To date, companies have exhibited a selective response to this need. Let us look at several areas that require such resources.

- *Training.* Here the response of companies has generally been positive. Companies have invested heavily in training programs for special areas such as quality awareness, statistical process control, and QC Circles. To go into strategic quality planning will require extensive training in the trilogy—how to think about quality. One can hope the response will continue to be positive.

- *Measurement of quality.* The quality crisis has required a major change in the basis for goal setting—the new basis requires measurement of market quality on an unprecedented scale. For example, some companies now have a policy that new products may not go on the market unless their reliability is at east equal to that of leading competitive products. Such a policy cannot be made effective unless the resources are provided to evaluate the reliability of competing products.

Beyond the need to expand quality-oriented marketing research, there are other aspects of measurement that require resources: establishing the scorekeeping associated with strategic quality planning (the quality equivalent of financial profit statements, balance sheets, and so on); extending measures of quality to the nonmanufacturing processes; and establishing means for evaluating the quality performance of managers, and fitting these evaluations into the merit rating system.

- *Quality improvement.* Here we have some puzzling contradictions. An emerging database tells us that quality improvement projects provide a higher return on investment than virtually any other investment activity. Yet many companies have not provided the needed resources.

  To be specific, that database comes mainly from the companies that have presented papers at the annual IMPRO conferences— conferences on quality improvement. Those published papers and related unpublished information indicate that in large organizations—sales of $1 billion or more—the average quality improvement project yields about $100,000 of cost reduction.[1]

  The same database indicates that to complete a project requires from $5,000 to $20,000 in resources. These resources are needed to diagnose the cause of the problem and to provide the remedy. The return on investment is obviously attractive. Nevertheless, many companies—too many—have failed to provide the resources and, hence, have failed to get the results.

  To go into strategic quality planning will require companies to create, for the quality function, a new role—a role similar to that of the financial controller. In all likelihood, this new role will be assigned to the quality managers.

  In part, this new role will involve assisting the company managers to prepare the strategic quality goals—the quality equivalent of the financial budget. In addition, to the new role will involve establishing the continuing means of reporting performance against quality goals. This role parallels the financial reporting role of the financial controller.

  Collateral with those two new responsibilities will be others, also of a broad business nature.

- Evaluation of competitive quality and of trends in the marketplace.

- Design and introduction of needed revisions in the trilogy of processes: quality planning, quality control, and quality improvement.

- Provision of training to assist company personnel in carrying out the necessary changes.

For many quality managers, such a new role will involve a considerable shift in emphasis: from technology to business management, from quality control and assurance to strategic quality planning. But such is the wave of the future. Those quality managers who choose to accept that responsibility, if and when it comes, can look forward to the experience of a lifetime. They will be participating fully in what will become the most important quality development of the century.

ENDNOTE

1. Eighteen case examples are cited in 1985 in Charting the course. *The Juran Report* 4 (Winter).

18

The Upcoming Century
of Quality

I propose to examine the stream of events that has brought the world of quality to its present state. I will also examine the role of ASQC relative to that world of quality. Finally, I will offer a prognosis of what lies ahead.

Managing for quality has had a long and fascinating history. I wish I had the time to tell you about it. Instead, here is a promissory note. Currently I am editing the book *History of Managing for Quality*. Many authors around the world have prepared chapters that tell how managing for quality evolved in their part of the world. That book, sponsored by the Juran Foundation, will be published next year by ASQC's Quality Press.

IN THE BEGINNING

So let us start with the state of affairs as it existed at the beginning of the 20th century. At that time, the United States had already emerged as an industrially developed nation. Starting with an agricultural base, it had expanded aggressively into many directions: mining, construction, manufacture, trade, and so on. Its industrial methods were largely derived from the European countries that had colonized North America.

The methods of managing for quality leaned toward informality, but formal organization for quality could be found in the large factories. In

Editor's note: This paper here in Chapter 18 was presented May 24, 1994, at the ASQC Annual Quality Congress (AQC), Las Vegas. It was Juran's final appearance at an AQC, as the 89-year-old quality leader said he will make no further public appearances beyond his 1994 schedule. The paper was published with the same title in 1994 in *Quality Progress* (August) 27(8):29–37.

those factories, the production managers and supervisors were responsible for meeting the quality specifications. Skilled craftsmen were generally in a state of self-control. They also provided quality assurance relative to their own work—self-inspection. Supervisors and craftsmen were used to train unskilled workers and to check their work. This checking was supplemented by the use of full-time inspectors.

In small shops, the owner was typically a master craftsman. He planned how work was to be done, including planning for quality. He trained the workers and then checked their work to ensure that quality had been achieved. As workers acquired skill and experience, he might reduce the frequency of checking their work.

In the early days of this century, it was unusual for a company organization chart to show a block relating to quality. There were inspectors, but they were scattered among the various production departments. In some large companies, there did exist departments for final inspection and test. These departments typically reported to the production superintendent or the plant manager.

One highly advanced concept of managing for quality was that employed by the Bell System, the telephone monopoly. Under its division of work, the system and product designs were done by Bell Telephone Laboratories, manufacture was done by Western Electric Company, and sales and customer service were provided by the regional telephone companies. Superimposed on all this was an advanced data system to report field performance, plus an inspirational concept of spirit of service.

When I joined the Bell System's Hawthorne plant in 1924, it lacked all kinds of things that we now say are essential to world-class quality: annual quality improvement, business quality management, strategic quality planning, statistical process control, and so on. Yet the equipment sent out by Hawthorne enabled the telephone companies to provide world-class telephone service. How did Hawthorne manage to do it? By brute force and at great cost. The production department priorities were to meet schedules and maintain piecework earnings. Understandably, defects abounded. It then took a massive inspection effort to find and remove those defects.

That was the inspection system at its best. In many companies, it was not at its best. In such companies, many defects escaped to show up as field failures, requiring repair by customers or by manufacturer's service. Some might recall that the early automobiles were sold with tool kits.

THE CENTURY OF PRODUCTIVITY

Let us now embark on a journey through the 20th century. It has brought much turbulence and change to the world of quality. Future historians, however, will likely record the 20th century as the Century of Productivity. Yet quality and productivity are so closely intertwined that our look at the world of quality must take into account the events relating to the world of productivity.

THE TAYLOR REVOLUTION

The driving force of the Century of Productivity was the movement known as scientific management. It was launched by the American engineer and manager Frederick W. Taylor. It made a basic change in managerial practice—the separation of planning from execution. The premise behind the change was that the workers and supervisors of that era lacked the education needed to do planning. Hence, Taylor gave the planning function to managers and engineers. He limited the supervisors and workers to the function of executing the plans.[1]

Taylor's system was stunningly successful in raising productivity, and it was widely adopted by American companies. It probably was the major reason that the United States became the world leader in productivity. Taylor's original applications were in the production departments of the factory. In due course, his followers (today known as industrial engineers) extended their activities to nonproduction functions and later to service industries.

Adoption of the Taylor system soon stimulated some unwelcome side effects. It upset the balance that had previously existed between quality and productivity. The upper management emphasis on productivity became intense. Factory supervisors were forced to make productivity their top priority. The associated piecework systems generated a corresponding priority among the workers. The priority on quality went down due to shortcuts during production, shipping of unfit products, and so on.

RESPONSE TO THE TAYLOR REVOLUTION

The upper managers responded by revising the organization. They moved the inspectors out of the production departments and into a central inspection department headed by a chief inspector. To provide added independence, the chief inspector now reported to the plant manager or to the vice president for manufacture. Those central inspection departments became the quality workhorses during the first half of the 20th century.

In due course, the central inspection departments grew into the quality departments that today are a feature of so many organization charts. Often enough they are headed by a vice president for quality who reports directly to the chief executive officer (CEO). It is a far cry from the days of the early 1900s. It is tempting to smile benignly on today's quality managers: You've come a long way.

Events in the service industries followed a different course. Their approach to managing for quality had been less systematic than that of the manufacturing sector. Service companies tended to rely more on supervisory review and less on formal systems of inspection and test. In addition, the service industries were wary of adopting the Taylor system. As a result, they lagged behind manufacture in raising productivity. They did, however, avoid much of the resulting damage to quality.

Creation of central quality departments also led to two developments that have done a lot of damage:

- Many upper managers concluded that quality is the responsibility of the quality department. This belief made it easier for departments such as production to give top priority to other parameters.

- Upper managers became detached from the quality function. Many concluded that by delegating quality to the quality manager, they could devote their own time to other matters. As they did so, they became progressively less informed about quality. Then when the crisis came, they lacked the knowledge needed to choose a proper course of action.

In retrospect, the use of inspection to attain quality involved inherent weaknesses, such as high costs and shaky habits. Nevertheless, it made companies competitive in quality on the condition that their competitors used the same strategy. That condition was largely met until the Japanese quality revolution came over the horizon.

An important handicap to progress in managing for quality was lack of communication among companies. Early in this century, there was no professional society oriented to quality. The occasional published papers focused mainly on technological topics, such as metrology. The conferences of the engineering societies sometimes included sessions devoted to quality. For example, my first published paper was presented at a session of a regional conference of the American Society of Mechanical Engineers

(ASME). All the papers at that session focused on inspection and test. About 50 people attended.

THE EFFECT OF WORLD WAR II

World War II had a profound effect on the American approach to managing for quality. I recently examined that effect in a paper published in *Quality Progress*.[2] Here are some key points of that paper.

The United States became involved in World War II during the late 1930s, first as a supplier to the allies, and then in 1941 as a combatant. The government created the War Production Board (WPB) to harness the civilian economy to the war effort. One department of the WPB had the job of helping industry meet the quality requirements of military goods. The focus of that effort was to offer free training courses in the use of statistical tools, notably control charts and sampling tables based on probability theory. These tools had evolved within the Bell System during the 1920s.

The WPB courses gave many companies their first exposure to statistical tools. For various reasons, the effect on the war effort was minimal. There were, however, residual effects of other sorts. One was the creation of quality specialists who were assigned to make use of the new tools. These specialists prepared training manuals and conducted in-house training courses. Some were young enthusiasts who went further. They established data systems, investigated abnormal conditions, initiated quality planning, prepared procedures manuals, conducted quality audits, published reports, and so on.

Collectively such activities came to be known as quality control engineering. Large companies tended to create departments of quality control engineering to house these new specialists. Such departments were not made subordinate to the chief inspectors. Instead, a new office—the quality control department—was created and headed by a quality control manager. This new department then presided over the inspection department and the quality control engineering department. The quality control manager was assigned to report to the plan manager or to the vice president for manufacture.

A second residual effect of the World War II training courses was the creation of ASQC. All attendees relished the chance to meet for two weeks and share experiences with people who faced the problems of quality control in other companies. For most attendees, this opportunity was unprecedented. The attendees then proceeded to create quality control societies in their respective areas to enable such sharing to continue. These local societies then merged to form ASQC.

THE EFFECT OF THE SHORTAGES

During the war, goods for the military received priority in allocation of facilities, materials, skilled manpower, and service of all sorts. Production of many civilian products came to a halt, including automobiles, household appliances, and others. All the while, employees in defense factories were working overtime and building up a great hoard of purchasing power.

By the end of the war in 1945, a massive shortage of civilian goods had built up. It then took years to refill the pipelines. During those years, the top priority of the companies was to meet schedules so as to secure maximum share of market. The quality of products deteriorated to scandalous levels. (Quality always goes down during a time of shortages.) The shortages also attracted the entry of new competitors whose inexperience contributed further to the decline in quality.

By the time the pipelines finally filled up, the lowest-quality producers had disappeared. The survivors, however, were forced to take steps to repair the damage to their quality reputations. One of those steps was to strengthen the status of the quality control department to help it deal with the now-entrenched habit of giving top priority to meeting schedules. To provide this new status, the department name was changed (typically) to quality assurance department. The chief was given (typically) the title of quality manager, and he typically reported to the vice president for manufacture.

Considering that, early in the 20th century, the organization charts were devoid of anything oriented to quality, this was a high status indeed.

THE JAPANESE QUALITY REVOLUTION

By far the most important event that followed World War II was the Japanese quality revolution, which opened the way for Japan to become an economic superpower.

Japan's efforts to achieve greatness through military conquest had failed. Now it would have to be done through trade. Lacking natural resources, this meant importing materials, processing them into finished goods, selling these goods, importing more materials, and so on. The major obstacle to creating such an upward spiral was Japan's reputation as a producer of shoddy goods.

To improve that reputation required some fundamental changes in habit patterns. The Japanese CEOs were prepared to make such changes—the shock of losing the war had opened up their minds. So they set out to improve their quality reputation. Through the Keidanren (Japanese Federation of Economic Organizations) and JUSE the companies acted collectively:

- They sent teams abroad to learn how foreign countries achieved quality.

- They translated foreign literature into Japanese.

- They invited two American experts, W. Edwards Deming and me, to give lectures.

Deming's lectures were on statistical methods, especially the control chart developed by Walter A. Shewhart. My lectures were on managing for quality, especially on the concept and methodology of annual quality improvement. Let me here deal with a widespread misconception. Some people believe that had these two Americans not given their lectures, the Japanese quality revolution would not have happened. In my view, this belief has no relation to reality. Had Deming and I never gone there, the Japanese quality revolution would have taken place without us.[3]

Each of us did bring to Japan a structured training package the Japanese had not yet developed. In that sense, each of us gave the Japanese a degree of jump start. But we also did the same for many other countries, none of whom succeeded in building such a revolution. That is why I tell my audiences that the unsung heroes of the Japanese quality revolution were the Japanese managers.

THE AMERICAN RESPONSE

The Japanese quality revolution brought great benefits to American consumers, but at the expense of other parts of the economy:

- Manufacturers lost large shares of market.

- Huge numbers of jobs were exported.

- The national trade balance was badly upset.

Early American efforts to respond to the Japanese quality revolution consisted mainly of:

- Keeping the imports out through restrictive legislation and quotas, criminal prosecutions, civil lawsuits, and appeals to "Buy American." These efforts yielded some relief, but did nothing to improve American competitiveness in quality.

- Solving the companies' quality problems by exhorting the workers to make no mistakes: to "do it right the first time." This simplistic approach was persuasive to many upper managers who, at the time, thought that the primary cause of the company's quality problems was the carelessness and indifference of the workforce.

- Training supervisors and specialists in statistical methods. The stimulus for this came from a widely viewed telecast titled "If Japan Can . . . Why Can't We?" It included a discussion of the Japanese success in quality and implied strongly that this success was solely the result of Japanese use of statistical methods for quality control. The telecast was influential in persuading companies to train many employees in basic statistical methods for quality control. Such training has undoubted merit. It provides the trainees with a useful set of tools. Yet it was premature. The companies had not defined their quality goals or the strategies needed to reach those goals. In a sense, the personnel were given a remedy when the diseases had not yet been diagnosed.

- Undertaking quality improvement on a project-by-project basis. I plead guilty to creating the videocassettes that stimulated this response.[4] Some companies achieved notable improvements; others did not. The decisive variable was the degree of personal leadership provided by upper managers.

In retrospect, the American responses of the 1970s and 1980s were inadequate and disappointing. The good news is that some U.S. companies did reach world-class quality. In addition, there were enough of them to prove that it can be done within the American culture, and to show how it can be done.

LIFE BEHIND THE QUALITY DIKES

A further mighty development during this century has been the growth of public suspicions and fears relative to the negative side of industrial progress. These fears are evident in multiple trends, all of them quality related:

- Growing concern about damage to the environment

- Fear of major disasters and near disasters

- Action by the courts to impose strict liability

- Growth of consumer protection organizations

Collectively these trends are traceable to mankind's adoption of technology and industrialization. Technology confers wonderful benefits on society, but it also makes society dependent on the continuing performance and good behavior of a huge array of technological goods and services. This is the phenomenon of "life behind the quality dikes"—a form of securing benefits but living dangerously.[5] Like the Dutch, who have reclaimed so much land from the sea, Americans secure benefits from technology. They need protective dikes in the form of good quality, however, to shield society against service interruptions and to guard against disasters.

These concerns have led to legislation that, at the outset, was bitterly opposed by U.S. industrial companies. Since then it has become clear that the public is dead serious about its concerns and is willing to pay for good dikes. In addition, the ingenuity of companies has begun to find ways to reduce the costs of providing solutions. Americans seem to be well on the way to dealing with these prickly problems.

WHERE ARE WE NOW?

The United States has already passed the most difficult milestone: having role models. Enough U.S. companies have gotten to world-class quality to prove that it can be done in this culture. In addition, companies have identified how the role models did it—what they did that was different from before. Companies have also learned from the numerous failures: why they failed and what not to do.

Scaling Up

The United States does have a massive problem of scaling up, and some progress is being made. The success stories are being disseminated. Successful companies are shrinking their supplier bases, and a major criterion for supplier survival is to get to world-class quality. Self-assessment using the Malcolm Baldrige National Quality Award criteria is helping suppliers identify their strengths and weaknesses.

The biggest single obstacle to scaling up is the absence of upper management leadership. Many, perhaps most, U.S. upper managers still don't understand the actions needed to achieve world-class quality. Neither do they understand their role in bringing it about—what are the nondelegable actions that upper managers must take, personally. (See the sidebar "CEOs' Nondelegable Roles.")

CEOs' Nondelegable Roles

In the article, "Made in USA—A Renaissance in Quality," J. M. Juran details what he calls the nondelegable roles of chief executive officers (CEOs) that relate to quality improvement.

"The new impetus for quality," he writes, "will be limited only by the pace at which our CEOs accept responsibility for their nondelegable roles. There are seven steps that a responsible CEO must take to achieve quality in any organization. They are strikingly similar to the steps that CEOs already routinely take in managing for financial results. To lead a revolution in managing for quality, every CEO must:

- Set up and serve on the company's quality council, the quality equivalent of the finance committee.

- Establish corporate quality goals, including quality improvement goals, and make them a part of the business plan.

- Make provisions for training the entire company hierarchy in managing for quality.

- Establish the means to measure quality results against quality goals.

- Review results against goals on a regular basis.

- Give recognition for superior quality performance.

- Revise the reward system to respond to the changes demanded by world-class quality."[1]

Prior to presenting his paper, "The Upcoming Century of Quality" at the ASQC Annual Quality Congress, Juran was asked which of the seven nondelegable tasks was the most important. His concise response: "It's an inseparable package."

1. J. M. Juran. 1993. Made in USA—A renaissance in quality. *Harvard Business Review* (July–August).

Buzzwords

To make matters worse, much of our society seems to be mesmerized by buzzwords, such as "excellence" or "reengineering." Often these are merely attractive new labels for old, well-known concepts. Some upper managers, however, are not aware that those concepts are old and well-known. So there is a market for buzzwords, and the opportunists know this. The media amplify the effect. They are ever on the lookout for new hot topics. If they can't find a hot one, they warm up a cold one.

It is tempting to dismiss the game of buzzwords as an innocent diversion from the serious, grim realities of managing enterprises. But experience shows otherwise. During the exhortation era of the 1980s, with its colorful banners and slogans, gullible managers lost years of potential progress as well as their credibility.

As for buzzwords, how about total quality management (TQM)? It is astounding how that term is tossed about without defining what it means. To me, TQM consists of those actions needed to get to world-class quality. Right now, the most comprehensive list of those actions is contained in the Baldrige Award criteria. The quality field has endured some bad press relative to TQM, and much of it is traceable to a failure to explain the meaning of TQM to the journalists.

Notice also the importance of distinguishing the basic quality goals from the means for reaching those goals. For operating managers, the basic goals are to cure the sick, educate the students, provide for national defense, and produce salable products. TQM and its many components—annual quality improvement, business process management, statistical process control, and so on—are all means for reaching the basic goal.

The Taylor System

The Taylor system is still very much with us. As a result, companies are failing to use a huge underemployed asset: the education, experience, and creativity of the workforce. Companies generally agree that the Taylor system is obsolete and should be replaced, but they don't agree on what should replace it. There are many options, all of which have been undergoing test. The options include:

- Creating the conditions for worker self-control

- Creating the conditions for work self-inspection

- Job enlargement, both horizontal and vertical

- Self-directed teams

Each option involves extensive transfer of work from supervisors and specialists to the workforce. As a result, each is meeting much cultural resistance. In my view, replacing the Taylor system is an idea whose time has come. So the Taylor system will be replaced despite the cultural resistance. I believe that all of these options will grow, but that the major replacement for the Taylor system will be self-directing teams of workers.

The Crisis of Opportunity

Earlier this year, I was invited to attend a worldwide conference of Xerox Corporation executives. As a part of their forward planning, they had come up with a concept called crisis of opportunity. It was quite intriguing.

Most human beings prefer a peaceful, predictable life despite the fact that life includes much turbulence. So when things go bad, and then from bad to worse, most people tend to delay making a responsive change until a crisis forces them to act. By that time, much damage has already been done and a sense of urgency has closed in. Few options remain, and none of them is attractive.

The concept of crisis of opportunity is to act on opportunities and not to wait for a crisis before doing so. Instead, the approach is to go after opportunities when things are going well. People can all agree that the best time to be looking for a job is when they are already comfortably employed. The critical difference between responding to an opportunity versus a crisis is taking an initiative versus acting defensively.

Opportunities for improvement abound, but they provide no wake-up calls. So companies must take positive steps to find them. They are then faced with a decision on priorities. To what extent are they willing to invest in improvement? Until the 1980s, priorities favored quality control over quality improvement by a wide margin. The major exception was in the area of new product development. Companies are now faced with making a drastic revision in priorities.

There should be no letup on quality improvement. Many U.S. companies have accepted the concept of annual improvement, and some have become proficient at it. Yet making improvements annually is no longer good enough. In addition, companies must improve the planning process to shut down the hatcheries that in the past have created so much chronic waste.

SOME BACKWARD GIANT INDUSTRIES

Progress among U.S. industries has varied widely. The manufacturing sector, having endured the worst crisis, has made the most progress. The service industry giants—health care, education, and government—have been slow to respond but now show signs of progress. Some islands of excellence have emerged and are serving as role models for scaling up.[6,7]

A development of great promise has been the formation of local alliances. These consist of numerous organs of society: government, industry, academia, chambers of commerce, and so on, all local to some geographic area. The activities of these alliances include committee meetings, luncheon discussions, conferences, and other forms of sharing experiences. Many of them have created local quality awards that are presented at memorable award ceremonies. The interchanges among people from such diverse activities are most informative and stimulating. They also provide opportunity for wide dissemination of knowledge about quality problems and solutions.

THE ROLE OF ASQC

Let me now turn to ASQC as it has evolved during this century.

ASQC Origins

The origin of ASQC is traceable to the training courses conducted by the WPB during World War II. Attendees at those courses relished the opportunity to meet with others in the same field. On return to their own areas, they created local societies that then merged to form a national society. So ASQC was born in 1946, 48 years ago.

During its formative years, ASQC groped to find its scope of activity. The major question was whether to focus on the quality function generally or on the application of statistical methods to control quality. This question was resolved when a study showed that most of the membership had interests beyond statistics.[8]

During those early years, the statistical advocates were rather naive with respect to managing for quality. But they exhibited enthusiasm and even euphoria relative to the new statistical tools: control charts, sampling tables, and probability theory. These tools had been developed during the mid-1920s by a team in the Bell System. (As it happens, you are reading words from the sole surviving member of that team.) In addition, the statistical advocates were quite vocal and influential. An example is seen in the evolution of the awards created by ASQC. The first national ASQC award was the Shewhart medal. It is statistics related and was established in 1948. The second national award, the Edwards medal, is oriented to managing for quality. It was created in 1959, 11 years later.

The Awkward Years

During its early years, ASQC exhibited all the features of a young society: large sails and a small rudder.

The Society income came mostly from membership dues. That is the second worst form of society income. The worst is government subsidies. The organization structure of ASQC vested the bulk of the decision-making in the elected officers. With few exceptions, the elected officers lacked experience in managing an enterprise. Their full-time jobs were those of middle managers or specialists in industrial companies.

The full-time staff was limited to doing housekeeping chores. These offered no inspiring career opportunities, so moral was low and turnover was high.

Progress toward solving these problems was interrupted during the late 1970s and early 1980s. A procession of opportunistic presidents plus some mismanagement converged to create a financial crisis that threatened to bankrupt ASQC. Heroic measures had to be taken. The society survived, amid deep concern by the membership and a wrenching experience for the staff.

That procession of opportunistic presidents deserves some comment. As set out in the constitution and bylaws, ASQC is a democratic society. In practice, the national nominating committee chooses the national officers, since a single slate is presented to the membership.

In my experience, the great majority of ASQC officers have been dedicated professionals. The presidents have increasingly included people of statesmanship stature. The exceptions have included opportunists and occasional lowlifes. For such people to become presidents is a disgrace that only the nominating committee can avoid. In turn, the nominating committee should consist of statesmen and no one else. Selection of the nominating committee is clearly one of the most critical decisions faced by the ASQC leadership.

During the 1980s, external forces converged to solve ASQC's financial problems. The crisis of international competition raised quality to an unprecedented level of priority. ASQC membership soared. There emerged a huge demand for training and consulting services. In turn, this stimulated attendance at ASQC's conferences and training courses. Publication of books grew from a trickle to a torrent, and book sales grew by orders of magnitude. (Some of these books should never have seen the light of day.) There sprang up a cottage industry of consultants, with an associated surge in ASQC's advertising revenues. The Society's accounts have recently been showing delicious annual surpluses.

ASQC and Service to Society

Most of us have an instinctive urge to contribute to public service. The professional society is one mechanism for doing that, and for some people, it is the chief mechanism.

In its early years, ASQC was preoccupied with service to its members. Service to society ranked a distant second. I once tried to quantify the proportions by analyzing the membership of ASQC's committees. I found that in 1969, there were 630 people listed as members of various Society boards, councils, committees, and so on. Of these 630 people:

- 555, or 88 percent, served on bodies devoted mainly to internal Society matters.

- 75, or 12 percent, served on bodies devoted mainly to external affairs.[9]

I don't know what the proportions should be, but 88 to 12 seems too lopsided. This situation has not escaped the attention of outsiders. During a breakfast I had in July 1983 with the late Kaoru Ishikawa, Japan's quality pioneer, he made the observation: JUSE serves society; ASQC serves its members.

Another effect of looking inward was that ASQC was seldom invited to participate in discussion of national affairs. There was little indication that it had a contribution to make. This has since undergone a change for the better. For example, during the congressional hearings on creating the Baldrige Award, ASQC was invited to testify.

Recently, when ASQC revised its vision statement, it included a specific item of being useful to society. That was good news to me. The U.S. economy has numerous unsolved quality problems, and ASQC is uniquely situated to assist in their solutions, provided it mobilizes to do so. More recently, I learned that ASQC is poised to create pilot efforts to provide quality training to the teachers and administrators of our schools. Such projects merit the support of all of us. They also require the support of professional staff. To my knowledge, the number of quality professionals on ASQC's staff is well below the level in other professional societies of comparable size. ASME and ASQC have comparable numbers of members, but the professionals on the ASME staff outnumber those in ASQC by more than an order of magnitude.

ASQC and Upper Management

In its early years, ASQC had few contacts with upper managers. The two groups had little in common. To ASQC, quality had top priority, but the focus was on techniques and tools. To upper managers, the focus was on company goals and results. Quality, though desirable, did not have top priority. An added fact of life was that upper managers prefer to meet with other upper managers. At the time, ASQC's membership was essentially devoid of people in senior managerial posts.

More recently, there has been some convergence of interests. Quality had risen dramatically in importance, forcing upper managers to raise the priority of quality and to create vice presidents for quality. In turn, ASQC membership now includes such vice presidents, and ASCQ has broadened its scope to include managing for quality. ASQC has also begun to take positive steps to create linkages with upper managers. The annual Total Quality Forum was established in 1989. It has brought CEOs of major companies into an initiative to raise awareness of the role of quality in the economy.

I would like to see ASQC get more involved in relations with upper managers. This could be done through committees to identify the major quality problems as seen by upper managers and to mobilize ASQC's resources to help deal with these problems. I see no present likelihood of inducing CEOs to become active in such committees. ASQC's membership, however, now includes vice presidents for quality who are able to reflect the views of CEOs and who can be induced to be active on such committees. In fact, there is precedent for such an approach. One such committee has been active in The Conference Board. Its chairman has been David Luther, who is now president of ASQC.

RESEARCH IN THE QUALITY FUNCTION

There is great need for research in the quality function, especially in managing for quality. ASQC has recognized this need and in 1987 created the nonprofit American Quality Foundation. I have recently reviewed the principal research project undertaken by that foundation: the International Quality Study.

The concept was to identify the best practices in managing for quality in Canada, Germany, Japan, and the United States. Questionnaires were designed and sent to a sample of companies in several industries: automotive, banking, computers, and health care. The responses to those questionnaires became the database for the study. The conclusions were then published in a series of reports.

The study was carried out by the consulting arm of a major accounting firm, under an agreement with American Quality Foundation. This firm also provided the funds, which were substantial.

I learned that there had been no site visits to the companies. When I tried to secure a copy of the questionnaire, I was informed that it was restricted, but if I brought the accounting company some consulting business, they would permit me to see the questionnaire.

I drew the following conclusions:

- The research was of dubious value, given the dubious state of the database.

- There is nothing wrong with a consulting company undertaking such a study with its own funds and then using the findings to help market its services.

- It is entirely inappropriate, however, for a nonprofit foundation to lend its name to such a venture.

Meanwhile, the American Quality Foundation has been shut down. ASQC is now participating with the National Science Foundation in a promising project to encourage people in academia to team up with business managers to study issues of importance.

A NATIONAL QUALITY CENTER

There has been much discussion about the merits of creating a national quality center for the United States. Some of this is stimulated by organizations that would love to become such a center. Additional stimulus comes from those who look sideways at the role of JUSE.

JUSE was created right after World War II as a nonprofit corporation. Its mission was to help in Japan's reconstruction after its crushing defeat. At the outset, it was supported by subsidies and by the work of volunteer committees. Its first managing director, Kenichi Koyanagi, understood the importance of changing Japan's quality reputation as a producer of shoddy goods, so he focused the activities of JUSE on quality. JUSE then played an increasing role in conducting training courses, sponsoring conferences, publishing books and journals, providing consulting services, administering the Deming Prizes, and so on. These activities played a major role in helping Japanese managers create the Japanese quality revolution. Those same activities have also made JUSE self-supporting financially.

JUSE is now the de facto quality center of Japan. It reached that status by earning it. It has a near monopoly in the quality field, with limited competition from Japan Standards Association and Japan Management Association.

The United States has no de facto national quality center. The country does carry out the same activities as JUSE, but these are scattered among many entities: consultants, industrial associations, universities, community colleges, local governments, the National Institute of Standards and Technology (NIST), which administers the Baldrige Award, the Federal Quality Institute, and still others, including ASQC.

Can any of these earn a de facto status of national quality center? It might be too late; some organizations have become quite competent and have put down deep roots. In any case, the likely key parameters can be identified:

- An organization not-for-profit

- A staff that includes some of the leading professionals in the field

- Conducting of research at the cutting edge

- A high priority on service to society

Meeting those parameters is, in any case, a challenge to ASQC. Right now, it meets only the parameter of being not for profit.

THE UPCOMING CENTURY OF QUALITY

Let us now turn to the 21st century. I am wary of going on record as to what lies ahead. Last year, at the annual NIST conference, Deputy Secretary of Commerce David J. Barram quoted my prediction at the 1966 European conference in Stockholm. I had told that conference: "The Japanese are headed for world quality leadership and will attain it in the next two decades because no on else is moving there at the same pace."

As Barram was talking, I thought I heard a small voice saying, "You ought to quit while you are ahead."

Nevertheless, I suspect that future historians will refer to the 21st century as the Century of Quality. Certainly there are some mighty forces that have become drivers for quality:

- Intense international competition in quality as demonstrated by the Japanese quality revolution

- Relentless demands arising from the concept of life behind the quality dikes

Prognosis: The United States

I believe that the United States is now well-poised to respond to these forces. Role models have shown that world-class quality is attainable in this culture. America has an immense job of scaling up, but some powerful forces are urging that it do so. In addition, U.S. companies now understand what the role models did to attain world-class quality, and they are disseminating those lessons learned.

The lessons learned from the role models make it clear that attaining world-class quality requires making some revolutionary changes in managing for quality:

- The entire managerial hierarchy must be trained in how to manage for quality.

- The upper managers must personally take charge of management for quality, much as they have long done in managing for finance. (This puts a limit on what they may delegate. We have identified the nondelegable roles of upper managers.)[10]

- The business plan must be enlarged to include quality goals.

- Managing for quality must be integrated into managing the business.

- Quality improvement must become an ongoing process, year after year.

- New measures must be evolved to enable upper managers to follow the progress of parameters such as customer satisfaction, competitive quality, performance of business processes, cost of poor quality, and so on.

- The workforce must be given the training and empowerment needed to enable them to participate widely in job planning and improvement.

- The reward system must be revised to take account of the changes in job functions and responsibility.

That is an extensive list of musts, but I believe Americans are on the road to accepting them as a way of life.

In looking ahead to the next century, let us also look briefly at the situation in Japan and Europe.

Prognosis: Japan

The Japanese have been improving quality for over four decades, and they show no signs of letting up. Their quality torch has been passed successfully through several turnovers of upper managers. They are quite aware that their achievements in quality are the chief reason for their status as an economic superpower. I believe that they will remain among the world quality leaders during the next century. Nevertheless, the Japanese face a serious threat that is waiting in the wings: the threat of "Buy American."

There are, of course, some consumers who favor imported goods, especially in the world of fashion. But many other consumers prefer to buy American, all other things being equal. During the 1960s and 1970s, other things were not equal, so the urge to buy American was overcome by the superior quality and value of Japanese products.

More recently, during the 1980s, the gap between Japanese and American quality was narrowed noticeably by some of our companies. That enabled those companies to recapture some of the market share they had lost. We can expect the quality gap to continue to narrow in the years ahead. That will translate into growth in market share as customer perception catches up with the facts. The more U.S. companies narrow the competitive gap in quality, the stronger will be the urge to buy American. I believe that some of this has already taken place, thereby helping to reverse the export of jobs as well as the trends in share of market.

There is also a further stimulus to buy American. The Japanese have alienated the U.S. government and U.S. companies by their restrictions on importing American goods. I suspect that this alienation extends to the American public as well. Beyond the effect on imports from Japan, it would not surprise me if the urge to buy American will in due course affect the market share of Japanese-owned companies that produce goods here in the United States.

Prognosis: Europe

In Europe, the national approaches to managing for quality vary greatly due to local history and culture. They have role models, but their major preoccupation is with registration to ISO 9000.

ISO 9000 is a label for a series of international standards for quality systems that were published by the International Organization for Standardization. The standards are voluntary; they are not a legal prerequisite to selling products in Europe. They have been so cleverly marketed, however, that whoever hopes to sell products in Europe must become registered as meeting the criteria of ISO 9000. Registration to ISO 9000 has become a de facto license to market in Europe.

The ISO 9000 standards have a degree of merit, as the criteria define a comprehensive quality system. The registration process might well get rid of the plague of multiple assessments that has burdened companies in the past. The criteria, however, fail to include some of the essentials needed to attain world-class quality:

- Personal leadership by upper managers

- Training the hierarchy in managing for quality

- Quality goals in the business plan

- A revolutionary rate of quality improvement

- Participation and empowerment of the workforce

All in all, my prognosis for Europe is gloomy. Already there is evidence of a lag: The European quality awards have gone mainly to American-owned subsidiaries despite their small numbers. In my view, many European companies are in for a massive letdown. They will all get registered to ISO 9000, but this alone will not enable them to attain world-class quality.

AND NOW, SAYONARA

The publicity for this AQC presentation said that this will be my final appearance before an ASQC audience. That is essentially correct. I still have some all-day seminars to conduct this year in various cities around the United States. Collectively they will conclude my last hurrah. In December, I will be 90 years old and will have completed 70 years in the field of managing for quality, less four years devoted to service in the federal government during World War II.

Starting in 1995, I will devote my time to tackling a huge backlog of neglected family and personal matters. I will also get into the formidable job of writing my memoirs—I have promised that to my grandchildren. In addition, I hope to be granted the time to sneak in a few books and papers on the subject of managing for quality. So I will remain fully occupied, but I will be free from deadlines that must be met. You can be sure that in December of this year, I will be shouting, "Free, free at last!"

Although I will remain fully occupied, I will miss the excitement of action in the arena and the association with managers who face the realities. I have been facing a different reality, so I have been backing off from consulting engagements. As a result, the active world has been receding from me and I am becoming increasingly out of touch. My future writings will relate to history rather than to current events.

I am looking forward to those memoirs. They will make clear the nature of the journey I have traveled. During some of that journey, I met Samuel Johnson's definition of a lexicographer: a harmless drudge. But much of that journey has been challenging in the extreme.

As related to quality, my journey began in 1924, when as a youngster out of engineering school, I joined the Hawthorne Works of the Bell System. There the powers that be tossed me into what they called the Inspection Branch, I had no idea what they did there, and I didn't care. What mattered was that for the first time in my life, I became financially secure—I had a steady job at steady pay.

During those 70 years, the subject of quality grew and grew, both in importance and complexity. It exposed its practitioners to the turbulence that accompanies a series of convulsions. That growth and turbulence are still in progress.

My association with ASQC began at the beginning. I was one of many founding members of the Society. In the decades that followed, I became quite active in some of its functions. I have served on some of its committees, attended most of its congresses, addressed many of them, contributed numerous published papers to its journals, perhaps over 200, and engaged in extensive correspondence with many members.

I welcomed those opportunities to contribute to a good cause. Yet I found that I was being repaid. Sharing experiences with other Society members gave me inputs that I was then able to put to good use when writing books, preparing training materials, or providing consulting service to clients. Beyond those tangible repayments, I relished the exhilaration of contributing to the common good.

All of you attending this Congress have an interest in the subject of managing for quality. Some of you are fully immersed in it. I believe I can safely promise you that it will continue to grow during your lifetime and will offer exciting challenges as well as drudgery. I hope that during your own journey, you, too, will avail yourself of the opportunities provided by ASQC and other professional societies to gain from sharing experiences with others in the field. And I hope that you, too, will come to relish the exhilaration of contributing to the common good.

ENDNOTES

1. Juran, J. M. 1973. The Taylor system and quality control. "Management Interface." *Quality Progress* (May through December) 6(5–12). See Chapter 11 of this book.
2. Juran, J. M. 1991. World War II and the quality movement. *Quality Progress* (December) 24(12).
3. Juran, J. M. 1993. Made in USA—A renaissance in quality. *Harvard Business Review* (July–August).
4. Juran, J. M. 1980. *Juran on quality improvement.* a series of 16 videocassettes plus associated manuals.Wilton, CT: Juran Institute.
5. Juran, J. M. 1969. Mobilizing for the 1970s. *Quality Progress* (August) 11(8). See Chapter 10 of this book.
6. Berwick, D. M., A. B. Godfrey, and J. Roessner. 1990. *Curing health care: New strategies for quality improvement.* San Francisco: Jossey-Bass.
7. Godfrey, A. B., D. M. Berwick, and J. Roessner. 1992. Can quality management really work in health care? *Quality Progress* (April) 25(4).
8. Juran, J. M. 1951. Directions for ASQC. *Industrial Quality Control* (November) 8(3).
9. Juran, J. M. 1974. ASQC and public services. *Quality Progress* (July) 7(7).
10. Juran, J. M. 1993. Made in USA—A renaissance in quality. *Harvard Business Review* (July–August).

Index